Shackerley Marmion

The dramatic works of Shackerley Marmion

With prefatory memoir, introductions and notes

Shackerley Marmion

The dramatic works of Shackerley Marmion
With prefatory memoir, introductions and notes

ISBN/EAN: 9783742870001

Manufactured in Europe, USA, Canada, Australia, Japa

Cover: Foto ©Andreas Hilbeck / pixelio.de

Manufactured and distributed by brebook publishing software (www.brebook.com)

Shackerley Marmion

The dramatic works of Shackerley Marmion

THE DRAMATIC WORKS OF SHACKERLEY MARMION.

WITH PREFATORY MEMOIR, INTRODUCTIONS,
AND NOTES.

MDCCCLXXV.

EDINBURGH: WILLIAM PATERSON.
LONDON: H. SOTHERAN & CO.

TO

THE RIGHT HONOURABLE

John, Lord Coleridge,

OF OTTERY ST. MARY,

DEVON,

LORD CHIEF JUSTICE OF THE COURT OF COMMON PLEAS,

ONE OF A FAMILY EMINENT IN LITERATURE,

A DISTINGUISHED LAWYER AND AN UPRIGHT JUDGE,

THIS VOLUME IS INSCRIBED

BY

HIS OBLIGED AND FAITHFUL SERVANTS

THE EDITORS.

CONTENTS.

	Page
INTRODUCTORY NOTICE AND MEMOIR,	ix
HOLLAND'S LEAGUER,	1
A FINE COMPANION,	99
THE ANTIQUARY,	197

PREFATORY NOTICE.

The name of the author of the following plays, three in number, has been variously spelt and its correct pronunciation consequently rendered doubtful. On the title-page of the first play, printed in 1632, he is called "Schackerley Marmyon, Master of Arts;" next year, on the second, he is entered as "Shakerley Marmyon;" and, thirdly, in 1641, he appears as "Shackerly Mermion, Gent." Although Mr Singer, in his elegant reprint of this author's Poem of Cupid and Psyche, which emanated from the Chiswick Press in 1820, inclines to call him Shakerley Marmion, our bias, guided by the preponderance of authority, is in favour of his being designated "Shackerley Marmion."

Shakerly, however, was an ancient family name in England. Francis, fifth Earl of Shrewsbury, who died on 25th September 1560, according to Collins,* took as his second wife "Grace, daughter of Robert Shakerley of Little Longdon in Derbyshire, Esq., but had no issue by her." Lodge says she was the widow of Robert Shakerley of Holme in Cheshire.

The name was territorial, and the chief of the family was Sir Jeffrey Shakerly of Shakerly, in the county of Lancaster. His eldest son George married Anne, youngest daughter of Sir Walter Bagot of Bagot, who died 15th February 1704, in the sixtieth year of his age.

Shackerley Marmion, it is surmized by Singer, "was descended from the ancient and noble family of the Marmions of Scrivelsby," in whom was

* Collins' Peerage by Sir E. Brydges, Vol. III., page 23.

vested the hereditary right to appear at the coronation of the Sovereigns of England as Champion. Of Mr Singer's assertion there is no legal evidence, but it is certainly true that the Office of King's Champion was inherited by the Marmions of Scrivelsby.

The Marmions, Lords of Fontney in Normandy, came over with William the Conqueror, being represented in the person of Robert de Marmion, who obtained a grant of the castle and town of Tamworth, in the county of Warwick, as well as of the manor of Scrivelsby in Lincolnshire, the tenure of the latter being hereditary service as Royal Champion, at coronations; an office which it is said his ancestors had exercised in relation to the Dukes of Normandy. The family became extinct in the 20th Edward I., Philip de Marmion, the fifth Baron, having died without male issue. His grand-daughter, Mazera, having been married to Alexander de Freville, he, in right of his wife, succeeded to Tamworth Castle. At the coronation of Richard II., Sir Baldwin de Freville, Knight, their grandson, then holding Tamworth Castle, appeared in virtue of the tenure to perform the duty of Royal Champion—that is, to ride, completely armed, into Westminster Hall, upon a barbed steed, and there to challenge the combat with whomsoever should dare to oppose the King's title to the Crown, a service which the Barons de Marmion, his ancestors, had theretofore performed; but the preference was given to Sir John Dymoke, to whom the Manor of Scrivelsby had descended by an heir female of Sir Thomas Ludlowe, Knt., by Joane, youngest daughter and coheir of the said Philip, the last Baron Marmion of Tamworth. The representative of that family is till the present day Hereditary Champion of England. The Earls

Ferrers are the descendants, and possess the estates of the family of Freville.

The form and ceremony observed in introducing the Champion on the day of the Coronation of James II. is given in a History of his Coronation, " illustrated with exquisite Sculptures, and published by his Majesty's especial command, by Francis Sandford, Lancaster Herald of Arms, anno 1687 :"—

" Before the second course was brought in, Sir Charles Dymoke, Knt., the King's Champion—son and heir of Sir Edward Dymoke, Knt., who performed the like service at the coronation of his Majesty Charles II.—completely armed in one of his majesty's best suits of white armour, mounted on a goodly white horse, richly caparisoned, entered the hall in manner following, viz. :—

" Two trumpets, with the champion's arms on their banner.

" The Serjeant trumpet, with his mace on his shoulder; two serjeants at arms, with their maces on their shoulders.

" The champion's two esquires, richly habited ; one on the right hand, with the champion's lance carried upright; the other on the left hand, with his target, and the champion's arms depicted thereon.

" York Herald, with a paper in his hand, containing the words of the challenge.

" The champion on horseback, with a gauntlet in his right hand, his helmet on his head, adorned with a great plume of feathers, white, blue, and red.

On his right " The Earl Marshall in his robes and coronet on horseback, with marshall's staff in his hand." On his left " The Lord High Constable in his robes and coronet on horseback, with the constable's staff."

"Four pages, richly apparelled, attendants on the Champion.

"The passage to their Majesties' table being cleared by the Knight Marshall, York herald, with a loud voice, proclaimed the Champion's challenge, viz. :—

"'If any person, of what degree soever, high or low, shall deny or gainsay our Sovereign Lord King, &c., &c., &c., to be right heir to the imperial crown of this realm of England, or that he ought not to enjoy the same, here is his Champion, who saith that he lieth, and is a false traitor, being ready in person to combat with him; and in this quarrel will adventure his life against him on what day soever he shall be appointed.'

"And then the Champion threw down his gauntlet. The gauntlet having lain some short time, the said York herald took it up, and delivered it again to the Champion.

"Then advancing in the same order to the middle of the hall, the said herald made proclamation as before, and the Champion threw down his gauntlet; which, after having lain a little time, was taken up by the herald and delivered to him again.

"Lastly, advancing to the foot of the steps, York herald, and those who preceded him, going to the top of the steps, made proclamation a third time, at the end whereof the Champion again cast down his gauntlet, which after some time being taken up and redelivered to him by the herald, he made a low obeisance to his Majesty. Whereupon his Majesty's Cup-bearer bringing to the King a gilt bowl of wine, with a cover, his Majesty drank to the Champion, and sent him the said bowl by the cup-bearer, accompanied with his assistants, which the Champion—having put on his gauntlet—

received, and retiring a little space, drank thereof,
and made his humble reverence to his Majesty;
and, being accompanied as before, departed out of
the hall, taking the said bowl and cover with him
as his fee."

In the British Museum is a MS. purporting to
be a Mandate of Henry VI. to R. Rolleston,
Keeper of his Majesty's Wardrobe, to deliver to
P. Dymoke, such furniture, &c., as King's Champion on the day of the Coronation, as his ancestors
were accustomed to have.*

Philip de Marmion was twice married. By his
first wife his territorial lordship of Tamworth
passed to the representative of his eldest daughter
Joane, and latterly vested in the ancient family of
Freville; thereafter by descent it came to the Lords
de Ferrers. In this line it is understood that
whatever right there may be to the Barony by
tenure it is vested in their present representative,
but it is very improbable that any attempt will
ever again be made to raise any claim to an honour
of this description, after the decision against the
late Lord Fitzharding, who, in virtue of his possession of Berkeley Castle, unsuccessfully asserted
a right to sit in the House of Lords. Serious
doubts have been entertained of the soundness of
the decision given by that very capricious tribunal—
if it can be so termed—a Committee of Privileges.
To console the claimant for his want of success
he was gratified by Government with a modern
Barony of Fitzharding—one of the old titles of
the Earls of Berkeley. This has been mentioned
to shew that the claim which was brought before
the House of Peers at the beginning of this cen-

* For pedigree and further account of the Marmions of
Scrivelsby see Banks' "Dormant and extinct Baronage of
England," Vol. I., 4to, Lond. 1807.

tury by another descendant of Philip de Marmion to the dignity of a Baron was unfounded, and could not be maintained in virtue of his descent from Joane, Lord Marmion's youngest daughter by his second marriage, whose grand-daughter, marrying Sir John Dymoke, Kt., thereby brought the Manor of Scrivelsby into the family, in which it remains.

Although the family of Dymoke have, from time to time, exercised the office of King's Champion down to the coronation of Her Majesty, Queen Victoria, they had no claim to the Peerage. Nevertheless Lewis Dymoke, having been advised that he had such claim, in July 1814, for the first time petitioned the Crown for a Writ of Summons, which petition having been referred to the Attorney-General, the case was heard in the usual manner in the House of Lords; but before any judgment was pronounced the claimant died, and the application has never been renewed.

"With respect to this claim," says Sir Harris Nicolas, in a Synopsis of the Peerage of England, Vol. ii., Art. Marmion, "it is to be observed, that though the Manor of Scrivelsby was held by the service of performing the office of King's Champion by Robert de Marmyon, in the reign of William the Conqueror, he was not by seizure thereof a Baron, but by seizure of the Castle and Barony of TAMWORTH, which he held of the King *in capite* by Knight's service; so that, if at this period Baronies by Tenure were admitted, the possessor of the Manor and Lordship of Tamworth—which in the division of his property fell to the share of Joane, his eldest daughter, wife of William Mosteyn, and, on her death S. P. to Alexander Freville, husband of Joan, daughter and heir of Ralf Cromwell, by Margaret or Mazera, the next sister of the said Joan de Mosteyn—would possess the claim to the Barony possessed by Robert de Marmyon above mentioned, he having derived his dignity from that Barony, instead of from the seizure of the Manor of Scrivelsby. Moreover, if Philip Marmion, the last Baron, had died seized of a Barony in fee, Lewis Dymoke, the claimant, was not even a co-heir of the said Philip, though he was the descendant of one of his daughters and co-heirs."

Sir Walter Scott, in a note upon his poem of Marmion, thus remarks as to the name:—"I have not created a new family, but only revived the titles of an old one in an imaginary personage." He goes on to say :—" It was one of the Marmion family, who, in the reign of Edward II., performed that chivalrous feat before the very Castle of Norham which Bishop Percy has woven into his beautiful ballad 'The Hermit of Warkworth.'" An account of this feat will thus be found in Leland :—

"The Scottes came yn to the marches of England, and destroyed the castles of Werk and Herbotel, and overran much of Northumberland marches.

"At this tyme, Thomas Gray and his friendes defended Norham from the Scottes.

"It were a wonderful processe to declare, what mischefes cam by hungre and asseges by the space of xi yeres in Northumberland; for the Scottes became so proude after they had got Berwick, that they nothing esteemed the Englishmen.

"About this tyme there was a greate feste made yn Lincolnshir, to which came many gentlemen and ladies; and amonge them one lady brought a heaulme for a man of were, with a very riche creste of gold, to William Marmion, Knight, with a letter of commandement of her lady, that he should go into the daungerest place in England,

and ther to let the heaulme be seene and known as famous. So he went to Norham; whither within 4 days of cumming, cam Philip Moubray, guardian of Berwicke, having yn his bande 40 men of armes, the very flour of men of the Scotish Marches.

"Thomas Gray, capitayne of Norham, seynge this, brought his garison afore the barriers of the castel, behind whom cam William, richly arrayed, as al glittering in gold, and wearing the heaulme, his lady's present.

"Then said Thomas Gray to Marmion, 'Sir Knight, ye be cum hither to fame your helmet: mount up on yowr horse, and ryde like a valiant man to yowr foes even here at hand, and I forsake God if I rescue not thy body deade or alyve, or I myself wyl dye for it.'

"Whereupon he toke his cursere, and rode among the throng of ennemyes; the which layed sore stripes on him, and pulled him at the last out of his sadel to the grounde.

"Then Thomas Gray, with al the hole garrison, lette prick yn among the Scottes, and so woudid them and their horses, that they were overthrowan; and Marmion, sore beten, was horsid again, and, with Gray, persewed the Scottes yn chase. There were taken 50 horse of price; and the women of Norham brought them to the foote men to follow the chase."

Shackerley Marmion was born in January 1602 at Aynho, near Brackley, in the county of Northampton, of which place his father was Lord of the Manor, and the possessor of a considerable estate there. He was initiated in letters, under the mastership of Richard Boucher or Butcher, as he was commonly called, at the free school, at Thame, in Oxfordshire; from thence, when about sixteen years of age, he was sent to Wadham College, of which, in 1617, he became a gentleman commoner, and continued there until he took the degree of M.A. in 1624. Anthony Wood says of him: "he was a goodly proper gentleman, and had once in his possession seven hundred pounds per annum at least, but died—as the curse is incident to all poets—poor and in debt." Oldys, in his MS. notes on Langbaine, says it was our author's father, and not himself, who squandered away this fortune; and this seems probable, inasmuch as Aynho was sold, according to Singer, "to Richard Cartwright of the Inner Temple in 1620," at which time he was only eighteen years of age, and apparently a careful student.

When left to his own resources he sought to push his fortune, like many other reduced gentlemen, in the Low Countries; but the contention for promotion was so great, that Marmion waited in vain for preferment, so he threw aside the pike, and returned to England, where he had recourse to his pen as a better means to attain that fame and fortune he as a soldier had expected to win. Sir John Suckling, who had also served in the Low Countries under Gustavus Adolphus, in turn came back to his own country, where, at his own charge, he raised a troop of horse for the King's service, so richly and completely mounted that the cost has been estimated at £12,000. Into this troop Marmion was admitted by his friend Sir John, and shortly thereafter they proceeded towards Scotland in the memorable but ill-fated expedition against the Scottish Covenanters, 1638-39. Marmion, however, reached no farther than York, when, falling sick, he was, by the care of his friend and brother-in-arms, removed by easy stages to London, where he died at the beginning of the year 1639.

Besides several minor Poems scattered about in different publications, he wrote

> Cupid and Psyche; or, an Epic Poem of Cupid and his Mistress, as lately presented to the Prince Elector. Lond. 1637. 4to; and
> The Three Comedies which follow, viz. :—
> Holland's Leaguer, . . . 1632
> A Fine Companion, . . . 1633
> The Antiquary, ... 1641

To him has also been attributed, but without sufficient evidence :—

> The Crafty Merchant, or the Soldier'd Citizen. A Comedy. *Not Printed.*
> The Faithful Shepherd. A Pastoral.

There is a copy of his "Fine Companion" in the Grenville collection in the British Museum, "marked" for acting, the character of the handwriting being about fifty years later than the date of the piece. There are numerous verbal alterations, and a good deal of "cutting" noted throughout and on the margins; but unfortunately the MS. interpolations of the longer passages deleted have been removed, the fragments of wafers to which these more important alterations have been attached being the only vestiges left of their having existed.

Marmion's very beautiful Legend of Cupid and Psyche, a work upon which his poetic fame must more immediately rest, has been carefully edited for modern readers, by W. S. Singer, Esq. He takes the text from the first edition, to which is prefixed commendatory verses by Richard Broun, Francis Tuckyr, Thomas Nabbes, and Thomas Heywood.

A second edition appears to have been issued in folio in 1638.

Another edition, which in this way may be

termed the third, subsequently appeared under this title :—

"Cupid's Courtship: or the Celebration of a Marriage between the God of Love and Psiche. Licensed October 29, 1666. Roger L'Estrange. London, printed by E. O. for Thomas Dring, at the White Lion in Fleet-street, near Chancery-lane. 1666. 16mo."

The commencing title is: A Moral Poem on the Marriage of Cupid and Psiche, pp. 80. Title, two Addresses by Friends, F. T. and T. H., the Argument and the Mythology occupying other 8 pages.

The Argument and its Explanation, which occur in all the editions, are as follows :—

"THE ARGUMENT.

There was inhabiting in a certain city a King and Queen, who had three daughters; the elder two of a moderate, mean beauty, but the youngest was of so curious, so pleasing a feature, and exact symmetry of body, that men esteemed her generally a goddess, and a Venus of the earth. Her sisters being happily married to their desires and dignities, she only, out of a super-excellency of perfection, became rather the subject of adoration than love. Venus, conceiving an offence, and envious of her good parts, incites Cupid to a revenge, and severe vindication of his mother's honour. Cupid, like a fine archer, coming to execute his mother's design, falls in love with the maid and wounds himself. Apollo, by Cupid's subornation, adjudges her in marriage to a serpent. Upon which, like Andromeda, she is left chained to a rock, her marriage being celebrated rather with funeral obsequies than hymeneal solemnities. In this inconceivable afright she is borne far away by the west-wind to a goodly fair house, whose wealth and stateliness no praise can determine. Her husband, in the deadness and solitude of night, did oft-times enjoy her, and as he entered in obscurity, so he departed in silence, without once making himself known unto her. Thus she continued for a long season, being only waited upon by the ministery of the Winds and Voices. Her sisters came every day to seek and bewail her; and though her husband did with many threats prohibit her the sight of them, yet natural affection prevailed above conjugal duty, for she never ceased with tears to solicit him, till he had permitted their access. They no sooner arrived, but instantly corrupt her, and with wicked counsel deprave her understanding, infusing a belief that she had married and did nightly embrace a true serpent: nor are they yet contented to turn the heaven of her security into the hell of suspicion, but with many importunities proceed, exhorting her to kill him, which she also assents unto. Thus credulity proves the mother of deceit, and curiosity the stepmother of safety. Having thus prepared for his destruction, the scene is altered, and she acts the Tragedy of her own happy fortunes: for coming with an intent to mischief him, so soon as the light has discovered what he was, she falls into an extremity of love and passion, being altogether ravished with his beauty and habiliments; and while she kisses him with as little modesty as care, the burning lamp drops upon his shoulder, whereupon her husband furiously awakes, and having with many expostulations abandoned her falsehood, scorns and forsakes her. The maid, after a tedious pilgrimage to regain his love and society, Ceres and Juno having repulsed her, freely at the last offers up herself to Venus, where through her injunctions and imperious commands she is coarsely treated, and set to many hard and grievous tasks: as first, the separation of several grains, with the fetching of the Stygian water and the Golden Fleece, and the Box of beauty from Proserpine; all which by divine assistance being perform'd, she is reconciled, and in the presence of the gods married to her husband: the wedding is solemnized in Heaven.

"THE MYTHOLOGY; OR, EXPLANATION OF THE ARGUMENT.

By the City is meant the World; by the King and Queen, God and Nature; by the two elder sisters, the flesh and the will; by the last, the Soul, which is the most beautiful, and the youngest, since she is infused after the body is fashioned. Venus, by which is understood Lust, is feigned to envy her, and stir up Cupid, which is Desire, to destroy her; but because Desire has equal relation both to Good and Evil, he is here brought in to love the Soul, and to be join'd with her, whom also he persuades not to see his face, that is, not to learn his delights and his vanities; for Adam, though he were naked, yet he saw it not, till he had eaten of the tree of Concupiscence. And whereas she is said to burn him with the dispumation of the lamp, by that is understood that she vomits out the flames of desire which were hid in her breast; for desire, the more it is kindled, the more it burns, and makes, as it were, a blister in the mind. Thus, like Eve, being made naked through desire, she is cast out of all happiness, exil'd from her house, and tost with many dangers. By Ceres and Juno both repulsing of her is meant that neither wealth nor honour can succour a distressed soul: In the separation of several grains is understood the act of the Soul, which is recollection, and the substance of that act, her forepast sins: By her going to Hell, and those several occurrences, are meant the many dangers of despair: by the Stygian water, the tears of repentance; and by the Golden Fleece, her forgiveness. All which, as in the Argument is specified, being by Divine Providence accomplish'd, she is married to her spouse in Heaven."

JAMES MAIDMENT.
W. H. LOGAN.

April 1875.

HOLLAND'S LEAGUER.

A

Hollands Leaguer. An excellent comedy as it hath bin lately and often acted with great applause, by the high and mighty Prince Charles his servants; at the private house in Salisbury Court. Written by Shackerley Marmyon, Master of Arts.

——*vult hæc sub luce rideri;*
Indicis argutum quia non formidat acumen.

Printed at London by I. B. for Iohn Grove, dwelling in Swan Yard within Newgate, 1632.

Of this play Langbaine says:—" An excellent Comedy often acted with great applause, by the High and Mighty Prince Charles his Servants, at the Private House in Salisbury Court, printed quarto, Lond. 1632. The author of this play has shewed his reading, having borrow'd several things from Juvenal, Petronius Arbiter, &c."

In the notice of this piece in the Biographia Dramatica it is said that besides being acted at Salisbury Court, it was acted at Court before the King and Queen, but no authority is given for this latter statement. The notice goes on further to say,—" This piece met with great applause. The story was printed the same year in 4to; but there is no incident in this play taken from it, except a detection of the sin of pandarism."

The situation of Holland's Leaguer, a well-known brothel, was what forms a part of the present Holland Street, Blackfriars.

There was a copy of this " Story," which is very scarce, in George Daniel's Library, sold in 1864 by Sotheby.—This copy was recently in the possession of Bernard Quaritch, Bookseller, Piccadilly, and in his catalogue it is thus described:—

" Holland's Leaguer, or a Historical discourse of the life and actions of Dona Britanica Hollandia, the Arch-Mistris of the wicked women of Eutopia, wherein is detected the notorious sinne of Pandarisme, and the execrable life of the luxurious Impudent, *with the rare frontispiece of the celebrated brothel, the last line of the metrical inscription being, as usual, cut into, fine copy in morocco extra, blind tooled, gilt edges. Sm. 4to, printed by A. M. for Richard Barnes*, 1632, £7, 15s."

Geneste in his quaint precis of the plot thus notes:— " The Lord Philautus is self-conceited to the last degree, he is encouraged in his folly by Ardelio, who is his Steward and parasite. Philautus is brought to his sober senses by Faustina. She turns out to be his sister. The bulk of the play consists of an under-plot with comic characters: the 4th act passes chiefly before a brothel, which is repeatedly called the Leaguer, and sometimes a castle or fort. Trimalchio and Capritio (two Gulls) with the Tutor of the latter, and Ardelio, are taken up by a pretended constable and watchman, as they are coming from the Leaguer."

The word "Leaguer," used to signify a brothel, occurs more than once in "the Knave in grain new vampt," a comedy by J. D. Acted at the Fortune playhouse, 1640.

In Glapthorne's comedy "the Hollander," is this passage :—

"Have you not constant
She souldiers in your citadelle? none such
Had Holland's Leaguer; Lambeth Marsh is held
A nunry to your Colledge."

Of the actors who personated the several characters in this play nothing is known, in so far as the Editors have been able to trace.

TO THE READER.

Courteous Reader, for so I presume thou art,—if otherwise, thou losest the title of being styled ingenious, for there are none but favour learning if they so much as pretend to it, but I hope I need make no apology, either to gain thy favour or to credit the work, it has so often passed with approbation, that I have hopes it will continue it. If there be any so supercilious to condemn it before they read it, let them rest content with the title, and not enter into the Theatre, unless they intend to behold the florales. However my Muse has descended to this subject, let men esteem of her only as a reprover, not an interpreter of wickedness: *Ocultare peccantis promulgare ludentis est.*

Aristippus, being compelled to dance in purple against the dignity of a philosopher, made an excuse that the baits of sin had no power on a good nature; and Plato, having composed wanton verses, affirmed that the more plain they were the more honest; and your former writers in their accurate discovery of vice, have mingled their precepts of wisdom. If thou shalt accept this as it was simply meant, the applause it has obtained shall not so much crown it as thy acceptation.

SHACKERLEY MARMYON.

DRAMATIS PERSONÆ.

PHILAUTUS,	*a Lord enamoured of himself,*	William Browne.
ARDELIO,	*his parasite,*	Ellis Worth.
TRIMALCHIO,	*a humorous gallant,*	Andrew Keyne.
AGURTES,	*an Impostor,*	Matthew Smith.
AUTOLICUS,	*his disciple,*	James Sneller.
CAPRITIO,	*a young Novice.*	Henry Gradwell.
MISCELLANIO,	*his Tutor.*	Thomas Bond.
SNARL,	*friends to Philautus,*	Richard Fowler.
FIDELIO,		Edward May.
JEFFRY,	*tenant to Philautus,*	Robert Hunt.
TRIPHŒNA,	*wife to Philautus.*	Robert Stratford.
FAUSTINA,	*sister to Philautus.*	Richard Godwin.
MILLESCENT,	*daugher to Agurtes.*	John Wright.
MARGERY,	*her maid,*	Richard Fouch.
QUARTILLA,	*gentlewoman to Triphœna,*	Arthur Savill.
BAWD,		Samuel Mannery.

Two Whores. Pandar. Officers,

PROLOGUE.

Gentle spectators, that, with graceful eye,
Come to behold the Muse's colony,
New planted in this soil: forsook of late
By the inhabitants, since made fortunate
By more propitious stars; though on each hand
To overtop us two great Laurels stand:
The one, when she shall please to spread her train,
The vastness of the globe cannot contain:
Th' other so high, the Phœnix does aspire
To build in, and takes new life from the fire
Bright poesy creates; yet we partake
The influence they boast of, which does make
Our bayes to flourish, and the leaves to spring,
That on our branches now new poets sing:
And when with joy he shall see this resort,
Phœbus shall not disdain to styl't his Court.

ACT. I. SCENE I.

FIDELIO, SNARL.

Fid. What, Snarl, my dear Democritus, how is't?
You are a Courtier grown, I hear.
Snar. No sir;
That's too deep a mystery for me to profess.
I spend my own revenues, only I have
An itching humour to see fashions.
   Fid. And what have you observ'd since you came hither?
   Snar. Why, they do hold here the same maxim still:
That to dissemble is the way to live.
But promotion hangs all upon one chain,
And that's of gold; he that intends to climb
Must get up by the links; and those are tied
Together with the thread of my Lord's favour.
   Fid. So, sir?
   Snar. And all desire to live long and healthy:
But ambition and luxury will not permit it.
   Fid. I hope you do not share in their desires?
   Snar. There is other preposterous dealing too;
For nature cannot find herself amongst them,
There's such effeminacy in both sexes,
They cannot be distinguished asunder.
And for your times and seasons of all ages;
Your best astrologer cannot discern them,
Not spring from autumn; you shall have a lady,

Whose cheek is like a screw, and every wrinkle
Would look like a furrow, yet with a garnish
Is so filled up and plaister'd that it looks
As fresh as a new painted tavern, only—
   Fid. Hold there! you'll run yourself out of breath else.
And now resolve me of the Lord Philautus:
Is all that true that is reported of him?
   Snar. Who, he? the most besotted on his beauty;
He studies nothing but to court himself:
No musick but the harmony of his limbs,
No work of art but his own symmetry
Allures his sense to admiration,
And then he comes forth so bath'd in perfumes,
Had you no sense to guide you but your nose,
You'd think him a musk-cat, he smells as rank
As th' extreme unction of two funerals.
   Fid. My sense will ne'er be able to endure him.
   Snar. Such men as smell so, I suspect their savour.
   Fid. Is none his friend to tell him of his faults?
   Snar. There want not some that seek to flatter him,
For great men's vices are esteem'd as virtues.
   Fid. O, they are still in fashion! in them
A wry neck is a comely precedent:
Disorder, disagreement in their lives
And manners is thought regular, their actions
Are still authentic, if it be received;
To be illiterate is a point of state.
   Snar. But the worst thing which I dislike in him,
Which he does more by words than action:
He gives out that the ladies dote upon him,
And that he can command them at his pleasure,
And swears there's scarce an honest woman.
   Fid. How?
   Snar. It is not well to say so, but, by this light,

I am of his mind too.
  Fid. You are deceived,
There are a thousand chaste.
  Snar. There was an age
When Juno was a maid, and Jove had no beard,
When miserable Atlas was not oppressed
With such a sort of deities, and each
Dined by himself: before ushers and pages
Swarmed so, and banquets, and your masques
    came up
Riding in coaches, visiting, and titles,
So many plays, and Puritan preachings,
That women might be chaste: now 'tis impossible.
Now should I find such a prodigious faith,
I'd honour't with a sacrifice.
  Fid. 'Tis ill
To be incredulous, when charity
Exacts your belief: but let that pass!
What will you say, if I find out a means
To cure him of his folly?
  Snar. Then I pronounce
The destruction of bedlam, and all mad folks
Shall be thy patients.
  Fid. Nay, I'll do it,
I'll make him in love and do it!
  Sna. That's a cure
Worse than any disease. I can as soon
Believe a fire may be extinct with oil,
Or a fever cooled with drinking of sack.
  Fid. Suspend your judgement, till I confirm you.
  Snar. No more! stand by, here comes the parasite.
That is Narcissus and this is his echo.
  Fid. What is he?
  Snar. One that feeds all men's humours that feed
    him,
Can apprehend their jests before they speak them,
And with a forced laughter play the midwife

To bring them forth, and carries still in store
A plaudit when they break wind, or urine.
He fits his master right, although he ne'er
Took measure of him, and though he has not been
Far from home yet will lie like a traveller.
He'll rather vex you with officiousness
Than you shall pass unsaluted : his business
Is only to be busy, and his tongue's still walking,
Though himself be one of the worst moveables :
A confus'd lump leavened with knavery.
Stand by a little, and let's hear his discourse !

Act I. Scene II.

Ardelio, Jeffry, Fidelio, *and* Snarl.

Ard. Jeffry, come hither !
Jef. Sir, I wait upon you.
Ard. Jeffry, you know that I have ever been
Indulgent to your knaveries.
  Jef. I thank your worship, you have ever been
    my friend.
Ard. Winked at your faults.
Jef. True.
Ard, And the reason is,
Because I still am welcome to thy wife.
  Jef. Your worship may be welcome there at all
    times.
Ard. Honest Jeffry, thou shalt lose nothing by it,
You know my authority in the house : my Lord
Puts all the care into my hands, has left me
The managing of his estate, because
I know the way to humour him.
  Jef. That is an evident token of your worship's
    wisdom.
Ard. And none of them have any place or being,
Without my suffrance.

Jef. Sir, you are of power to disperse us like
   atoms.
Ard. Therefore I expect the reverence is due
   unto my place.
Jef. And reason good.
Ard. Well, for thy honest care,
I mean to substitute thee under me
In all inferior matters, for I mean
To take my ease, and pamper up my genius
As well as he.   Only for entertainment,
Or anything belongs unto the kitchen,
Let me alone.
   Jef. Yes, sir, your providence
Has shewed itself sufficiently that way.
   Ard. I'll take the air in his coach, eat of the
   best,
And for my private drinking I will have
My choice of wines, fill'd out of vessels whose age
Has worn their countries name out, and their own,
Like some unthankful hospital or college,
That has forgot the founder.
   Snu. To what purpose,
I wonder, should nature create this fellow?
He is good for nothing else, but to maintain
The mutiny of the paunch against the members;
Keep him from his whore, and his sack, and you
Detain him from his centre.
   Ard. By the way,
I will acquaint thee with a secret, Jeffry.
   Jef. What's that, sir?
   Ard. I do love a pretty wench well.
   Jef. 'Tis the only gentle humour that is extant.
   Ard. I will not leave my recreation that way
For a whole empire! 'tis my *summum bonum*,
My sole felicity, tickles my conceit.
But, not a word.
   Jef. Not I, by any means, sir!

Ard. And for this cause, I mean t' apply my-
self
Wholly to my venery. I feel this heat
Renews my blood and makes me younger for it.
And thou shalt keep one for me at thy house.
   Jef. Where! at my house?
   Ard. Ay, there! a heavy burden
Of fleshly desires daily grows upon me
And ease works on my nature; once a week
When I am ballasted with wine and lust,
I'll sail to my Canaries.
   Jef. And unlade there.
   Ard. Wilt keep her for me and let none come
near her?
   Jef. I have had such favour at your worship's
hands,
That should good fortune come in human shape
To tempt your mistress, I'd not let her in.
   Ard. I'll procure thee the lease of thy house free,
And when I have done, I'll see it sha'nt stand
empty.
Hast thou any good rooms for stowage there?
   Jef. Spare rooms enough, sir; why do you ask?
   Ard. Because I will convey away some house-
hold stuff.
That's not amiss?
   Jef. No, sir!
   Ard. 'Tis quite against my nature to see any
vacuum,
Besides, 'tis not an age to be honest in.
   Jef. That's the highway to poverty.
   Ard. I mean to make the benefit of my place
therefore,
And when I have done I'd fain see all your artists,
Your politicians with their instruments
And plummets of wit, sound the depth of me.
   Jef. It lyes not in the reach of man to fathom it.

Ard. Were I set in a place of Justice now,
They would admire me, how I should become it:
Cough on the bench with state, sit in my nightcap,
Stroke out an apophthem out of my beard,
Frame a grave city face, jeer at offenders,
Cry out upon the vices of the times,
O *tempores, O morums!*
 Sna. How the rank rascal
Is over-grown with flesh and villany!
 Ard. This getting of money is a mystery,
Is to be learned before a man's alphabet,
No matter how, 'tis supposed he that has it
Is wise and virtuous, though he be obscure,
A fugitive, and perjur'd, anything,
He and his cause shall neither want for friends.
He is the chick of the white hen, old Fortune:
What e'er he treads upon shall be a rose,
He shall be invited to his capon and custard,
Ride to the Sheriffs a feasting on his foot-cloth,
Possess the highest room, have the first carving,
With please you eat of this or that, my noble,
My right worshipful brother? Your rich men
Shall strive to put their sons to be his pages,
And their wives to be his concubines.
 Jef. Shall marry young ones a purpose for him.
 Sna. Very likely.
 Ard. No more, be gone! I hear my Lord a coming.
I'll send thee my wench; mark me, keep her close!
 Jef. Believe me, not a breath of air comes near her,
But what steals in at the window.
 Ard. 'Tis well said.
 Jef. But stay, sir, will she not be too great a charge
To keep her to yourself? What if you hired her
By the month as your factors do beyond sea,
And when she is grown old and leaky, sir,

Mend her i'th dock and fraught her o'er for Holland.

Ard. Ay, o'er the water, 'twas well thought upon,
I think an she were trimmed up, she would serve
At last for such a voyage well enough.
What wilt thou say, when I have done with her,
If I do make thee master of my bottom ?

Jef. Who, me ? The devil shall be the pilot first,
Ere I come near their quicksands, their base roads :
They have a dangerous quay to come into.

Ard. What e'er the key be, still the door's kept fast.

Jef. As strict as an alderman's at dinner time.
Ay, and the way to hell is grown so narrow,
A man's in danger to pass o'er, for if
We reel beside the bridge, straight we shall fall
Into a lake that will foully dight * us,
Darker and deeper than Styx or Cocytus.

Ard. Well rhymed, Jeffry ! this knave will come in time,
By being often in my company,
And gleaning but the refuse of my speech,
T' arrive at some proportion of wit.
But, to avoid suspicion, be gone !   [*Exit Jeffry.*
Now would I see the man that should affront me.
My Lord will straight be here, I'll entertain him,
And talk as superciliously, and walk
As stately as the Warden of a college,
Until I have made a right pupil of him.

ACT I. SCENE III.

SNARL, FIDELIO, *and* ARDELIO.

Sna. How now, Ardelio ! what ? so melancholy ?

Ard. Faith, all this day I have been so employed
With setting things in order, and provisions,

---

* Dirty us.—"Dight," in Scotch, means to wipe down.

I can compare my pains to nothing less
Than a Lord General's.
 Sna.   Why, what's the matter?
 Ard. Things must be ordered, and there's nothing
Done unless I oversee it; my industry
Must marshall the dishes, put the stools in rank,
See the wood set upon the carriages,
Sharpen the knives: all these witness my care,
The very shining of the candlesticks
Acknowledge my directions.
 Snar.   'Tis much!
The strange activity that some men have
To dispatch business.
 Ard. Why, sir, did you never
Hear how Apelles pictured Homer spewing,
And all the poets gaping to receive it?
 Snar. Yes, and what then?
 Ard.   In the same manner do I,
Upon the hushers, the clarks, and the butlers,
The cooks, and other officers, 'mongst whom
I find to be a drought of understanding,
Shower down the dregs of my counsel.
 Snar. They are like to be well edified.
 Ard. Here comes my Lord! make room for my
  Lord's Grace!

Act I. Scene IV.

PHILAUTUS, TRIPHŒNA, TRIMALCHIO, ARDELIO,
  SNARL, FIDELIO.

 Ard. God save your Honour! may your flourish-
  ing youth
Enjoy an everlasting spring of beauty,
And know no autumn.
 Phil. Thanks, good Ardelio!
Your wishes have effect: this is the tree

Under whose shadow Flora builds her bower,
And on whose branches hangs such tempting fruit,
Would draw fair Atalanta from her course;
An altar on which Queens should sacrifice
Their scorned loves. Nature will scarce believe
It is her own invention, and repines
She has no way to be incestuous.

 Triph. Mr Trimalchio, I am sick to hear him,
I can't abide these repetitions,
And tedious encomiums of himself!
Let you and I walk a turn in the garden.

 Trim. You are the only garden of my delight,
And I your dear Adonis, honoured lady.

       [*Exeunt Trimalchio, Triphœna.*

 Phil. Ardelio, tell me how this suit becomes me!

 Ard. Exactly well, sir, without controversy,
And you wear it as neatly.

 Phil. Nay, I have
A reasonable good tailor: I hope he has not
Surveyed me so long but he knows my dimensions.
I think I may venture i' th' presence with it.

 Ard. I' th' presence? Ay, and love were th' presence,
You'd thrust Ganymede out of his office.

 Phil. What think you, gentlemen?

 Fid. We all do wish,
Your beauty or your vanity were less,
For, by this means, that which would else commend
 you
Proves your disgrace: you take the edge of praise off
Is due to you by too much whetting it.

 Phil. I should prove too injurious to myself,
Should I pass over, with a slight regard,
This building nature has solemnised
With such magnificence, to which I owe
The loves of ladies, and their daily presents,
Their hourly solicitations with letters,

Their entertainments when I come, their plots
They lay to view me, which, should I recount,
'Twould puzzel my arithmetic, and to answer
Their unjust desires would ask the labours
Of some ten stallions.
    Ard. And make all jades of them?
    Fid. You are the centre of all women's love then?
    Phil. 'Tis true I have a strange attractive power
Over your females; did you never hear of
Three Goddesses that strove on Ida hill,
Naked before a shepherd, for a ball
With an inscription " let the fairest have it?"
    Fid. And what of those?
    Phil. Bring them all three before me!
If I surprise them not all at first dash,
If they fall not together by the ears for me,
Nay, if they run not mad, and follow me
As if they were drunk with a love potion,
Ne'er trust a prognosticator again.
    Snar. But how if you should chance to meet
        Diana?
Take heed of her, it is a testy girl,
A profest virgin.
    Phil. 'Tis my ambition
To meet with her, to bath my limbs with her
In the same well, shoot in her bow, dance with her,
And get the foremost of her troupe with child,
And turn the rape on Jupiter.
    Snar. Fine, y' faith!
    Fid. It seems that you are of opinion
There is no text of womankind so holy,
But may be corrupted, though a Deity.
    Phil. Ardelio, tell me what thou dost think of them.
    Ard. Who, I? hang me should I be questioned
Now for my faith concerning articles
Of women's chastity, I should be burnt
For a rank heretic. I believe none of them.

Fid. But I think otherwise; and can justify it.
What, if I bring you now unto a beauty
As glorious as the sun, but in desire
Cold as the middle region of the air,
And free from all reflection of lust?
   Phil. But shall I speak with her, and tempt her
     to it?
   Fid. You shall converse with her, and she shall feed
Your sense with such discoursive influence,
And a voice sweeter than the Lydian tunes,
Jove would bow down his ear to, yet her blood
Shall run as cold as julips through her veins;
The spring tide of her youth shall swell with more
Delights than there be drops in April, yet she
As chaste as Salmacis, amidst the streams.*
Her eye shall sparkle like the diamond,
And be as pure, her kisses soft and melting
As the south wind, but undefil'd as Heaven:
And you shall feel the elemental fire
Of her unspotted love, and grieve, and swear
She is so celestial and divine a creature,
That's only hot in her effect, not nature.
   Phil. Why such a one would I converse withall;
The conquest will be greater. Shall I see her?
   Fid. I'll bring you to her.
   Ard. He has a strong belief.
I have no such confidence. She may be Lucrece
And he a foolish Colatine † to brag of her;
But most of them in playing fast and loose
Will cheat an oracle. I have a creature
Before these Courtiers lick their lips at her
I'll trust a wanton haggard ‡ in the wind.
This lady is his sister and my mistress,

---

* A fountain of Caria, near Halicarnassus, which rendered effeminate all those who drank of its waters.
† Tarquin.
‡ A wild-hawk—metaphorically, a loose woman.

Yet both unknown to him—some few years since,
Her father jealous of my love, because
I was a gentleman of no great fortune,
Sent her away, and charged her by an oath
To marry none till seven years were expired,
Six parts of which are gone, yet she remains
Constant to what she promised, though his death
Has partly quit her. To live in her sight
And not enjoy her is a heavenly torment,
But unsufferable, I must live apart
Till the prefixed minute be expired.
In the meantime I'll work by some good means,
To win his love, and draw him from his folly.
But first by him I'll try her constancy:
I must prepare her for his entertainment,
Because she will admit no company,
Nor will be known to any but myself.
Come sir, let's go! by that which shall ensue,
You shall affirm what I relate is true.

Act I. Scene V.

Agurtes, Autolicus.

Agu. 'Tis a dull age this! Fame casts not her eyes
On men of worth: Captains and commanders,
Victorious abroad, are vanquished at home
With poverty and disgrace; they look as bad
As Brutus, when he met his evil genius:
Worse than they had been frighted from the ruins
Of Isis' temple; and you, sir, for your part,
That have been brought up under me at my elbow,
A daily witness unto all my projects,
That might have got experience enough
To cozen a whole State if they had trusted you,
Now to be wanting to yourself, worn out,
No name or title but on posts and trenchers,
And doors scored with a coal, instead of chalk.

Are my hopes come to this?
    Aut. What should I do?
I have no thriving way to lie and flatter,
Nor have I such dexterity of wit
As you have, blest be heaven! to convert
Black into white.
    Agu. Nay, if you have no will
Nor power to free yourself, you must resolve
To stick in the dirt still.
    Aut. Nor can I promise
The death of any by the stars. I have
No rich man's funeral to solemnise,
That left a gilt ring for my legacy,
And his old velvet jerkin to survive him.
I have no secret boils within my breast,
For which I am feared, no suit in law to follow,
No accusation 'gainst a great man,
No house to let to farm, no tender wife
To prostitute, or skill to corrupt others,
And sleep amidst their wanton dialogues.
    Agu. I cry you mercy! you would fain be styled
An honest politic fool, see all men's turns
Served but your own; so leave off to be good.
For what is now accounted to be good?
Take a good lawyer or a good attorney,
A citizen that's a good chapman:
In a good sense what are they? I would know
Why a good gamester, or a good courtier?
Is't for their honest dealing? Take a good poet,
And if he write not bawdy lines and raptures,
I'll not give a pin for him.
    Aut. Would you have me
Act the plagiary and seek preferment,
To be the drunken bard of some black stews
And think my destiny well satisfied,
When my shame feeds me, and at length expect
A legacy bequeathed me from some Bawd,

In lieu of my old service, or according
To the proportion of my Hernia?
 Agu. Well, I perceive that I must once more take
  you
To my protection, which if I do
I'll teach you better rules. You shall no more
Commit your misery to loose papers,
Nor court my Lord with panegyrics, nor make
Strange anagrams of my Lady. You shall not need
To deal for stale commodities, nor yet
Send forth your privy bills without a seal
To free you from your lodging, where you have
Lain in most part of the vacation.
You shall no longer run in score with your hostess
For brown toasts and tobacco, but you shall leave
Your open standings at the ends of lanes,
Or your close coverts in tobacco shops,
Where you give strict attendance like a sergeant,
Until some antedated country cloak
Pass by, whom you most impudently may
Assault to borrow twelvepence; but bear up
Stiffly and with the best.
 Aut. How shall that be done?
 Agu. We will not call Tiresias* from the dead
To show us how, as he did once Ulysses.
You must resolve to learn virtue from others,
Fortune from me.
 Aut. For that I'll make no scruple.
 Agu. I have a bird i'th' wind, I'll fly thee on him:
He shall be thy adventure, thy first quarry.
 Aut. What's he?
 Agu. A golden one that drops his feathers,
That has received his patrimony, gives money
For all acquaintance. When he first came up,
His only search was for prime curtezans
And those he entertained for mistresses,

* A blind soothsayer of Thebes.

Only sometimes to drink a health to them.
The ladies too would use him for a cooler,
But they suspect his silence, yet he uses
Their names and titles as familiarly,
As he had bought them. Thou shalt hook him in
And crack him like a nut.
    Aut. Is he not the son
To the rich usurer that died so lately?
    Agu. The same, that heaped up money by the bushel;
And now this studies how to scatter it.
His father walks to see what becomes of it,
And that's his torment after death.
    Aut. When shall I see him?
    Agu. He is to meet me here within this hour,
Then take you an occasion to pass by,
And I will whisper to him, privately,
And praise thee, beyond Pyrrhus or Hannibal.
You must talk and look big, 'twill be the grace on't.
    Aut. What, shall I turn a roarer?
    Agu. Anything,
Broker or pandar, cheater or lifter,
And steal like a Lacædemonian.
Observe what I do, and fill up the scene.

            Enter BOY.

How now! What news?
    Boy. Sir, there's some five or six without to speak with you.
    Agu. How! five or six?
    Boy. Yes, sir, and they pretend
Great business.
    Agu. What manner of men are they?
    Boy. They look like pictures of antiquity,
And their cloaks seem to have bin the coverings
Of some old monuments.
    Agu. They are my Gibeonites,

Are come to traffic with me? Some design
Is now on foot, and this is our Exchange time.
These are my old projectors, and they make me
The superintendent of their business.
But still they shoot two or three bows too short,
For want of money and adventurers.
They have as many demurrers as the Chancery,
And hatch more strange imaginations
Than any dreaming philosopher: one of them
Will undertake the making of bay salt
For a penny a bushel to serve the State.
Another dreams of building water-works,
Drying of fens and marshes, like the Dutchmen.
Another strives to raise his fortunes from
Decayed bridges, and would exact a tribute
From ale-houses and sign-posts; some there are
Would make a thorowfare for the whole kingdom,
And office, where nature should give account
For all she took and sent into the world.
But they were born in an unlucky hour,
For some unfortunate mischance or other
Still come athwart them : well I must into them
And feast them with new hopes, 'twill be good sport
To hear how they dispute it *pro* and *con.*
In the meantime, Autolicus, prepare
To meet my Courtier.
    Aut. I have my cue, sir.

Act II. Scene I.
Agurtes, Trimalchio.

Agu. 'Tis near about the time he promised.
  Trim. Boy,
Go and dispatch those letters presently!
Return my service to the Lady Lautus,
And carry back her watch, and diamond.

Ask if the duchess has been there to-day,
And if you chance to see the Lord, her brother,
Tell him I'll meet him at the Embassador's.
  Boy. I shall, sir.
  Aug. What! M. Trimalchio?
You are punctual to your hour.
  Trim. Sir, for your sake
I can dispense with my occasions.
You'll not imagine what a heavy stir,
I had to come to-day.
  Agu. Why, what's the matter?
  Trim. No less than seven coaches to attend me—
To fetch me *nolens volens.*
  Agu. Pray from whom?
  Trim. The Lord Philautus, and some minor nobles,
Whose names I am loth should clog my memory.
They strove for me as the seven Grecian cities
Were said to wrangle about the blind poet.
  Agu. How got you rid of them?
  Trim. I had the grace
To go with none of them; made an excuse
T' avoid their troublesome visitations.
  Agu. How do they relish your neglect of them?
  Trim. I know not, yet I still abuse them all.
  Agu. How? not abuse them?
  Trim. I mean laugh at them.
Some passages, some sprinkling of my wit,—
No otherwise for which you little think
How I am feared amongst them, how the ladies
Are took with my conceits, how they admire
My wit and judgment, trust me with their secrets
Beyond their painter, or apothecary.
I'll tell you in a word, but 'twill perplex you:
I am their Lasanophorus.*

  * Λάσανον. Cloaca, sella familiaris: locus aut vas ad deponendum ventris onus, *apud Hesych. et Poll.* i. 10. cap. 9.

Agu. Their piss-pot carrier.
Trim. Their winged Mercury, to be employed
On messages, and, for my company,
They swear it is the element they move in.
Agu. You are happy, Signiour Trimalchio.
Trim. I thank my fates, they have not altogether
Envied me. The fruition of such gifts
Are worth the taking notice of, besides
Some special helps of our own industry.
I lately studied the Economics.
Agu. What's that?
Trim. The ordering of my family.
I have reduced it to a certain method.
Agu. As how?
Trim. I'll tell you. Since my father's death
First thing I did I cashiered his old servants,
And, to avoid confusion and expense,
I left the country to revel it here,
I' th' view of the world, and in the sight of
    beauties;
And have confined myself unto some certain
Appendices, some necessary implements,
My single page, my groom, my coach, my foot-boy,
And my two penitentiary whores.
Agu. And these
Are all your inventory?
Trim. Stay, who comes here?

Enter AUTOLICUS.

Agu. O, 'tis Autolicus!
My noble friend and brother of the sword.
His stomach and his blade are of one temper,
Of equal edge, and will eat flesh alike.
He walks there melancholy; to shew that worth
Can pass unregarded, be proud to know him!
He is the shrewdest pated fellow breathing,
The only engineer in Christendom,

Will blow you up a carak like a squib,
And row under water: th' Emperor.
And Spinola by secret intelligence
Have laid out for him any time this ten years,
And twice he has escaped them by a trick.
He is beyond Dædalus, or Archimedes,
But lies concealed like a seminary,
For fear the state should take notice of him.
Machavill for policy was a dunce to him,
And had he lived in Mahomet's days he had been
His only counsellor for the Alcoran!
He is newly come from Holland:

   Trim. My body
Is all of an itch to be acquainted with him;
Pray speak to him for me.

   Agu. Nay more; he is able
To make you a perfect statesman in a month,
Able to be employed beyond the line.

   Trim. You will for ever thrall me to your service.

   Aug. Heark ye, Autolicus! here's a gentleman,
Who though he be the Phœbus of the court,
So absolute in himself, that the desires
Of all men tend towards him and has power
Enough to wander in the Zodiac
Of his own worth, yet craves your acquaintance.

   Aut. I take it, Senior Trimalchio.

   Trim. Do you know me then?

   Aug. By an instinct, sir, men of Quality
Cannot lie hid.

   Trim. Indeed, my father's name
Was Malchio, for my three additions
Of valour, wit, and honour, 'tis enlarg'd
To Mr Trimalchio: this is wonderful.

   Agu. Alas, 'tis nothing, sir, if you knew all.
No ambuscado of the enemy,
No treachery, or plot, but he foresees it.
He was the first brought o'er the mystery

Of building sconces here in England,—a trade
That many live upon.
   Trim. A good commonwealth's man.
   Agu. But this is certain, once in a strait leaguer
When they were close besieged, their ammunition
And victuals most part spent, he found a means
To yield the town on composition.
   Trim. Stand bye a while! I must reward his virtues.
Sir, will you please t'inlarge your disposition,
T'accept a courtesy to bind me to you.
   Aut. I do not use to sell my liberty,
But that I see your face promise true bounty.
   Trim. Have you skill in the face, sir?
   Aut. I were not fit else to be styl'd traveller.
   Trim. How do you find my looks inclin'd to State?
   Aut. Sir, you have won me to power out of my thoughts,
And I must tell you plain they are too loose,
Too scattered to pretend such an acumen,
Too much displayed, and smooth. You must ha' quirks
And strange meanders in your face t'express
A State subtilty. I'll make it plain
Hereafter by demonstration in the optics.
   Trim. Who would have lost the opportunity
Of getting such a friend? Came you from Holland?
   Aut. Yes, very lately.
   Trim. Pray what news from Holland?
   Aut. Holland's beleagured!
   Trim. What, all Holland beleaguered?
   Aut. And will hold out as long as Busse or Boloign,
They have their moat and drawbridge. I have given them
Besides a draught of a fortification,

Will hold them play this twelvemonth for they keep
Their passage open, and want no supplies,
For whosoever comes, they pay them soundly.
The French have made many onslaughts upon them
And still been foil'd.

   Trim. Is there such hot service there?

   Aut. Crossing the lines a bath to it! I had like
Been scorcht to death by the intemperature
Of the climate, 'tis the only Zona Torrida
In the whole microcosm of man or woman,
If you shall once come near the height of it
'Twill melt you like lightning.

   Trim. Shall's build a sconce there?

   Aut. If you please.

   Trim. Agreed! Who is the leader of these factious troops?

   Aut. A woman!

   Trim. How! a woman?
Now by this hand an Amazonian,
A Tomarus,* a right Penthisile.†
I'll view this leaguer by this light, and swim
Like a Leander o'er the Hellespont
That shall divide me from these heroines.

   Agu. 'Tis well resolved! you are not married, sir?

   Trim. No, pox! I know them too well for that!
I can use them for recreation or so.

   Agu. What think you of a rich widow?

   Trim. I'll none of them!
They are like old clothes that have been worn.

   Agu. I like you, that you care not for such relics;
But yet I think I have a match will fit you.
An orphan, a young heir that has some thousands,
Besides her possibilities, if you
Can win her she is at her own disposing.

   * Tmarus. A soldier, in Virgil.
   † Penthesilea, an amazonian queen, slain by Achilles, or, as some say, by Pyrrhus.—*Virg. Æn.* i. 495.

There's one that knows her.
    Trim. By instinct, it may be.
    Aut. But for the pattern of true modesty,
'Tis seldom known, riches and virtue meet
In such a mixture.
    Trim. Will you bring me to her?
    Agu. Ay, and perhaps persuade her to't, you know
    not.
Let us secure this business first of all,
And then we'll meet at the Leaguer.
    Aut. 'Tis good counsel.
    Trim. And I'll confirm
All with a jointure.
    Agu. Well, 'tis done.
I'll tell you more of her; she is one
Whose tender years have not yet aspired
The height of wickedness, but may be brought
To commit venery in her own language,
And be content with one man; has not robbed
Young boys of their voices, knows not her flights
And doubles, nor her labyrinths, through which
The Minotaur, her husband, shall ne'er track her,
Cannot indite with art nor give a censure
Upon the lines are sent her, has no agents,
No factors, pensioners, or champions,
Nor has her tears fixed in their station,
To flow at her command, and so confirm
Her perjury; not large in her expense, nor one
That when she is dressed will call a conventicle
Of young and old to pass their judgments on her,
As if her life were guaged upon the matter.
Nor carries an Ephemerides about with her,
To which she ascribes your forked destiny;
Nor is her body crazy, neither takes she
Physic for state, nor will rise up at midnight
To eat her oysters, and drink wine till lust
Dance in her veins, and till the house turns round

And she discern not 'twixt her head and tail;
Nor holdeth strange intelligence abroad
To furnish her discourse with, neither takes she
Her journey once a year to th' Bath, nor is
So learned as to judge betwixt your poets
Which of them writes best and fluent, nor yet
Is grown an antiquary, to decide
Matters in heraldry; she has no fucus
To catch your lips like birdlime, nor yet uses
Restoratives more than the help of nature.
I'll speak the noblest words I can, of you;
So many women on a mere report
Do fall in love with men before they see them.

 Trim. Nay, when I see her I am sure of her.
I have a little haste, I am to meet
A Countess at th' Exchange within this hour;
Besides I have a catalogue of business,
If I could think on't. So I take my leave.
Farewell, gentlemen.

 Aut. Farewell, sir!

 Agu. Farewell, sweet Monsieur Coxcomb!
This wench I so commended is my daughter,
And if my skill not fails me, her I'll make
A stale, to take this courtier in a freak.

Act II. Scene II.

Fidelio, Faustina.

 Fid. Is there no means t'absolve you of your oath?
The blame on me, let the bright day no longer
Envy the darkness that conceals such beauty.
You are no votary, and yet force your youth
To such a strict and solitary life,
Which others, bound by vow, cannot perform.
I wonder at the temper of your blood,

So differing from your sex, when your old women
Do burn with lustful thoughts as with a fever,
Yet you go on in the old track of virtue,
Now over-grown with seeds of vice.
  Fau. Sweet, hear me!
It is a penance that I live reserved,
Because my love to you was made abortive;
But when due time shall perfect in her womb,
And bring it forth anew unto the birth,
I will surrender up myself and it
To your dispose. Let it suffice the while,
I am no haunter of your public meetings,
No entertainer nor no visitor;
Nor did I ever trust my wand'ring eyes
To view the glittering vanity of the world,
Nor ever yet did sit a guilty witness
To a lascivious and untuned discourse,
Sounding to their fantastic actions.
  Fid. But I must beg one favour at your hands,
And suffer no repulse.
  Fau. What is't?
  Fid.   It may offend you.
  Fau.   It shall not.
  Fid. Then know that I have boasted of your
    beauty;
Nay more, exposed thy virtues to the trial.
  Fau. You have not prostituted them on stalls,
To have the vulgar fingers sweat upon them,
As they do use upon your plays and pamphlets?
  Fid. I am engaged to bring a Lord to see you.
  Fau. A Lord?
  Fid. And you must use all art for his content,
With music, songs, and dancing, such as are
The stirrers of hot apetites.
  Fau. Prophane
And idle wretch, to cast away thy hopes
Upon a pandarly profession!

Or didst thou think that I could be corrupted
To personate a strumpet's dalliance?
I grieve for thee. Begone! henceforth I'll live
Immured for ever, as an anchorist,
From him and thee, since thou hast wrong'd my love.
 Fid. Mistake me not, the difference 'twixt the poles
Is not so great as betwixt me and baseness:
Nor is't a sinister intent to make
Your favours stale and common as a drug,
Which are so dear to me, that both the Indies
Are not of equal value to engross,
But for a noble and peculiar end.
 Fau. This seems to me a paradox.
 Fid.   'Tis true.
 Fau. If it be so, 'tis granted! speak it free.
 Fid. Then if it please you to grant relief
To my desires, take them in brief;
I would have you first express
All the skill that comeliness
Can invent, to make you seem
Fair and pleasant, as love's Queen,
When she Anchises came to kiss
On the banks of Simois.
Call the graces, and suborn
Them thy beauty to adorn,
Thy face the table where love writes
A thousand stories of delights:
Make it all over, smooth and plain,
But see you shadow it with disdain,
Weave a net out of thy hair,
A subtle net that may ensnare
Such fond souls as shall aspire
To come near the holy fire
Of thine eyes, which were of late
By Cupid's torch illuminate.

Use all the delusive art
That may captivate his heart.
   Fau. What's your intent in this?
   Fid. I'll have him punished!
He casts aspersions of disloyalty
On all your sex, and you shall vindicate them
When he is plunged in love irrevocable,
As conquered by thy all-subduing look;
Then you shall bind him to conditions,
As I shall first instruct you, shall redeem
Him from his folly and next clear your honour.
   Fau. Your will's a law, and shall not be withstood,
When my ill's quited with another's good.

Act II. Scene III.

Agurtes, Autolicus, Margery.

   Agu. Margery, go call your mistress!
   Aut.   What is she?
   Agu. My daughter's maid, a wench fit for the purpose,
Cunning as a whore. Besides, I have provided
A bed and hangings, and a casting bottle,*
And once a day a doctor to visit her.

Enter Millescent.

Millescent, come hither! know this gentleman.
Captain, here lies our venter, this is she,
The rich Antonio's daughter, the great heir
And niece to the grand Sophies of the city;
That has been wooed and sued to by great Lords,
Aldermen's sons, and agents of all sorts.

---

* A bottle used for sprinkling perfumes, introduced about the middle of the sixteenth Century.—Also called a "casting-glass," in Ben Jonson, and Privy-purse expenses of Queen Mary.

Thus we have spoke thy praise, wench—has not seen
The man she likes yet, but her fortunes may
Ordain her to some better choice, to the making
Of some deserving man, which must needs be
Trimalchio and no other; how lik'st thou her?

   Aut. Hang me, so well, I think you may go on
In a right line, she is worthy of a better:
Few of your modern faces are so good.

   Agu. That's our comfort, she may put a good face on't.

   Mil. Let me alone, sir, to be impudent,
To laugh them out of countenance, look skirvy,
As a citizen's daughter new turned Madam.

   Marg. I warrant you, sir, my mistress and I
Have practised our liripoop* together.

   Agu. Thou must insinuate strange things into her,
Both of her virtue and nobility,
The largeness of her dowry, besides jewels,
Th' expected death of her old grandmother
That has a blessing for her, if she marry
According to her mind, keep him at distance,
Make him believe 'tis hard to have access,
And wait the happy hour, to be let in
At the back door.

   Marg. Aye, and the fore-door too.

   Aut. Thou hast a noble wit, and spirit, wench,
That never was ordained for any skinkard†
T' engender with, or mechanic citizen,
Unless it were to cuckold him; thou shalt
Be still i' th' front of any fashion,

---

* In the present instance, "liripoop" may be considered synonymous with the modern cant term, "a lark"—a piece of fun.—"Practised our liripoop"—seen life.
   "There's a girle that knows her lerripoope"
                           Lilly's Mother Bombie.

† Tapster.

And have thy several gowns and tires, take place,
It is thy own, from all the city wives
And summer birds in town, that once a year
Come up to moulter, and then go down to th'
 country
To jeer their neighbours, as they have been served.
 Agu. Nay more, if you can act it handsomely,
You'll put a period to my undertakings,
And save me all my labour of projecting,
As putting out my money on return,
From aqua pendente, or some unknown place
That has as much ado to get a room
I' th' map as a new Saint i' th' kalender.
'Twill dead all my device in making matches,
My plots of architecture and erecting
New amphitheatres, to draw the custom
From playhouses once a week, and so pull
A curse upon my head from the poor scoundrels.
'Twill hinder too the gain of courtiers,
Put on by me to beg monopolies,
To have a fixed share in the business.
Nor need I trample up and down the country,
To cheat with a Polonian, or false rings,
Nor keep a tap-house o' th' Bank side, and make
A stench worse than a brewhouse, 'mongst my
 neighbours,
Till I am grown so poor, that all my goods
Are shipt away i'th bottom of a sculler.
And then be driven t' inhabit some blind nook
I' th' suburbs, and my utmost refuge be
To keep a bawdy house, and be carted.
 Mil. Ne'er fear, sir.
 Agu. 'Tis well! speak for thyself, girl.
 Mil. If I do not, let me be turned to ashes
And they be buried in an urn so shallow,
That boys may piss into it. Let me deal
In nothing else but making sugar cakes,

Ointments and dentifrices. Let me serve
Seven years' apprenticeship, and learn nothing else.
But to preserve and candy. Let me marry
With a pedant, and have no other dowry
Than an old cast French hood. Let me live
The scorn of chambermaids, and, after all,
Turn a dry-nurse.

Aut. You shall have trophies, wenches,
Set up for you in honour of your wits,
More than Herculean pillars, to advance
Your fame to a non ultra, that whoever
Shall read your history may not attempt
To go beyond it.

Agu. Well, prepare yourselves
To entertain him!

Aut. Faith! you need not doubt them
To manage the business.

Mil. Let us alone!

Agu. We leave the charge to your discretion.

ACT II.   SCENE IV.

Enter TRIPHŒNA *and* QUARTILLA.

Quar. Madam, in troth this grief does not become you,
'Tis an ill-dressing for so good a face,
Yet you pursue it with such eagerness,
As if you were ambitiously sad.
'Tis some invincible malignity
Makes her untractable, deaf to all comfort.
What might I guess the cause of this disaster?
Her monkey and her dog are both in health,
I thank my providence! only her monkey
Is a little costive, but I'll physic him.
Sure her intelligence arrived too late
About the last new fashion, or the crime

Lies in the sempster, or it must needs be
Some other grand solecism in her tailor,
What if it prove a capital offence
Committed by the tire-woman? but I believe
Some skirvy lady put it in her head,
To practice a State melancholy, that first
Begins in an imperious revolt,
And frowning, and contempt of her own husband,
And what she might recover by the law
In case of separation, or a nullity,
Which she already has took council of:
Come, it is so?

   Tri. Nay, tell me now, Quartilla,
Can I behold the current of that love
Should flow to me with a prodigious course,
Run back to his own head, to have a husband
That should grow old in admiration
Of the rare choice he made in me, at last,
As if there were a barrenness and want
Of my perfections, dote upon himself?
I could plot against him! pri'thee, Quartilla,
How long hast thou been chaste?

   Quar. This chastity
Is quite out of date, a mere absolute thing,
Clean out of use, since I was first a maid.
Why do I say a maid? Let Juno plague me,
If I remember it, for I began
Betimes, and so progrest from less to bigger,
From boys to lads, and, as I grew in years,
I writ my venery in a larger volume.

   Tri. Where's my brother?

   Quar. With his tutor, forsooth.

   Tri. I think that dull Prometheus was asleep
When he did form him. Had he but so much
As the least spark of salt that is in me,
He would see me righted.

   Quar. He is very obtuse,

And so are many of your elder brothers.
I carried all the wit from mine. When I
Was young, I'd have looked a captain in the face,
Answered him in the dialogue, and have stood
On tiptoe to have kissed him. But for your brother,
Do not despair, good madam! what although
His breeding be a little coarse, he may be
A Lord in's time, now he has means enough!

Tri. I sent for him up hither to that purpose;
But yet I am ashamed to have him seen,
Or show him publicly.

Quar. You have provided
A tutor to instruct him, a rare man,
One that has poisoned me with eloquence,
I fear he will make my belly swell with it.

Tri. Go call the novice hither, and his tutor!
        [*Exit Quartilla.*
And now I think on't, Mr Trimalchio
Shall take him strait to Court with him, to learn
And imitate his fashions, suck from him
The quintessence of education.
He is the only man I know, and for
His face, it is the abstract of all beauty.
Nor does his voice sound mortal; I could dwell
For ever on his lip, his very speech
Would season a tragedy: nay more, there is
A natural grace in all his actions.

Act II. Scene V.

Enter Triphœna, Quartilla, Capritio, *and*
Miscellanio.

Tri. What, are you come? 'Tis well, advance
 yet forward!
We ever told you what a hateful vice
This bashfulness was counted.

Quar. You forget
The theorems we told you. Lord, how often
Shall we enforce these documents upon you?
    Cap. May not a man buy a brazen face, think you,
Among all this company?
    Quar. By no means,
Your tradesmen will not part with them; there are
Many i'th' city have such furniture,
But they do keep them for their own wearing.
    Mis. Stand bye a while, let me salute these
        ladies!
Hail to these twins of honour and of beauty.
    Quar. Sir, you transgress in your opinion,
If you consider both; alas, my beauty
Is much exhausted.
    Mis. Lady, you are deceived,
For you are amiable, or else I have
In vain so often exercised my judgment
In the distinction of faces.
    Quar. I shall
Be proud to be so seated in your favour.
    Tri. But tell me, Signiour Miscellanio,
What think you of your pupil?
    Mis. Troth, I found him
As rude as any chaos, so confus'd
I knew not which way to distinguish him.
He seemed to me, not to participate
Of any gentle nature; never, I think,
To fashion out a Mercury with such
A crooked piece of timber, was attempted
By a true traveller: but I hope in time
To rectify him, for *labor vincit omnia.*
    Tri. Does he come on well, is there any hope
He will receive his true dye, his right tincture?
    Mis. I warrant you, that I'll make him in time
A perfect cavaliero: he shall wear
His clothes as well, and smell as rank as they,

And court his mistress, and talk idly: that's
As much as can be required in a true gallant
T'approve him one: nay, more too, he shall dance
And do the half pomado,* play at gleek,†
And promise more than e'er he will perform,
And ne'er part with a penny to a tradesman
Till he has beat him for't: shall walk the streets
As gingerly as if he feared to hurt
The ground he went on, whilst his cast down eye
Holds commerce with his leg: shall utter nothing
Whate'er he thinks, yet swear't whate'er it be.
Nay more, he shall vow love to all he sees,
And damn himself to make them believe it,
Shall fawn on all men, yet let his friend perish,
For what he spends in one day on his punk
For coach-hire. These are special properties,
And must be often practised to remember,
He shall never rise till it be ten o'clock,
And so be ready against dinner-time.

 Cap. 'Slight! and my father had not been an ass,
I might have been able to have writ this down.

 Tri. Pray let me hear how he has profited.

 Mis. Salute these ladies as you were instructed.
You must conceive the coldness of his courtship
As yet points but one way; you may suppose it
To his disdainful mistress, when he shall come to
The *cape de bone speranza* of her love,
He may vary like the compass of his compliment.

 Cap. Lady, the fates have led me to your service
To know myself unworthy of your favours.
You let me so far win upon your bounty,
That what I utter in humility
May not cause my contempt, or have my love

---

 * Vaulting on a horse without the aid of stirrups.

 † A game of cards, played by three persons with forty-four cards, each hand having twelve, and eight being left for the stock. A gleek was three of the same cards in one hand together.

Shak'd off because 'tis ripe, but let me hang by
The stalk of your mercy; the remnant of whose
    life
Lies in your power.
    Mis. Your oath now to confirm it,
If she should chance to doubt or press you to it.
    Cap. That's true indeed. By the structure of
       your breasts,
And by the silken knot that ties your hair
Upon the top of your crown, I protest it.
    Quar. If he can persevere, 'tis excellent.

          Enter TRIMALCHIO.

    Trim. Where be these noble ladies?
    Tri. Sir, you are come in the most happy hour!
I was wishing for you.
    Trim. I am in haste,
And only come to see you : there's a banquet
Stands ready on the table, and the Lords
Swear they will not sit down, until I come.
    Tri. You still are in such haste when you come
       hither.
    Trim. I think I must retire myself; I am
So sued and sought to where I come, I am grown
Even weary of their loves. Last night at a masque,
When none could be admitted, I was led in
By the hand, by a great Lord, that shall be nameless,
And now this morning early, in his chamber,
A fencer would needs play with me at foils;
I hit him in three places, and disarmed him.
    Quar. Why, now my dream is out! I lay last
       night
Upon my back, and was adream'd of fighting.
    Tri. Sir, will you please to know these gentle-
       men?
My brother and his tutor.
    Trim.   I must crave pardon,

Is this your brother?
   Tri. Yes.
   Trim. I must embrace him.
I never saw a man, in all my life,
I so affected on the sudden. Sure
There's some nobility does lurk within him
That's not perspicuous to every eye:
He promises so fair, I should have known him
To be your brother, had you not told me so.
   Mis. Your method now of thanks.
   Cap. Right noble sir,
I have so often times been honoured
And so much madefied—
   Quar. That word I taught him.
   Cap. With the distilling influence of your bounty,
That I must blame myself and my hard fortune,
That has envied me the ability
To render satisfaction.
   Mis. Very well.
   Tri. Sir, you must pardon him! he is but a novice,
Newly initiated, and 'tis his fault,
That he is bashful.
   Trim. Is that all? I'll take him
To court with me, where he shall be acquainted
With pages, laundresses, and waiting-women,
Shall teach him impudence enough.
   Tri. 'Tis my desire.
   Quar. His tutor has taught him the theory,
Only he wants the practike.
   Trim. I pray you, sir,
Without offence, may I demand of you,
What do you profess?
   Mis. Why, sir, anything
Within the compass of humanity;
To speak or act, no Pythagorean
Could ever think upon so many shapes

As I will put you in; the French, the Spanish,
Or the Italian garb—not any one
But jointly all. I'll make a perfect man
Out of the shreds of them.
   Quar. Besides the riding
Of the great mare; nay, sir, his very carvings,
Even to the dissecting of a capon,
Are lectures of anatomy.
   Trim. I shall
Be proud to know him.
   Mis. Now I collect myself,
Sure I have seen you, sir, in Padua,
Or some face near like yours.
   Trim. I have indeed
Received letters of invitation
From one that's son to a Magnifico,
Who is informed that I am very like him.
   Mis. There was the mistake then.
   Trim. Sir, had I power
O'er my occasions, which now are urgent,
I would most willingly employ the time
In survey of your virtues.
   Mis. Sir, it has been
The scope I ever aimed at in my travels
To seek out and converse with such as have
With foreign observations advanced
Their natural endowments, and I thank
My stars I have been ever fortunate
To be beloved amongst them, and that you
Are one I make no question.
   Trim. Sir, you need not.
   Mis. My mind was ever larger than to be
Comprised within the limits of my country.
And I congratulate my fate, in that
I come so near the virtue of that planet
That ruled at my nativity: whose nature,
Which e'er it be, is ever to be wand'ring.

Trim. Sir, I must be abrupt, but for my promise
Unto some noble friends that do expect me,
I could not easily be drawn away
From one in whom so many several graces
Are so apparent, therefore I entreat you
Not to impute it to my lack of judgment,
Or neglect of your worth.
    Mis. By no means, sir.
Friendship is turned into an injury
When it usurps authority, conceive me,
O'er a friend's business; some other time
Shall serve to give a mutual testimony
Of love between us, and how much I honour you.
    Quar. When will you do this?
    Cap. I am practising.
    Triph. Prithee, Quartilla, help me stave them off.
Although they have no mercy on themselves
Yet we must use some conscience.
    Quar. Gentlemen,
You'll break your wits with stretching them. Forbear,
I beseech you!
    Trim. My wit it never fails me,
I have it at a certainty: I'll set it
To run so many hours, and, when 'tis down,
I can wind it up like a watch. But I fear
I have deceived the time too long. Ladies,
I'll take my leave of your fair beauties. You have
No service to enjoin?
    Triph. You'll take my brother
Capritio with you.
    Trim. If he please, and his tutor.
    Mis. My suffrage shall consent to anything
Her ladyship approves.
    Quar. You must remember
You prove not refractory to your discipline,

'Twill be much for your improvement.
   Trim. I'll bring him
Unto a captain, shall set both our faces
To look like the very Janus of a statesman,
And so farewell. Come, sir!
                      [*Exeunt Trimalchio, Capritio.*
   Triph. I told you, Signiour,
What a rare man he was.
   Mis. In all my travels
I have not met the like; not any one
Was so mellifluous in his discourse.
I think when he was young, some swarm of bees
Did light upon his lips, as it was fained
Of Hesiod.
   Triph. Let's in, for I shall mourn
And melancholy be till his return.

Act III. Scene I.

Philautus, Ardelio.

   Phil. Ardelio, we are now alone, come tell me
Truly, how does the vulgar voice pass on me?
   Ard. Why sir, the shallow currents of their brains
Run all into one stream, to make a deep,
To bear the mighty burden of your fame.
   Phil. And 'tis all true they say?
   Ard. That you are most fair,
A most exact, accomplished, gentle Lord,
Not to be contradicted, 'tis a truth
Above all truths, for where is any truth,
That is agreed upon by all, but this?
   Phil. Such is the force of beauty, there is nothing
Can please without it, and whoever has it,

As there be few, is adjudged happy in it.
 Ard. All this is true.
 Phil. Then he that has a pure
And sublim'd beauty, 'tis a thing sensible,
And cannot be denied, must be admired,
And free from all detraction.
 Ard. This is true.
 Phil. He that excels in valour, wit, or honour,
He that is rich or virtuous, may be envied,
But love is the reward of beauty : no object
Surprises more the eye, all that delight us,
We ascribe beauty to it.
 Ard. All this is true,
 Phil. Look high or low ! 'tis true. Why are the stars
Fixed in their orbs, but to adorn the heavens ?
And we adore their beauty more than light.
Look on the arts, how they tend all to beauty,
'Tis their only end. He that builds a house
Strives not so much for use as ornament,
Nor does your orator compose a speech
With lesser care to have it elegant
Than moving; and your limner does observe
The trim, and dress, more than the rules of painting.
 Ard. All truth, and oracles.
 Phil. Look on a fair ship,
And you will say 'tis very beautiful.
A General rejoices in the title
Of a fair army. I'll come nearer to you ;
Who were thought worthy to be deified,
But such as were found beautiful ? For this cause,
Jove took up Ganymede from Ida hill
To fill him wine and go a hunting with him.
 Ard. 'Tis too much truth to be spoke at one time.
 Phil. It shall suffice, but yet you know that man

May safely venture to go on his way,
That is so guided, that he cannot stray.

Enter FIDELIO.

How now! hast thou obtained in thy request?
   Fid. I have with much entreaty gained your
     admittance.
   Phil. Let me embrace my better genius.
   Fid. I do not use the profession.
   Phil.   'Tis an art
Will make thee thrive; will she be coy enough?
To tell you true, I take a more delight
In the perplexity of wooing them,
Than the enjoying.
   Fid.   She is as I told you.
   Phil. If she be otherwise than I conceive,
A pox on the augury.
   Fid.   But hark you, sir,
You need not be known who you are.
   Phil.   For that,
Trust to my care; come, let us go about it!
Some men may term it lust, but, if it hit,
The better part shall be ascribed to wit.

ACT III. SCENE II.

TRIMALCHIO, CAPRITIO, AGURTES, AUTOLICUS.

   Trim. How goes our matters forward?
   Agu.   Very well, sir,
For I have made your entrance open; told her
All that I can to grace you, that you are
Exactly qualified, unparalleled,
For your rare parts of mind and body, full
Of rare bounty, and that she likes best in you.
She holds it a good argument you will
Maintain her well hereafter, marry else

She is natural covetous, but that's
A point of housewivery, she does not care
You should spend much upon yourself, and can
Dispense with house keeping, so you allow her
To keep her state, her coach, and the fashion;
These things she means to article beforehand.
I tell you what you must trust to.
 Trim.   Very well, sir.
 Agu. Now see that you be circumspect, and fail not
In the least circumstance; you may do somewhat
Extraordinary, at the first meeting.
For when she has conceived of your good nature,
The less will be expected.
 Trim.   Why, the captain
Has put me in a form.
 Agu.   Of words he has,
But you must do the deeds.
 Trim.   Ay, so I will!
For look you, sir, I have the several graces
Of four nations, in imitation
Of the four elements, that make a man
Concur to my perfection.
 Agu.   As how?
 Trim. I am in my compliment, an Italian,
In my heart a Spaniard,
In my disease a Frenchman,
And in mine appetite an Hungarian.
 Agu. All these are good and commendable things
In a Companion, but your subtle women
Take not a man's desert on trust, they must
See and feel something. What you give her now,
You make her but the keeper, 'tis your own,
You win her by it; I should be loth to see you
Out-done with courtesies: what if some gull,
That has more land than you, should interpose it,

And make eclipse between you? 'Tis a fear!
Therefore you must be sudden and dispatch it,
For she is ticklish as any haggard,
And quickly lost; she is very humoursome.
   Trim. I'll fit her then! I am as humoursome
As herself, I have all the four humours.

> *I am hot, I am cold.*
> *I am dry, and I am moist.*

   Agu. I must be like the Satyr, then, and leave you,
If you are hot and cold.
   Trim. O you mistake me.

> *I am hot in my ambition,*
> *I am dry in my jests,*
> *I am cold in my charity,*
> *And moist in my luxury.*

   Aut. Sir, for the gentlewoman that is with her,
Not so much in the nature of a servant
As her companion; for 'tis the fashion
Amongst your great ones, to have those wait on them
As good as themselves. She is the sole daughter
To a great knight, and has an ample dowry.
Apply yourself to her, though it be nothing
Else but to practice courtship, and to keep you
From sleep and idleness.
   Cap.   I shall be ruled
By you in anything.
   Aut.   You shall not do
Amiss then. What? You may get her good will,
And then object it to your friends; you can
Advance yourself without their counsel.
   Cap.   .   Counsel?
I still scorned that.
   Trim. Captain, a word with you;

Were I not best look like a statesman, think you?
   Aut. What, to a woman? 'twere a solecism
In nature, for you know Cupid's a boy,
And would you tire him like a senator,
And put a declamation in his mouth?
'Twere a mere madness in you! Here they come!
See what a majesty she bears. Go meet her!

ACT III. SCENE III.

TRIMALCHIO, CAPRITIO, AGURTES, AUTOLICUS,
    MILLISCENT, MARGERY.

   Trim. Stand by! it is my happiness invites me.
O that I could appear like Jupiter
Unto his Semele.
   Agn. Why, would you burn her?
   Trim. Yes, with my love I would. Most luculent
     lady,
After the late collection of my spirits,
Lost in the admiration of your beauty,
Let me crave pardon.
   Mille.   Sir, for what?
   Trilm. My boldness.
   Mile.   I apprehend none.
   Trim.   You must pardon me,
For I am jealous of the least digression:
And you may justly frown.
   Mille.   I should be loth
To acknowledge so much from you.
   Trim. Lady, you have those fair additions
Of wealth and parentage, join'd to your virtues,
That I may justly suspect your disdain.
But, by my hopes, I do not court your fortunes,
But you.
   Mille. Believe me, no deserving man
Shall be the less esteemed for that, where I find

Ability to govern what I bring him,
'Tis that I value : things that are without me,
I count them not my own.
    Trim.   'Tis a speech, lady,
Worthy an Empress. I am a made man,
Since you have cleared the heaven of your brow :
Now by that light I swear, a brighter day
Ne'er broke upon me.
    Agu. Sir, I hope this lady
Shall have no cause to repent your admittance ?
    Mille. Sir, for my part, since virtue is my guard,
I do not only keep my doors still open,
But my breast too, for gentlemen of merit.
    Trim. Now by this air, that does report your voice
With a sound more than mortal; by your fair eyes,
And as I hope to be enrolled your servant,
I honour the meanest stitch in your garment.
    Mille. I would not wish you place your love upon
A thing so mean, so likely to be cast off.
    Trim. O, divine counsel! that so rare a beauty
Should mix with wisdom : these words are not lost.
I am your slave for ever. I'll go hire
Six poets to sing your praise, and I myself
Will be the seventh to make up the consort.
    Aut. You see your friend there, Mr Trimalchio,
Is like to speed, and fairly on his way
To much happiness. I would not willingly
That any should miscarry in a plot
That I have a hand in : You must be sudden
I told you, if you meant to be a favourite
To fortune and your mistress, and be bold.
    Cup. If I had spoke to her, the brunt were past.
    Aut. Aye, then the ice were broke ; now she makes towards you !

'Tis the best time, let no occasion slip.
 Cap. Lady, advance the pinnacle of your thoughts,
And enlarge the quadrangle of your heart,
To entertain a man of men.
 Aut.   A man
Of means, sweet lady, that I can assure you.
 Marg. He's so much the more welcome, I assure you.
 Aut. You are welcome by this means, do you mark that?
 Cap. Some three thousand a-year, or thereabouts.
Alas, I value it not, 'twill serve to trifle
In pins, and gloves, and toys, and banquets.
 Marg.   'Tis much
One of such tender years should step so soon
Into the world.
 Cap. Indeed, the spring of my courtship
Has been somewhat backward, but I will strive
To redeem it: I have some seeds a-growing
Shall make m' ere long spread like a gentleman,
And you shall say so too.
 Marg.   I do believe it.
 Cap. Nay, whe'er you do or no, 'tis no great matter.
 Aut. Be not capricious.
 Cap.   My name's Capritio.
There be in town of the Capritios,
Come from our house, that shall approve it so.
 Aut. What will you say, if I show you a way
To get a general credit?
 Cap.   Can you do it?
 Aut. I can and will. I'll have you, out of hand,
The master of a good horse and a good dog,
And be known by them.
 Cap.   Will that do it?
 Aut.   Will it?

Why, when you once have matched your horse, or
    dog,
The adverse party being a man of note,
'Twill raise an inquisition after you.
" Who's is the horse?" says one, " Mr Capritio's!"
" What he?" says another, " a noble gentleman!"
'Twill draw the eyes of a whole shire upon you,
Besides the citizens that go down to bet.
    Cap. Why, this is rare indeed!
    Aut. And then 'twill furnish you
With fitting discourse for any man's table.
A horse and a dog, no better a subject
To exercise your tongue in, many ladies
Talk in that dialogue; besides, there being
A kind of near relation in the nature
Of you and those beasts, the good qualities
That are in them may be thought to be yours.
    Cap. I'll buy me a dancing horse that can caper,
And have him called Capritio, by my name!
    Aut. You may do so.
    Cap.   Lady, by your leave, I will.
    Mar. Sir, what you please.
    Aut.   Her desires go with yours.
Observe but what a wife she's like to prove,
That is no more imperious being a mistress.
    Cap. Brother, come hither!
    Trim.   I am busy here.
How do you like the fabric of this watch?
    Mil. Pray, let me see it!—a rare piece of work!
    Trim. It cost me twelve pound, by this light, this
        morning.
    Mil. But that it was so dear I would have begged
        it.
    Trim. 'Tis at your service, lady.
    Mil.   I'll make use of
Your courtesy, with many thanks, sir.
    Trim.   Nay, but

You must not have it.
 Mil. Will you go from your word?
 Trim. I'll give you as good, but this is none of
  mine;
By this hand, I borrowed it.
 Mil.   You said you bought it.
 Trim. I said so indeed.
 Mil.   You should do well to buy you
A better memory, as I shall hereafter,
To keep at distance from you.
        [*Exit Millescent.*
 Agu.   Is she gone?
 Trim. Gone in a fume.
 Agu.   How did you anger her?
 Trim. She would have begged my watch, and I
  excused it.
 Agu. She beg your watch? She scorns to beg
  anything;
She has more than she can tell what to do with.
Perhaps she longed for yours, and would receive it
As a courtesy. Why would you shew it her
Unless you meant to part with it?
 Trim.   I know not:
I think my wit was cramped.
 Agu. You must ne'er look for
The like occasion offered you; why, this
Was such a time to win her love! a gift
Would put her every hour in mind of you.
 Trim. What shall I do?
 Agu.   Best send it after her.
 Trim. Do you carry it; tell her withall, I'll send
  her
A coach and four horses, to make her amends.
 Agu. Give me the watch! if I do make all good
Will you perform your promise?
 Trim.   By my life!
I'll send them without fail immediately.

Agu. I'll after her and see what I can do.
            [*Exit Agurtes.*
   Cap. Stand for a watch? here, take this diamond!
Nay, do not wrong me, I have sworn you shall,
Were it as good as that which was made precious
By Berenice's finger, which Agrippa
Gave his incestuous sister, you should have it.
What! do you think I am an ass? No, sir,
'Tis he has taught me wit.
   Ant. And are you happy,
That can be wise by other men's examples?
   Cap. What! should I lose my mistress for a toy?
   Trin. Lead on, good brother! I am all of a sweat,
Until some gale of comfort blow upon me. [*Exeunt.*

ACT III. SCENE IV.

PHILAUTUS, FIDELIO, FAUSTINA.

Fid. You see that I have brought you to the treasure,
And the rich garden of th' Hesperides;
If you can charm those ever watchful eyes
That keep the tree, then you may pull the fruit,
And, after, glory in the spoil of honour.
   Phil. Prithee, let me alone with her.
   Fid.   I'll leave you. [*Exit Fidelio.*
   Phil. Lady, my preface is to know your name.
   Fau. Faustina, sir.
   Phil.   I may be happy in you.
I have a sister somewhere of that name,
That in her youth did promise such a feature,
And hopes of future excellence: she had
A beauty mixed with majesty, would draw
From the beholders love and reverence.
And I do ill, methinks, with unchaste thoughts
To sin against her memory. This task

Would I were rid of; but I'll venture. Lady,
You are not blind, I conceive.
    Fau. No sir, I have not
Yet seen a thing so strongly sensible,
To hurt my eyesight.
    Phil. Then I hope you can
Take notice of a gentleman's good parts,
Without a periphrasis.
    Fau. What's that ?
    Phil. A figure,
Needless at this time to explain my deserts,
So easy and apparent to be seen.
    Fau. I dare not envy, nor detract, where worth
Does challenge due relation of respect:
Nor is my wit so curious, to make
A gloss or comment on your qualities.
    Phil. 'Tis too much labour, 'twere a task would dull
The edge of rhetoric, to describe them rightly;
Nor would I have them dwell upon your tongue,
But fixed in your thoughts, there let them move,
Till they meet in conjunction with your love;
Nature would boast so sweet a sympathy.
    Fau. I should be sorry, if my understanding
Moved in so poor a circle as your praise;
I have not leisure to take notice of it.
Is this all you have to say ?
    Phil. No, I have more;
But love is slow to dictate to my vows;
And yet those sacred and divine impulsions
Strike truer than my heart, and, by his power
That has inflamed me, here I swear I love you.
    Fau. Your oaths and love are made of the same air,
Both die in their conception: quickly uttered,
And as easily not believed.
    Phil. Nay, now you wrong

My true intent.
  Fau. Suppose I grant you love me.
What would you infer?
  Phil. That you should speak the like,
And with the same affection.
  Fau. If your love
Be not a bawd unto some base desire,
I do return the like.
  Phil. I know not how
You may interpret it, but sure the law,
And the command of nature, is no baseness,
A thing that Jove himself has dignified,
And in his rapes confessed the god of love
The greater of the two, whom Kings have stooped
   to.
We are allowed to enjoy some stolen delights,
So we be secret in't; for 'tis set down
By such as in this art have skilful been,
W'are not forbid to act, but to be seen.
  Fau. Upon these terms, I do deny you love me.
'Twas lust that flattered sin, made love a god,
And, to get freedom for his thefts, they gave
Madness the title of a deity.
For how can that be love, which seeks the ruin
Of his own object, and the thing beloved?
No, true love is pure affection,
That gives the soul transparent, and not that
That's conversant in beastly appetites.
  Phil. Tell me not of your philosophical love.
I am a fool to linger, women's denial
Is but easy cruelty, and they
Love to be forced sometimes.
  Fau. Pray, know your distance.
  Phil. Come, you dissemble, and you all are willing.
  Fau. To what?
  Phil. There's none of you but feel the smart
Of a libidinous sting; else wherefore are

Those baits and strong allurements to entice us?
Wherefore are all your sleekings, and your curlings,
Crispings, and paintings, and your skin made soft.
And your face smooth with ointments; then your gait
Confined to measure, and composed by art,
Besides the wanton petulancy of your eyes,
That scatter flames with doubtful motion,
Unless it were to prostitute your beauty?
　Fau. I'll give account for none, sir, but myself,
And that I'll speak: before my virgin zone
Shall be untied by any unchaste hand,
Nature shall suffer dissolution.
But whate'er others be, methinks your worth
Should not pretend to an ignoble action.
　Phil. Now, by this light, I think you'll moralize me.
　Fau. 'Tis my desire you should go better from me,
Than you came hither: you have some good parts
But they are all exterior, and these breed
A self-conceit, an affectation in you,
And what more odious? Some applaud you in it,
As parasites, but wise men laugh at you.
Will you employ those gifts that may commend you,
And add a grace to goodness, had you any,
In the pursuit of vice, that renders you
Worthy of nought but pity?
　Phil.　　　　　　　　I came as to
A whore, but shall return as from a saint.
　Fau. Then leave to prosecute the foggy vapours
Of a gross pleasure, that involves the soul
In clouds of infamy. I wonder, one
So complete in the structure of his body,
Should have his mind so disproportioned,
The lineaments of virtue quite defaced.

Phil. I am subdued! she has converted me.
I see within the mirror of her goodness,
The foulness of my folly. Sweet, instruct me,
And I will style thee my Ægeria.
    Fau. It is a shame, that man that has the seeds
Of virtue in him, springing unto glory,
Should make his soul degenerous with sin,
And slave to luxury, to drown his spirits
In lees of sloth, to yield up the weak day
To wine, to lust, and banquets.
    Phil. Here's a woman!
The soul of Hercules has got into her.
She has a spirit, is more masculine
Than the first gender: how her speech has filled me
With love and wonder! sweet lady, proceed.
    Fau. I would have you proceed and seek for fame
In brave exploits, like those that snatch their honour
Out of the talents of the Roman Eagle,
And pull her golden feathers in the field.
Those are brave men, not you that stay at home,
And dress yourself up, like a pageant,
With thousand antic and exotic shapes;
That make an idol of a looking glass,
Sprucing yourself two hours by it, with such
Gestures and postures, that a waiting wench
Would be ashamed of you, and then come forth
T' adore your mistress' fan or tell your dream,
Ravish a kiss from her white glove, and then
Compare it with her hand, to praise her gown,
Her Tire, and discourse of the fashion:
Make discovery, which lady paints, which not,
Which lord plays best at gleek, which best at racket.
These are fine elements!

Phil. You have redeemed me,
And with the sunny beams of your good counsel
Disperst the mist that hung so heavy on me:
And that you may perceive it takes effect,
I'll to the wars immediately.
    Fau. Why, then
I must confess I shall love you the better.
    Phil. I will begin it in your happy omen:
But first confess, that you have vanquished me.
And if I shall o'ercome an enemy
Yield you the trophies of the victory
    Fau. Please you walk in the while.
    Phil. I shall attend you.   [*Exit Faustina.*
Henceforth I'll strive to fly the sight of pleasure,
As of an harpy or a basilisk,
And, when she flatters, seal my ears with wax
Took from that boat, that rowed with a deaf oar
From the sweet tunes of the Sicilian shore.

Enter TRIMALCHIO, CAPRITIO, FIDELIO, ARDELIO,
    and SNARL.

    Trim. Are you for the war, indeed?
    Phil. Immediately.
Is there any of you will go along with me,
Besides this gentleman?
    Trim. I think, nobody.
    Phil. Ardelio, thou art my faithful servant.
    Ard. Alas sir,
My body is fat, and spungy, penetrable,
And the least cold will kill me.
    Sna. Yet his face
Is hatched with impudency, threefold thick.
    Ard. I am not for your trenches and cold cramps,
Their discipline will quickly bring me under;
I'll stay at home, and look to your business.
    Phil. Brother Capritio, what say you to it?
    Cap. Who, I? od's lid! I am not such an ass,

To go amongst them, like you volunteers,
That, frighted worse at home with debt and danger,
Travel abroad i'th' summer to see service,
And then come home i'th' winter, to drink sack.
I am none of those; I'll hardly trust myself
In the artillery yard, for fear of mischief.

Phil. Mr Trimalchio, you are young and lusty,
Full of ambitious thoughts.

Trim. 'Tis true, indeed,
That I am grown ambitious of honour,
And mean to purchase it.

Sna. But with no danger
Of life and hope.

Trim. I mean to hazard a limb for it.

Phil. Why, whither are you going?

Trim. To the Leaguer,
Upon the same employment that Hercules
Did once against the Amazons.

Sna. And I
Will stay at home and write their annals for them.

Phil. Stay all at home, and hug your igno-
  minies,
And whilst we spoil the enemy, may you
Be pil'd by pimps, cheaters intrench upon you.
Let bawds and their issues join with you. Marry
With whores, and let projectors rifle for you.
And so I leave you.

Trim. We shall hear of you,
By the next caranto, I make no doubt of it.

Act IV. Scene I.

Enter TRIMALCHIO *and* CAPRITIO.

Trim. Brother Capritio, are you well provided
With amunition? armed *cap à pie.*

To scale the fort of our Semiramis?
  Cap. I am appointed, brother.
  Trim.   Then let us on
And beat a parley at the gates. So, ho!

Enter PANDAR.

  Pand. How now, what bold adventurers be here?
What desperate rudeness tempts you to your ruin!
Here are no geese to keep our capitol,
But men of arms, you slaves, stout imps of Mars,
Giants, sons of the earth, that shall rise up,
Like Cadmus' progeny, to fight it out,
Till you are all consumed. Have you any gold?
'Tis that must break our gates ope; there are
    lock'd,
A score of Danaes, wenches of delight,
Within this castle, if I list to show you
Where Circe keeps her residence, that shall,
If she but lay her rod upon your necks,
Transform you into apes, and swine, you sheep's
    face.
If thou shalt once but drink of her enchantments,
She'll make a lion of thee.
  Cap.   Alas, sir,
I had rather look like an ass, as I am still.
  Trim. Be not too boistrous, my son of thunder!
We are well-wishers to thy camp, and thee.
Here is a freshman, I would have acquainted
With the mystery of your iniquity.
  Pan. I do embrace thy league, and return the
    hand
Of friendship. To thy better understanding,
I will discover the situation of the place.
'Tis of itself an island, a mere swan's nest,
Which had Ulysses seen, he would prefer
Before his Ithaca, and he whom fate
Shall bless to vanquish it, he may deserve

The name of a new conqueror. It has
The credit to be styled the *Terra florida*,
Of the best beauties in the town, my friend,
That repair hither upon the least summons,
Besides some that are constant to their trenches;
Venus in this house is predominant.
'Tis barren, I confess, yet wholly given
To the deeds of fructification. But those
Are barred from coming to perfection
With rheums, and diseases. You dormice!
What, must I read a lecture to you gratis?
   Trim. No, sir, here's money for you.
   Pand. You may enter,
And return safe, upon your good behaviour.

Act IV. Scene II.
Bawd, *Two* Whores.

   Bawd. Well, they may talk of Dunkirk or of Callis,
Enriched with foreign booties, but if ever
A little garrison, or sconce, as this,
Were so filled up with spoils, let me be carted.
   1 *Who.* And carry it so cunningly away,
Beyond the reach of justice, and of all
The jurisdiction in our own hand,
Like a free state.
   Bawd. Did not I purchase it?
And am I not the lady of the manor?
And who shall dare to question me? I hope,
I shall be able to defend my fort
From the invasion of the painted staff,
Or the tempestuous paper-engine, safe,
As a mole in a trench, and work at high midnight.
When their wise heads are laid, we'll raise the
   spirits
Of our dead pleasures, use the benefit
Of youth, and dance our orgies by the moonlight.

1 *Who.* I hope they need not to condemn us, we drive
As open trade as they, and vent as ill
Commodities as any; all that we utter
Is in dark shops, or else by candle-light.
   2 *Who.* We are become the envy of citizens.
   1 *Who.* It is reported that we study physic.
   Bawd. Why so?
   1 *Who.* The reason is, because we know
The several constitutions of men's bodies.
   2 *Who.* And some term us the Leaguer.*
   Bawd. We defy
The force of any man. Who's that knocks so?
Go bid the watch look out, and if their number
Be not too plural, then let them come in!
But if they chance to be those ruffian soldiers,
Let fall the port-cullis. All they can do
Is to discharge a volley of oaths at me.
I'll take no tickets nor no future stipends.
'Tis not false titles, or denominations
Of offices can do it. I must have money,
Tell them so! draw the bridge! (*Exit 1st W.*)
   I'll make them know
This is no widow's house, but Marcus Manitius
Is Lord of the Island. Who was't?
   1 *Who.* (*Re-entering*). The Constable!
   Bawd. What would he have?
   2 *Who.*   You know his business.
   Bawd. Pox on the Marshal and the Constable!
There cannot be a mystery in a trade,
But they must peep into it. Merciless varlets,
That know how many fall by our occupation,
And yet would have their venery for nothing.
A chambermaid can't have a ruff to set,
But they must be poking in it!

   * We will bind and hoodwink him so, that he shall suppose no other but that he is carried into the leaguer of the adversaries, when we bring him to our own tents.—*Shakespeare.*

Now, they have brought us under contribution,
They vex us more than the Venetians do
The whole corporation of courtezans;
But we must give good words. Shew them a room!

Enter ARDELIO.

Ard. There's hot service within, I hear the muskets
Play from the rampiers. I am valiant,
And will venture upon the very mouths of them.

Bawd. Mr Ardelio, you have been a stranger.
You are grown rich of late.

Ard. Who, I grown rich?

Bawd. Yes, somewhat pursey for want of exercise.

Ard. Well, I was wont to put in for a gamester,
But now I am quite thrust out of all play.

Bawd. We were wont to be your subjects to work on,
And since you scorn us, yet you cannot say
But you have found good dealing at our hands.

2 Who. We have been always bent to your worship's will,
And forward to help you on at all time.

Ard. Come, you are good wenches.

Bawd. Truly, sir, you know
I keep as good creatures at livery,
And as cheap too, as any poor sinner
Of my profession.

Ard. Hast thou e'er a morsel
That is not tainted or fly blown?

Bawd. Indeed I have
So much ado to keep my family sound,
You would wonder at it; and such as are so
They are taken up presently. But I have one,
I dare commend to you, for wind and limb.

Ard. Come, let me have her then.

Bawd. Please you walk in, sir! [*Exit Ardelio.*

Enter MISCELLANIO.

Mis. It's strange there is no more attendance given,
To usher in a man of my quality.
Are you the governess of this *Cinqueport*, lady?
　Bawd. The fortress, sir, is mine, and none come
　　here
But pay me custom.
Mis. Hast thou ne'er a pilot,
Or man of war to conduct a man safe
Into thy harbour? there be rogues abroad:
Piratical varlets that would pillage me.
　Bawd. Very well, sir.
　Mis. I thought at first, you would have bar'd
　　my entrance.
　Bawd. I do not use the fashions of those countries
That keep a stranger out four weeks at sea,
To know if he be sound. I make no scruple,
But give free traffic to all nations.
If you have paid your due, you may put in;
There is the way! I'll follow presently.
　　　　　　　　　　[*Exit Miscellanio.*
I think our soldiers are all come, let's in
And set the watch.

　　　　Enter TRIMALCHIO, CAPRITIO.

　Trim. Stay, punk! make room for us,
That have advanced our banners to thy walls,
Past all the pikes, the perdues, and the sentries.
'Tis a good omen! where's Bellona there,
And the daughters of Mars, those brave girls?
We are come to pay our homage to their smocks.
　Bawd. Nay, if you are unruly we shall tame you.
　Trim. Fear not, we are tributaries, punk.
　Bawd. Sir, do you speak with no more reverence
To me? it seems you know me not.
　Trim.　　　　　　　　　　　　I shall
Endeavour to preserve thy dignity.

Art thou that brave Hippolite,* that governs
This troop of Scythians? speak Orithyia,†
My Menalippe,‡ my Antiope!
We are sworn vassals to your petticoats.

   Bawd. Did you attempt but the least injury,
There be in readiness would vindicate
The wrongs and credit of my house.
   Trim.   I know
Thy power, punk, and do submit me, punk,
Tam Marti, quam veneri. 'Tis thy motto, punk.
   Cup. Would I could tell how to get out again.
   Bawd. How came you in? have you performed all
    duties?
   Trim. I threw thy Cerberus a sleepy morsel,
And paid thy Charon for my waftage over,
And I have a golden sprig for my Proserpine.
   Bawd. Then you are welcome, sir.
   Trim.   Nay, I do honour
Thee and thy house, and all thy vermin in't,
And thou dost well to stand upon thy guard
Spite of the statutes. 'Tis a castle this,
A fort, a metropolitan bawdy house:
A Cynosarges, such as Hercules
Built in the honour of his pedigree,
For entertainment of the bastard issue
Of the bold Spartan.
   Bawd. You have said enough, sir,
And, for requital, I will shew you in
Where you shall read the titles, and the prices.
   Trim. But here's a brother of mine is somewhat
    bashful:

---

* A queen of the Amazons, vanquished by Hercules, who gave her to his companion, Theseus, by whom she had a son called Hippolytus. She was also called Antiope.

† One of the Amazons.

‡ A sister of Antiope, taken by Hercules when he made war against the Amazons. He received as her ransom the arms and girdle of the Amazonian queen. *Juv.* 8. v. 229. This capture of the girdle achieved his ninth labour.

I'd fain deliver to thy discipline.

Bawd. What, is he bashful? that's a fault indeed. Come hither, chops! you must not be so shamefaced.

Trim. Lo! you there, sir? you shall come forth in print.

March on, my Calypso! come, sir, follow your colours! You shall have the leading of the first title.

ACT IV. SCENE III.

AGURTES *like a Constable:* AUTOLICUS, SNARL, *like Watchmen.*

Agu. Are your disguises ready?
Aut. I have mine.
Snar. Mine's in my pocket.
Agu. Put it on your face!
Now they are housed, I'll watch their coming forth,
And fright them in the form of a Constable!
If that succeeds well, then I'll change the person,
To a Justice of peace, and you shall act
My clerk, Autolicus. They say an officer
Dares not appear about the gates: I'll try it!
For I have made one drunk and got his staff,
Which I will use with more authority,
Than Mercury his all commanding rod,
To charm their steps, that none shall pass this way
Without examination. There stalks one!

[*Ardelio passes by.*

I'll first know what he is; now they drop away,
As if they leapt out from the Trojan Horse:
This is the autumn of the night. Who goes there?

Ard. A friend!
Aut. Friend or foe, come before the Constable.
Agu. Whence come you, friend?
Ard. And't please you, sir, I have
Been waiting on my niece home to her lodging.

Agu. Why, is your niece a Leaguer, a suttler,

Or laundress to this fort?

Ard. No, and it like you,
She lyes without the camp.

Agu. You lie like a pimp!
You are an apple squire,* a rat, and a ferret.
I saw you bolt out from that coney-berry.†

Ard. Mr Constable.

Agu. Out of the wind of me! what, do you think
You can put out the eyes of a gorcrow?‡
Fob me off so,—the Constable that have
The parish stock of wit in my hands? I am glad
That I have got you from your covert: you shall
Be searched! you shall along with me, sir!

Ard. Whither?

Agu. No farther than to prison, where you shall pay
But forty shillings for noctivagation.

Ard. I am undone then. There are forty old scores
I owe in town will follow after me.

Agu. What are you? what's your name?

Ard. Ardelio,
A Lord's servant.

Agu. Do Lords' servants do this?

Ard. Alas, a venial sin! we use to learn it
When we come first to be pages.

Agu. Stand by! there's one has got a clap too.

[*Miscellanio passes by.*

Mis. The shirt of Hercules was not so hot.

Sna. There's one sure has been hurt with a gronicado.

Agu. How now! who's there?

Mis. Here's nobody.

---

* A kept gallant. A person who waits on a woman of bad character.
† Cony-burrow—a place where rabbits make their holes in the ground. ‡ A carrion crow.

Agu. Nobody? my senses fail me then. Who is't? What man are you?
Mis. No man! you are deceived,
I cannot find I am a man! that part
Is dead, wherein I once was an Achilles.
Aut. Come nearer.
Mis. I cannot go; I have lost my nerves.
Aut. You shall be carried to the jail then.
Mis. Fitter for an hospital; I am condemned already
To fluxes and diet drinks.

TRIMALCHIO, CAPRITIO.

Trim. Murder, murder, Mr Constable! murder!
Agu. Who's that? Jeronimo's son's ghost in the garden?
Trim. O, Mr Constable, we have been so used,
As never two adventurous gentlemen
In the hands of their enemies.
Agu. What's the matter?
Trim. Let me take breath! I am at the last gasp.
We have escaped from the den of the Cyclops,
There was one ran a spit against my eyes.
Cap. Amongst the rest, there was a blink-ey'd woman
Set a great dog upon me.
Trim. They have spoiled us
Of our cloaks, our hats, our swords, and our money.
Snar. Your wits and credit were both lost before.
Cap. No, we had not our wits about us then.
Trim. Good sir, let's think on some revenge! call up
The gentlemen 'prentices, and make a Shrove Tuesday.*

* On Shrove Tuesday in each year, being their holiday, the 'Prentices of London exercised the right of attacking and demolishing houses of ill-fame, even prior to the date of their damaging "the Cockpit Playhouse in Drury Lane," on 4th March 1617.

Agu. By no means. I must suppress all violence.
Cap. My brother talked of building of a sconce,
And straight they seized our cloaks for the reckoning.
Trim. There I lost my hat and sword in the rescue.
Agu. 'Twas well done.
Trim. And whil'st some strove to hold my hands,
The others dived in my pockets. I am sure,
There was a fellow with a tann'd face, whose breath
Was grown sulphurous with oaths and tobacco,
Puffed terror in my face. I shall never be
Mine own man again.

BAWD *and* WHORES *from above.*

Bawd. Stop their throats, somebody!
1 *Who.* 'Twere a good deed to have made them swim the moat.
2 *Who.* Ay, to have stripped them, and sent them out naked.
1 *Who.* Let's sally out and fetch them in again!
Then call a court on them for false alarms.
Trim. Fly from their rage, sir! they are worse than harpies,
They'll tear us as the Thracians did Orpheus
Who's music, though it charmed the powers of hell,
Could not be heard amongst these. Mr Ardelio
And Miscellanio, I joy to see you,
Though ill met here.
Mis. Signiour Trimalchio!
Sir, you must pardon me. I cannot stoop,
I have the grincums in my back, I fear
Will spoil my courtship.
Trim. Mr Ardelio,
Who would expected to have met you here?
Ard. Nay, who would not expect it?' tis my haunt,

I love it as a pigeon loves a salt-pit.
  Mis. O me! my scholar too, how came he hither?
I did not mean t' impart this mystery.
How could he find it out?
  Trim. His own Minerva,
And my help, sir.
  Agu. Well, you must all together.
  Trim. Whither must we go?
  Agu. Marry, before a Justice!
To answer for your riot.
  Ard. Mr. Constable!
  Agu. I cannot dispense with it.
  Mis. Let us redeem our peace.
  Agu. Not before next sessions. Bring them away!
  Snar. Come, there's no remedy.

Act IV. Scene IV.

Bawd, Whores, Pandar.

  Bawd. Was ever such a treacherous plot intended
Against our state, and dignity?
  Pan. Had this
Passed with impunity, they might have sworn
Vengeance had run the country.
  1 *Who.* But I hope
They have no cause to boast their victory.
  Pan. Now, by this air, as I am a true soldier,
Bred under and devoted to your banner,
But that your pity did prevent my rage
They should have known no quarter, for this brow
Brooks no affronts.
  2 *Who.* Captain, you fought it bravely.
  Bawd. We'll have a stone graven with characters,
To intimate your prowess.

Pand. No, my dear Gorgons,
I will not have my fame wander without
The precincts of your castle: 'tis enough
It can be sheltered here within these walls,
And to recount with your acknowledgements
What this fort owes to my protection.
  Bawd. Captain, we must confess you are our
    guardian.
  Pand. Then let me sacrifice unto my humour.
All you this night shall be at my disposing
To drink and drab, 'tis the fault of your fortune
That do profess this trade, t' have somebody
To spend your purchase on: 'tis my decree,
What others riot, you should waste on me.

ACT IV. SCENE V.

AGURTES *like a Justice of Peace.*
AUTOLICUS *his clerk.*

  Agu. What, are they come?
  Aut.   Yes, sir.
  Agu. Then let me see
How I can act it; do I look like a Justice?
  Aut. As fearful as an ass in a lion's skin, sir.
  Agu. Here I begin my state. Suppose me now
Come down the stairs, out of the dining-room
Into the hall, and thus I begin. Brisco!
Call Brisco, my clerk!
  Aut. At your elbow, sir.
  Agu. Reach me my ensign of authority!
My staff I mean. Fy, fy, how dull you are,
And incomposed! Now set me in my chair,
That I may look like a cathedral Justice
That knew what belongs to an *Assignavimus*
And *Dedimus potestatis.* Nay, though we are
Of the peace, we can give *Priscian* * a knock.

* The grammarian.

Let me alone now to determine causes,
As free from error as the Pope ; old Minos
And Rhadamanth are not so skilled i'th' urn,
As I am in the statutes. I have them *ad unguem*.
Now if they enter, at their peril be it.
How dost thou like my action ?
   Aut.   Very well, sir.
   Agu. Let them come in !

Enter SNARL, *like a Constable,* TRIMALCHIO, CAPRITIO, MISCELLANIO, ARDELIO.

                        Now, Mr Constable,
I must commend your diligence. Come hither!
   Snar. Sir, I have brought four men before your Worship,
I found last night at midnight in the streets,
Raising a tumult.
   Agu. Brisco, be ready to take
Their examination. Good ! you found four men
At midnight. Whose men are they ?
   Trim. Our own men, sir.
   Agu. So it seems by your liveries.
Write that down! first they say, they are their own men.
   Ard. Sir, by your favour, I am not my own man.
   Agu. I thought they would not all be in one tale ;
I knew I should find them tripping, and I
Once come to sift them. You are not your own man ?
It argues you are drunk. Write his confession
Ex os tuum te indico : perge, Mr Constable.
   Snar. I hold it fit your Worship should examine
What they did there so late.
   Agu.   What did you there
So late ?
   Mis. Good Justice echo, we had business.
   Agu. Record, they say, they had business. They shall know

That I am Judge of Record, and what I do
Record shall stand, and they shall have no power
To plead not guilty in a *Scire facias*,
By a recognisance. I have my terms.
   Ard. Good your Worship, give us not such hard words.
   Trim. 'Tis almost as hard usage as the Leaguer.
   Agu. Then you came from the Leaguer?
   Trim.   You may read
Some adventures in our habit. We have seen,
And tasted the experience of the wars.
   Mis. They have made me of another religion,
I must turn Jew, I think, and be circumcised.
I may be anything, now, I shall lose a limb,
I may go seek my pension with the soldiers.
But, 'tis no matter, I'll turn valiant
And fight with the stump.
   Agu. You are a fighter then?
This doth appear to me to be a riot.
What think you, Mr Constable?
   Snar. I think no less.
   Agu.   Was *ad terrorem populum.*
   Snar.   I know not
What you mean, but I mean as your Worship means:
I did perceive they had been quarrelling.
   Agu. Why then, 'twas an affray, a sudden affray,
Directly against the state of Northampton.
The *Decimo tertio* of Harry the fourth clears the doubt. .
How do you traverse this, what do you answer?
   Ard. We make a question, by your Worship's favour,
Under correction, whether that which was
Done under foreign powers, in foreign lands,
Be punishable here or no.
   Agu. How prove you that?
   Ard. 'Tis a province by itself, a privileged place,

A strong corporation, and has factions
In court and city.
  Trim.   Is inhabited
With furies, that do multiply like Hydra;
An army of diseases can't suppress them,
Besides their many fallings t'other way.
  Agu. I should be loth t' infringe their liberties,
I'll send you to be tried, from whence you came,
  then.
  Cap. O, good your Worship, hang us up at home
  first,
Let us endure the rack or the strapado,
We do submit us to your Worship's censure.
  Agu. Have you provided sureties for the peace
  then?
  Ard. More need to provide somethings for my
  belly.
I think they mean to keep me for a race.
I'm fallen away quite, I was like a hogshead:
Now I am able to run through my hoops,
  Agu. What's he that halts before me? do you
  mock me?
'Tis ill halting before a cripple, sirrah.
  Mis. 'Tis sore against my will, I cannot help it.
Would I could run away with half my teeth.
  Agu. Can't a man have the venerable gout,
Or the bone-ache, but you must imitate him?
  Mis. Good Mr Justice.
  Agu. Mock your fellow rogues!
I'm none of those, that raised my fortunes with
Fiddling and tobacco. Make his Mittimus!
  Snar. And't please you, sir, here's one has brought
  a letter.
  Agu. From whom?
  Snar. From one Mistress Millescent.
The contents will inform you.

The Letter.

Noble Sir,—

I am sorry to interest my unstayd honour in the patronage of offenders, or to abuse the credit I have with you, in stopping the course of justice against them, whose youthful licentiousness would pollute the pen of a lady to excuse it. On the other part, I hold it the betraying of a virgin's sweet disposition, to withdraw her favours where she has once placed them, although there be some want of desert. I must confess 'tis an antipathy to my nature to see any gentleman suffer when I may prevent it. Howsoever I have found a disrespect from him, yet I forget it. For anger abides in the bosoms of women as snow on the ground; where it is smooth and level it falls quickly off, but remains where it is rough and uneven. That this may appear to be true, I would entreat you to dismiss those two gentlemen and their associates, Mr Trimalchio and Capritio, whose riotous looseness has made them obnoxious to your censure, and my suspicion. Thus not doubting the success of my letter, I rest in your favour as you may presume on mine, and your true friend, MILLESCENT.

Agu. This lady, that has writ on your behalf,
Is one I honour.

Trim. How should she hear of it?

Agu. It seems, your fault is quickly blown abroad.

Trim. I had rather seal a *nocerint universi*
For a thousand stale commodities,
Than she should know of it.

Agu. As for you two,
You may pay your fees and depart; you have
Your manumission for this lady's sake.
Master Constable you are discharged, and you may
Go along with them and receive their fees.

Mis. Though I say nothing, yet I smell something;
A lady send a letter? she is in love
With me, I'll pawn my life, and I ne'er knew it.
I'll get my back well, and go visit her.
   Ard. Now I have got my teeth at liberty,
And they e'er tie me to the rack again
Let me be choked.
                [*Exeunt Miscellanio, Snarl, Ardelia.*
   Agu. Well, I perceive you are
A favourite to this lady. What's your name?
   Trim. Trimalchio.
   Agu.   And yours?
   Cap.   Capritio.
   Agu. Two ancient names in Camden. Of what country?
   Cap. Of Norfolk.
   Agu.   The Capritios of Norfolk?
I think we shall be kin anon: my mother
Was a Capritio, and of that house.
Are you allied unto this lady?
   Trim.   No, sir,
But I have formerly been entertained
As a poor suitor to her grace's favour.
   Agu. I find by that, you are a man of fashion;
And would you then?—
   Trim. Nay, good sir, do not chide.
   Agu. Yes, I must tell you that you were to blame,
Having so fair a fortune before you, to wrong
A lady of her spirit; so rich and fair,
Of unreproved chastity, and one
So high in birth, nay, 'tis not possible
To speak her virtues, and present yourself
So lumpishly, nay perhaps fill her bed
Full of diseases.
   Trim.   Good sir, say no more!

I am a traitor, I have killed a man,
Committed sacrilege! Let her seek revenge
For these, or if less punishment will serve:
To have me beaten, I'll run naked to her.

   Agu. I will not press a good nature so far.
You two shall stay and dine with me. I'll send
My coach for your mistress; it shall go hard,
But I will make you friends, before we part.

ACT V. SCENE I.

PHILAUTUS, FIDELIO, FAUSTINA.

   Fau. Now let me bid you welcome from the wars,
Laden with conquest, and the golden fleece
Of honour, which, like Jason, you have brought
T' enrich your country, now indebted to you.
Had it not been a pity such a talent
Of virtue should be lost or ill employed?

   Phil. Lady, you are a good physician,
It was your counsel wrought this miracle,
Beyond the power of Esculapius.
For when my mind was stupified, and lost
In the pursuit of pleasures, all my body
Torn and dissected with close vanities,
You have collected me anew to life;
And now I come to you, with as chaste thoughts
As they were first adulterous, and yield
A due submission for the wrong I did
Both to yourself and sex.

   Fau.   Sir, for my part,
You have your pardon.

   Phil. You were born to quit me.

   Fid. But, when you know the author of your freedom,

F

You'll thank her more.
   Phil. Why, who is it?
   Fid. Your sister.
   Phil. Who? not Faustina? she told me so
      indeed,
Her name was Faustina. Let me look upon her,
As on the picture of all goodness, engraven
By a celestial finger, shall outwear
A marble character. I knew her not;
I am glad there is a scion of our stock,
Can bear such fruit as this, so ripe in virtue.
Where have you lived recluse? you were betrothed
To one Fidelio, but crossed by your father.
I have heard good reports of the gentleman.
   Fau. I never knew you flatter any man
Unto his face before.
   Phil.   Unto his face?
Where is he?
   Fid.   My name's Fidelio.
   Phil. I am transported, ravished! give me leave,
Good gods, to entertain with reverence
So great a comfort. Let me first embrace you.
Great joys, like griefs, are silent. Loose me
      now,
And let me make you fast. Here join your hands,
Which no age shall untie; let happiness
Distil from you, as the Arabian gums,
To bless you issue.
   Fid. Now I hope, sweet lady,
The time has put a period to your vow.
   Fau. 'Tis ended now, and you may take a com-
      fort,
That I could tie myself with such a law.
For you may hope thereby I shall observe you
With no less strict obedience.
   Fid. I believe you.
   Phil. And, for her dowry, I will treble it.

Enter SNARL.

Here Snarl is come to be a witness to it!
   Snar. My Lord Philautus, if I may presume
To congratulate your Honour's safe return,
I must confess I do it with my heart,
And all your friends long to participate
Your happy presence.
   Phil. Thanks both to them and thee.
   Snar. Master Fidelio, no less to you.
I see you happy in your mistress' favour,
And that's as much as I can wish to you.
   Fid. You have been always privy to my counsel.
Ask me no questions now, I shall resolve you
When we come in.
   Phil.   How fares our camp at home?
Trimalchio, and the rest?
   Snar.   I have been busy
In projecting for them; they must all be married.
I have seen the interlude of the Leaguer:
And we have played the Justice and the Constable:
I will not prepossess you with the sport,
But I will shew you such a scene of laughter.
   Phil. Where is Ardelio?
   Snar.   Your servant, Ardelio?
'Tis the notoriousest mixture of a villain,
That ever yet was bred under the dunghill
Of servitude: he has more whores at command
Than you have horses. He has stables for them,
His private vaulting houses.
   Phil.   Discharge him the house!
Take his accounts and office, and dispose them.
   Snar. Ever your Lordship's true and faithful servant.

ACT V. SCENE II.

MILLESCENT, MARGERY.

Mil. When was my father and the Captain here?
Mar. They are plotting abroad, I hope to see
you shortly
Honestly married and then turn virtuous.
Mil. 'Tis the course of the world now, Margery.
But yet I fear I have got such a trick,
When I was young, that I shall never leave it.
Mar. What help then? the poor gentleman
must suffer,
Good Trimalchio: 'tis his fate.
Mil.   I am thinking
What I shall do with him when I am married.
Mar. What do other women do with their
husbands?
Bring him up in obedience, make him besides
An implement to save your reputation.
Let him not press into your company
Without permission; you must pretend
You are ashamed of him. Let him not eat
Nor lie with you, unless he pay the hire
Of a new gown or petticoat; live with him,
As if you were his neighbour, only near him,
In that you hate his friends: and, when you please
To show the power you carry over him,
Send him before on foot, and you come after
With your coach and four horses.
Mil.   'Tis fitting so.

Enter MISCELLANIO.

Host now! what piece of motion have we here?
Would you speak with any body?
Mis.   My business
Is to the lady Millescent.

Mil.   What's your will?
Mis. Are you that lady?
Mil.   Yes, my name is so.
Mis. To you then I direct m'apology.
It seems your eye with approbation
Has glanced upon my person. I protest
I never was so dull in the construction
Of any lady's favour in my life:
I am ashamed of my error.
    Mil.   In what, sir?
I cannot call to mind that e'er I saw you.
    Mis. You have been still too modest to conceal it.
That was not my fault: you did ill to strive
To hide the flames of love, they must have vent:
'Tis not the walls of flesh can hold them in.
    Mis. What riddles have we here? that I should love you?
I would not have you think so well of yourself.
    Mar. Perhaps he has some petition to deliver,
Or would desire your letter to some Lord.
    Mis. I know not how, sure I was stupified!
I have ere now guessed at a lady's mind,
Only by the warbling of her lute-string,
Kissing her hand, or wagging of her feather,
And suffer you to pine for my embraces,
And not conceive it?
    Mil. Pray, be pacified.
This fellow will persuade me I am in love.
    Mis. Lady, you have took notice of my worth,
Let it not repent you. Be not stubborn
Towards your happiness. You have endured
Too much already for my sake, you shall see
Pity can melt my heart. I take no delight
To have a lady languish for my love.
I am not made of flint as you suspect me.
    Mil. I would thou wert converted to a pillar,

For a memorial of this impudence.
　Mis. You shall know what 'tis to tempt me, here-
　　after,
When I shall let you perish for your folly.
I came to remunerate the courtesy
I received from your ladyship.
　Mil.　　　　　　　I know of none.
　Mis. I must acknowledge myself bound to you.
　Mil.　　　　　　　　　　For what?
　Mis. Your letter to the Justice, lady!
It free'd me from the pounces of those varlets,
When I was under the gripe of the law.
I know the only motive was your love.
　Mil. I cry you mercy! Were you one of them
That drew Trimalchio to those idle courses?
I am ashamed of the benefit. Leave me
That I may not see the cause of my sorrow.
But 'tis no matter, we shall leave you first.
　　　　　　　　　[*Exeunt Mil. and Margery.*
　Mis. They shall find I am no man to be slighted,
And that she has misplaced her affection.
When I have wracked the wrongs on my co-rival,
Trimalchio, look to thyself! were he removed
There might be hopes my valour shall make known
There is a difference. I'll straight to the tavern,
And when I once am hot with good canary,
I pronounce him dead that affronts my fury.

Act V. Scene III.

Ardelio.

　Ard. Turned out of service? the next turn will
　　be
Under the gallows, and have a ballad made of me.
The corruption of a cashiered serving-man
Is the generation of a thief. I fear
My fate points me not out to so good fortune;

My bulk will not serve me to take a purse.
The best thing I am fit for is a tapster,
Or else get a wench of mine own, and sell
Bottle ale and tobacco, that's my refuge.
They termed me parasite, 'tis a mystery
Is like a familiar, that leaves a man
When he is near his execution.
I have no power to flatter myself now,
I might have gone a wooing to some widow,
And had his countenance, but now the tenants
Look like their bacon, rustily, upon me.

Enter JEFFRY.

What, Jeffry? thou art the comfort of my woes.
Welcome, good Jeffry!
    Jef.   Thanks to your Worship.
    Ard. Where are my hangings, Jeffry?
    Jef.   Very well, sir.
Locked in a cypress chest for fear of moths.
    Ard. And all the other furniture, good Jeffry?
    Jef. They are kept safe and well aired for your
        Worship.
    Ard. Thanks, good Jeffry. I were in a sweet
        case,
If I had not conveyed some things away
To maintain me hereafter.
    Jef.   Why so, sir?
    Ard. I may go set* up bills now for my living,
Cry vinegar up and down the streets; or fish
At Blackfriars' stairs; or sit against
A wall, with a library of ballads before me.
    Jef. You are not out of service?
    Ard.   Turned a grazing
In the wide common of the world, Jeffry.
    Jef. Then are my hopes at best; I have no
        reason

* Paste.

To care for him any longer. A word with you,
What furniture do you mean?
 Ard.   Those that I sent,
The beds and hangings.
 Jef.   Did you send any such?
 Ard. I hope you will not use me so.
 Jef.   Your own words:
I must make the best benefit of my place.
You know 'tis not an age to be honest in,
'Tis only the highway unto poverty.
I know not how, I do not fancy you
Of late.
 Ard. I chose thee for thy knavish look,
And now thou hast requited me: of all
My evils thou art the worst.
 Jef.   No faith, sir!
You have a worse commodity at my house,
But you may save the charges of a writ;
I'll send her you without reprieve or bail.
I do you that favour.
 Ard. No, you may keep her still.
 Jef. Methinks you are much dejected with your fall,
I find an alteration in your face.
You look like an almanac of last year's date,
Or like your livery cloak, of two years' wearing,
Worse than the smoky wall of a bawdy house.
 Ard. Villain, dost thou insult on me!
 Jef.   No faith, sir!
Alas, 'tis not within the reach of man
To countermine your plots.
 Ard.   Well, slave, because
I'll rid my hands of thee, I'll give thee a share.
 Jef. You must have none without lawful proceeding,
And that I know you dare not.

Enter SNARL, *and* OFFICERS.

Snar. But I dare !
Have you been partners all this while in mischief,
And now fall out who shall be the most knave ?
  Jef. What do you mean ?
  Snar. I mean to search your house
For ammunition, no otherwise,
Which I suspect you send unto the Leaguer.
  Jef. Sir, I have nothing there, but one cracked
    piece
Belongs to this gentleman, can do no service.
She is spoiled in the bore.
  Sna. We'll have her new cast.
Come, bring them away !
  Ard. Nay, good sir, you know
That I was lately quit before a Justice,
And if I fall in a relapse—
  Sna. All's one
To me, but you must satisfy the law.
  Ard. Well then, I know the worst of it.

Act V. Scene IV.

AGURTES, AUTOLICUS, TRIMALCHIO, CAPRITIO.

  Agu. Master Trimalchio, 'tis an age since I saw
    you.
  Trim. I was ne'er out of town.
  Agu. Not out of town ?
We sought you all about the ordinaries,
Taverns, and bawdy-houses, we could imagine
You ever haunted.
  Trim. You might have found us then.
  Aut. Nay, more, we enquired at the play-houses.
  Agu. 'Twas once in my mind to have had you cried.
  Aut. We gave you lost.
  Trim. Well, shall I tell you, Captain ?
  Aut. Aye do, what is't ?

Trim. This gentleman and I
Have passed through purgatory, since I saw you,
If I should tell you all the passages
At the Leaguer.
    Aut. Thither we came to meet you,
And you were gone.
    Cap.   And then at the Justice's.
    Agu. Were you before the Justice?
    Trim.   'Tis such a story
Would fill a chronicle.
    Cap. We met with a party of the enemies,
Took all we had from us, and then it cost us
Forty shillings in fees at the Justice's.
    Agu. That was hard dealing.
    Cap.   The old boy and I
Grew to be kin at last.
    Trim.   He made me sure
To my mistress, before we parted.
    Agu.   How?
By what strange accident?
    Trim.   Honest Ardelio,
And Miscellanio, we were all together
In rebellion, and quit by a letter,
That came from my mistress.
    Agu.   Is't possible?
And Miscellanio turn traitor!
    Trim.   What?
    Agu. Would have your mistress from you, thinks
    the letter
Was sent for his sake.
    Trim.   That I'm sure he does not.
    Agu. Threatens and swears that he will fight for
    her.
    Trim. If he be weary of his life, he may.
Why, what can he pretend to her?
    Agu.   I know not
What has passed between them, but I am sure

He has been practising at the fencing-school,
To get a trick to kill you.
    Trim.   He kill me?
I'll kill him first.   I fight by geometry.
    Agu. How! By geometry?
    Trim.   Yes, sir.   Here I hold
My rapier, mark me, in a diameter
To my body; that's the centre, conceive me.
    Aut. Your body is the centre, very good.
    Trim. And my hilt, part of the circumference.
    Aut. Well, sir.
    Trim. Which hilt is bigger than my body.
    Aut. Than your whole body?
    Trim.   Yes, at such a distance.
And he shall never hit me whilst he lives.
    Aut. Where did you learn this? at the Leaguer?
    Trim.   No.
No, by this light, it is my own invention:
I learnt it on my travels.
    Aut.   Very strange!
You are a scholar?
    Trim. Nay, I would not be
Suspected of such a crime for a million.
But 'tis no sin to know geometry
And, by that, I can tell we shall ne'er fight.
    Aut. Not fight at all?
    Trim. I'll shew you in geometry,
Two parallels can never meet: now we two
Being parallels, for so we are, that is
Equal in wit and valour, can never meet,
And if we never meet, we shall ne'er fight.

Enter MISCELLANIO.

    Aut. To prove your axiom false, see where he
      comes!
    Trim. I do defy him.
    Mis.   Hang thee, blust'ring son

Of Æolus, defy me! I'll tie up thy breath
In bags, and sell it for a penny an ounce.
   Aut. Draw, sir!
   Mis.   Draw, if he dares!
   Cap. Sure, this is the second part of the Leaguer.
'Twere best for me to hide me in my cabin.
                                    [*Exit Capritio.*
   Mis. Will you resign your mistress?
   Trim.   No, I scorn it.
   Mis. Unless you'll have her tane away by force.
   Aut. I see, this cannot be ended without blood.
   Trim. Captain, a word with you.
   Aut.   What say you, sir?
   Trim. I am afraid he comes with the black art.
   Aut. How! you afraid? Do not say so for shame.
   Trim. He has lain with an old witch at Sweden,
And is grown stick-free.
   Aut. Fye! that you should say so.
   Trim. I'll be resolved of that before I fight.
   Aut. Why, do you think the witches have such
     power?
   Trim. Ay, marry do I. I have known one of
     them
Do more than that, when her husband has followed
Strange women, she has turned him into a bezar,*
And made him bite out his own stones.
   Aut.   'Tis strange!
   Trim. I'll tell you another as strange as that, of
     one
When a vintner has sent her but ill wine,
She has converted him into a frog,
And, then conjured him into one of his butts,
Where he has lived twelve months upon the lees,
And, when his old guests chance to come to see him,
He has croaked to them out at the bung-hole.

   * Beazar. A goat.—"Beazar-stone, used in physic as a cordial, breeds in the maw of the Beazar."—*Blount,* 1661.

Aut. This is miraculous!
Trim. There was a lawyer
That spoke against one of them at the bar.
Aut. What did she then?
Trim. Turned him into a ram,
And still that ram retains his profession,
Has many clients and pleads causes as well
As some lawyers in Westminster.
Aut. Do you think
That he has had recourse to any such?
Trim. I know not, but 'tis good to be mistrustful.
He may have advantage in the encounter.

Enter MILLESCENT, MARGERY.

Mis. There she comes! win her, and wear her.
Mil. Hold your hands!
I'll have no blood a prologue to my wedding.
Trim. Nay then, have at you. Hold me not, I say
I am as fierce as he.
Mil. Be pacified!
I thought you had been both bound to the peace.
Aut. Lady, it seems that these two gentlemen
Do stand in competition for your love.
Mil. Mr Trimalchio, I confess, has been
A former suitor, but with his ill carriage,
He has thus long prevented his good fortune,
Aut. Then let me make a motion.
Mil. What is it?
Aut. Will they both stand to it?
Trim. I agree.
Mis. And I!
Aut. Then let the lady dispose of herself.
Trim. She is mine already, I am sure to her
Before a Justice.
Mis. I will have no woman
Against her will.
Mil. No, sir, you shall not.

Since you are so peremptory, on your words then
That he shall sing a Palinodium,
And recant his ill courses, I assume
My love, Trimalchio.   [*Capritio peeps out.*
  Cap. Do we take, or are we taken?
  Trim. Nay, we do take.
  Agu. Who's that? Capritio! where have you
    been?
Come your ways forth, and lay hands on the spoil.
Go lead away that lady by the hand.
Now you may take occasion by the foretop,
Advance your own predominant the better,
And march away.
  Trim. Come, let us to the church.
          [*Trimalchio and Millescent exeunt.*

CAPRITIO, MARGERY.

  Mis. And what must I do now? be laughed at?
  Agu.   Would you
Hazard yourself for one, that cares not for you?
You may be glad you 'scaped. Recall yourself!
Were not you formerly engaged?
  Mis.   No never.
  Agu. Not to Mistress Quartilla?
  Mis.   Faith, we have toy'd
In jest sometime.
  Agu. Let it be now in earnest.
Make her amends, I know she loves you.
  Mis.   Well!
I will have her, and stand up for my portion
With the rest of my tribe.

ACT V. SCENE *the last.*

SNARL, PHILAUTUS.

  Sna. Stay here a little. They are gone to
    church,

And will return in couples. First, Trimalchio,
That giant in conceit, thinks he is matched
To some great heir, but shall embrace a cloud
Instead of Juno. Then her waiting-woman,
Her Iris, reflects upon Capritio,
And for my piece of fragmentary courtship,
My miscellany gentleman, 'tis his lot
To be cast upon Quartilla, with Agurtes
In his old Justiceship. All these march together,
Like the seven deadly sins, and, behind them,
Comes Autolicus, the clerk of the company.

Enter AGURTES *like a Justice,* TRIMALCHIO, MILLES-
CENT, MISCELLANIO, QUARTILLA, CAPRITIO,
MARGERY, AUTOLICUS *like a clerk.*

Aut. Look you, sir, here they come!
Trim. Make room! methinks
You should not stop the course of justice so.
My Lord Philautus, you are welcome from
The wars, and I from the church; I wonder
Who makes the better return, you have got
Honour, and so have I. But where's your wealth?
I can embrace five thousand pounds a-year.
That's nothing with you; I have no more wit
Than to be pil'd with pimps, and marry whores.
Yet I mean shortly to rank with your honour.
Here is my warrant, I have promised her,
To make her a countess, but that's nothing with
    you.
Nay, more than this, I can go on and leave
Some advancement behind me. *Ecce signum!*
Phil. 'Tis well! I am glad of your happiness,
And much joy to my brother, Capritio,
And his fair spouse.
Cap. She is according to
My heart's desire, sir.
Sna. Well, a word with you,

Master Trimalchio, and the rest.
 Trim.   What say you ?
 Sna. You were as good know it at first as at
last.
You are not the first that have been deceived.
 Trim. In what ? My wife ? I married her for
maid,
And whether she be one or no, I care not.
 Sna. Nay, should I hear a man that should abuse
her
In that, I would defend her with my sword.
But she and you must call this man your father.
 Trim. Ay, so she must, he gave her at the church.
 Sna. Nay, her own natural father, flesh and
bone;
I hope she'll not deny it.
 Mille.   No, indeed, sir,
I would not live to be so ungracious.
 Agu. I must acknowledge thee my child, or I
Should do thy mother wrong.
 Trim.   I do not think so,
You'll not make me believe that I took her
For a Lord's daughter, and a great heir. Where are
Agurtes and the Captain to justify it ?
Is he your father ?
 Mille.   He has ever bred me ;
And I have always called him so. I hope
It is no shame; my parentage is honest.
 Trim. Well, if he be, 'tis no disparagement
To marry a Justice's daughter.
 Snar.   Come, you have
Been carried hood-winked through this business,
Nor is the day clear before you. Mark me :
I'll open but one leaf in all the book,
And you shall see the whole discovery.
Come, sir, uncase.
   [*Agurtes and Autolicus pull off their disguises.*

Trim. Who have we here? Agurtes
And the captain! was't you that played the Justice,
And you his clerk?
   Snar. And I the Constable.
   Trim. Then you are a knot of knaves for your labour.
Now I perceive that I am plainly gulled.
   Cap. I am glad there's no man cheated but himself.
   Snar. Your arrow is one of the same quiver too.
   Trim. I'll none of her, by this light.
   Agu.   Why you may choose,
And yet I do not well see how you can choose.
She is your wife and you have married her,
And must allow her means to maintain her.
You may declare yourself unto the world,
And be laughed at: but keep your own counsel,
And who needs know of it?
   Phil.   Believe me, sir,
The gentlewoman is not to be despised,
Her wit and virtues are sufficient dowry.
   Trim. Nay, if you say so, then must I needs love her:
But by this hand I thought you would have jeered me.
   Phil. Hold on your course, march on as you came in,
And rest content, since fate has thought it fit,
To make your fortunes equal with your wit.

A FINE COMPANION.

Acted before the King and Queene at White-Hall, and sundrie times with great applause at the private-House in Salisbvry Court, by the Prince his Servants.
Written by Shakerley Marmyon.

——— *Lectori credere mallem,*
Quam spectatoris fastidia ferre superbi.—Hor.

London, Printed by Aug. Mathewes for Richard Meighen, next to the Middle Temple gate in Fleet Street, 1633.

THIS is a fair comedy of the day in which it was written. The plot, such as it is, has been seized upon by many writers since, so that, although fresh at the time, it does not now present much novelty to those who are conversant with stage-plays. It would seem to have been well received.

Durfey, in his comedy of "Sir Barnaby Whig, or no Wit like a Woman's" 1681, borrows from the present piece, without any promise of return, much of Captain Whibble's character and humour, with which to garnish and trick out his "Captain Porpuss."

Sir Ralph Dutton, to whom Marmion dedicates this piece, and whom he characterizes as "the truly noble, and his worthy cousin in all respects," was of an ancient family, dating from the time of William the Conqueror, and denominated from the town of Dutton in Cheshire. He was the seventh and last son of William Dutton, of Sherbourne, Esq., who served the office of Sheriff for the county of Gloucester in 1590 and 1601, by Anne, daughter to Sir Ambrose Nicholas, Knight, Lord Mayor of London. His brother John, (third son) became heir to his father's estate. Of him, Wood has this notice:—

"John Dutton, of Sherbourne, in Gloucestershire, Esq.—He was one of the Knights for that county, to sit in the said Parliament, 1640; but being frighted thence by the tumults that came up to the parliament doors, as other Royalists were, he conveyed himself privately to Oxford, and sate there. He was a learned and a prudent man, and as one of the richest so one of the meekest men in England. He was active in making the defence, and drawing up the articles of Oxon, when the garrison was to be surrendered to the parliament. For which, and his steady loyalty, he was afterwards forced to pay a round sum in Goldsmith's-hall at London." This means that he compounded for his estates by paying £5216, 4s. Wood also informs us that, however loyal he was at the beginning of the troubles, he thus expresses himself in his will, dated 14 January, 1655;—"I humbly request and desire, that His Highness, the Lord Protector, will be pleased to take upon him the guardianship and disposing of my nephew, William Dutton, and of that estate I, by deed of settlement, hath left him; and that His Highness would be pleased, in order to my former desires, and according to the discourse that hath passed betwixt us thereupon, that, when he shall come to ripeness of age, a marriage may be had and solemnized betwixt my said nephew, William Dutton, and the Lady Frances Cromwell, his Highness's youngest daughter, which I much desire, and (if it take effect) shall account it as a blessing from God."

Sir Ralph Dutton, Knight, to whom this play is dedicated, received his honour at Woodstock in 1624. In Charles the First's time he was gentleman of the privy-chamber in extraordinary, and High-Sheriff of Gloucestershire, in 1630; and, being zealously attached to the interests of his sovereign in the great rebellion, his estate was sequestered, for which a composition of £952, 17s. 1d., was paid, and he forced to fly beyond sea; but, being beaten back by contrary winds in his passage from Leith to France, he was cast away on "Brunt Island," and there died in the year 1646.— *See Collins' Peerage of England, cura Bridges.* He married Mary, daughter of Sir William Duncombe, of London, Knight, and by her had two sons, William and Ralph, the latter of whom was ancestor to the present Lord Sherborne.

TO THE TRULY NOBLE

and his worthy kinsman in all respects,

SIR RALPH DUTTON.

SIR.—We have great cause to triumph over the iniquity of the times, that in all ages there wants not a succession of some candid dispositions, who, in spite of malice and ignorance, dare countenance poetry, and the professors. How such an excellent, and divine part of humanity should fall under the least contempt, or arm the petulancy of writers to declaim against her, I know not: but I guess the reason, that having their souls darkned, and rejoicing in their errors, are offended at the lustre of those arts that would enlighten them. But the Fates have not so ill befriended our studies, as to expose them to contempt, without the protection of such, whose ability of judgment can both wipe off all aspersions, and dignify desert. Amongst the worthy patrons of learning that can best vindicate her worth, you are not the least; and because custom and respect to noble friends gives a priviledge to dedicate our endeavours where they may find admittance, I have made bold to present this piece unto you. It hath often pleas'd, and without intermission. If you shall second that applause by your kind favour, it shall not aspire to be more honour'd,

By him that is yours
in all observance,

SHACK. MARMYON.

DRAMATIS PERSONÆ.

AURELIO, *an elder brother disinherited.*
CARELESS, *his brother, the Fine Companion.*
DOTARIO, *an old gentleman, their uncle.*
FIDO, *their friend.*
SPRUSE, *a young Gallant.*
LITTLEGOOD, *an usurer.*
FONDLING, *his wife.*
LACKWIT, *their son.*
VALERIA, } *their daughters.*
ÆMILIA, }
CROTCHET, *a clown.*
WHIBBLE, *a captain.*
STERNE, *a lieutenant.*
TAILOR.
SEMPSTER.
HABERDASHER.
HOSTESS.
FOUR WENCHES.
FIDDLERS.
BOY.
ATTENDANTS.

PROLOGUE.

CRITIC, AUTHOR.

Crit. Are you the author of this play?
Auth. What then?
Crit. Out o' this poetry, I wonder what
You do with this disease, a seed of vipers
Spawned in Parnassus' pool, whom the world frowns on,
And here you vent your poison on the stage.
Auth. What say you, sir?
Crit. Oh, you are deaf to all
Sounds but a plaudit, and yet you may
Remember, if you please, what entertainment
Some of your tribe have had that have took pains
To be contemn'd, and laught at by the vulgar,
And then ascrib'd it to their ignorance.
I should be loth to see you move their spleens
With no better success, and then with some
Commendatory Epistles fly to the press,
To vindicate your credit.
Auth. What if I do?
Crit. By my consent I'll have you
Banisht the stage, proscrib'd, and interdicted
Castalian water, and poetical fire.
Auth. In that you wrong th' approved judgments of
This noble Auditory, who, like a sphere
Moved by a strong intelligence, sit round
To crown our infant muse, whose celestial
Applause she heard at her first entrance.
Crit. This way of poetry has deceiv'd many;

For 'tis not every one that writes a verse
Has washt his mouth in Helicon, or slept
On the two-topt Parnassus; there's great difference
Betwixt him, that shall write a lawful poem,
And one that makes a paper of loose verses
To court his looser mistress; there's much air
Requir'd to lift up the Dircœan swan,
When he shall print his tracts among the clouds:
Not as your ignorant poetasters use,
In spite of Phœbus, without art or learning,
T' usurp the stage, and touch with impure hands
The lofty buskin, and the comic style.

 Auth. This I confess; but when the prosperous gale
Of their auspicious breath shall fill our sails,
And make our high-borne thoughts swell like a tide:
And when our bolder Muse shall put on buskins,
And clap on her Talaria on her feet,
Then, like swift Mercury, she may aspire
To a sublimer region, with that force,
And bear that weighty burthen on her wings,
That she shall fear to crack her pinions.

 Crit. 'Tis this licentious generation
Of poets trouble the peace of the whole town;
A Constable can't get his maid with child,
A baker nor a scrivener lose his ears,
Nor a Justice of peace share with his clerk;
A Lord can't walk drunk with a torch before him,
A Gallant can't be suffer'd to pawn's breeches,
Or leave his cloak behind him at a tavern,
But you must jerk him for it.

 Auth.   In all ages
It hath been ever free for comic writers,
If there were any that were infamous,
For lust, ambition, or avarice,
To brand them with great liberty, though I

Disclaim the priviledge; no impure language,
As Stygian mud stir'd up with Charon's oar
Ne'er belcht so foul an air, shall ever mix
With our ingenious mirth, nor need we fear
Any their foul aspersions; whilst the wise
Sit to controul and judge, in whose clear eyes,
As we deserve, we look to stand or fall,
Passing prophaner people, and leave all
To be determined as you censure. Boy,
Go and subscribe it quickly what I say.

 Crit. He's grown contemptuous, and flings away
In a rapture; for this, when I am in,
If I can't laugh at 's play, I'll laugh at him.

A FINE COMPANION.

Actus I. Scena I.

Aurelio, Valeria.

Aur. 'Tis true indeed, our love is like our life;
There's no man blest in either till his end.
And he whom Fate points to that happiness,
A thousand passions mock his doubtful hopes,
Till virtue, that can never be extinct,
Shall rise above their rage, and call down Hymen,
Attended with as many several joys,
To triumph in the circle of our brow.
   Val. But that the fatal union of our hearts
Should breed such issues of extremity
In both our fortunes, yet the greatest grief
I feel, is in your wrongs, not in my own.
   Aur. Ne'er think of it! what though my father made me
A stranger to his loins, and cut me off
From my inheritance, because he thought me
A rival in his love, that fatal love
Whose jealousy prevail'd so in a wooer,
That it kill'd all affection in a father.
These ill-begotten thoughts he still maintain'd,
And cherisht to his death, whose period
Of life was the beginning of my mischief:
For he gave all the land unto my brother,
One less deserving. Would I could report
That he had any worth, his ill wrought mind,
Too apt for the impression of all vice,

As if he were to strive with his estate,
And had no other enemy, would make
A conquest of his ruin.   So negligent
Of what his father wrongfully bereft me,
That he spends all in riot, and so vainly,
As if he meant to throw it after him.
Only he has a foolish flashing wit,
Too weak to sustain, or prevent his fall,
But no solidity of mind or judgment.
And now imagines he can salve it up,
By being styl'd a "Fine Companion."
Let that entitle him to all my right,
Whilst I, secure in my imputed crime,
Think thee a better portion ; all my fault
Was honesty, and true affection.
 Val. And those still envious fate insults upon.
But we will live together, and what e'er
Shall interpose to poison our true love,
Still triumph o'er their malice.
 Aur.   Dear Valeria,
Had fortune pleas'd to place me in that means
My birth assur'd me, we had spent our life
Lull'd in the lap of peace, our days had run
Smooth as the feet of Time, free from all tumults.
 Val. And why not still ?
 Aur.   It may do so, but I
Have not a fortune equal to your virtues,
And to support the title of your worth.
 Val. My mind was never yet ambitious,
And there is nothing but your company
Can satisfy, or limit my desires.
 Aur. I love you better than to injure you.
I will resign you to some richer heir,
Whose heaps of wealth left by his greedy father,
Untoucht as is your goodness, may advance you,
And make you happy.   Think on't ! be not cruel
To your own self.

Aur. Oh, how have I deserv'd that you should think
So ill of me? You may divorce the ivy
The vine from her embraces, me you cannot.
Where is the care you wont to have of me?
What is my fault? you can be well without me,
And I shall please you best when I am absent.
    Aur. Nay, my Valeria, do not weep so sore!
Thy grief adds more to mine. It is enough
I part from thee, my heart with drops of blood
Pays tribute to the ocean of thy tears;
This treasure of thine eyes, if spent for those
That lye unterr'd, wanting their funeral rites,
And restless walk upon the Stygian strand,
So long as fate has limited their curse,
Would send them over to Elizium.
One grain of that same grief which clogs her heart,
Would lye in balance 'gainst the universe.
The joy and happiness of all mankind
Are given to me in her, and she was born
T' upbraid the world, and tell them they are false.
    Va. What shall I do when you are ravished from me?
Could Portia rather swallow glowing coals
Than burn with a desire of her lost Brutus?
Shall the example to those times descend
To shame my love? Could the Ægyptian Queen
Rather endure the poignant stings of adders
Than that of death which wounded Antony?
And must I then survive you? can I live,
When you that are my soul are taken from me?
Oh 'tis not now as when Penelope
Could stay ten years the coming of her love,
And span a tedious web of foolish thoughts,
In expectation.
    Aur. Faith that fled to heaven,
And truth, that after once men's hearts grew cold,

Would go no longer naked, now again
Are come to dwell with mortals. Here's a woman,
In whose comparison all wealth is sordid;
And since she proves so constant, fate itself
Shall not be blam'd for me that I forsook her.

Actus I. Scena II.

Enter LITTLEGOOD.

Lit. Are you so well resolv'd? but I may cross
   you.
  Val. Oh me, my father, I am quite undone!
I am no body.
  Lit. Yes, you are the wickedst,
The most ungracious child that ever lived
Under so good a government, but that
Shall turn to tyranny, since your discretion
Can not distinguish of the difference.
Have I—what should I say?—cherisht you up,
With tenderness and costly education,
To have you made a sacrifice to beggary,
To one that's cut off, disinherited,
The son of the people?
  Aur.   Pray, sir, forbear!
My wrongs do not permit you to abuse me.
  Lit. Sir! 'tis most basely done of you, to use
The charity and freedom of my house,
Thus to seduce my daughter: but for that,
If you can keep her as well from your mind,
As I can from your sight, you may, in time,
Learn to forget her. You were best go travel,
Repair yourself by some new found plantation,
Not think to supplant my issue. This place
Is moraliz'd with thrift and industry,
Suits not with men of your condition,
That have no stock but their gentry. Get you in!

And, for your part, sir, know my house no more,
I'll provide her a husband. So, farewell!

Aur. Howe'er I speed, comfort attend thee still,
And so my best Valeria, farewell!

Actus I. Scena III.

Careless, Fido.

Car. Ne'er tell me on't, a gentleman must shew himself to be a gentleman.

Fid. Ay, so he must, sir, but in you there's small resemblance of one.

Car. Come, you are an importunate ass! a dull, heavy fellow, and I must bear with you, must I? By this light! I will not live out of the blaze of my fortunes, though it last but a minute, to linger out a tedious siege of adversities.

Fid. Yet you may live with more credit, at a competent rate as your land will allow you.

Car. Land? There was my unhappiness to have any, I was born to none, 'twas merely thrust upon me, and now I cannot be quiet for it; 'tis like a wife that brings a thousand impediments; I must take an order, I cannot walk the streets in peace, your Magnifico stops his great horse to salute me, another treats of marriage, and offers me his daughter, your advocate racks me with impertinences, and to free my land from incumbrances troubles me ten times worse. What with friends and counsellors, fellows that seem to me of another species, I could resign my interest.

Fid. All this, sir, is a grace to you, if you conceive it.

Car. I'll sell all! 'twere a sin to keep it. When didst thou know an elder brother disinherited and the land continue with the issue? Now for me

H

to live thriftily upon it were no otherwise than to mock fate and contemn providence.

Fid. But now you know the danger, you may prevent it.

Car. What! should I doat upon casualities, trust scriveners with my money, fellows that will break, and all the wit in town can't solder them up again?

Fid. You may scorn my advice, but when 'tis too late—

Car. I tell thee, I'll keep no land, nor no houses, candle rents that are subject to fire and ruin, I can't sleep for fear of them. There's no danger in coin, 'twill make a man respected, drink, and be drunk, wear good clothes, and live as free as a Parthian.

Fid. But when all's gone, where's your respect and gentility then?

Car. Where is't? why, in my blood still; we'll both run one course ne'er out of the vein, I warrant thee.

Fid. If you can hold in this vein 'tis more lasting than a mineral.

Car. Prithee, good honest, old patcht piece of experience, go home and wear thyself out in contemplation, and do not vex me with problems. They can do no more good upon me, than a young pitiful lover upon a mistress that has the sullens.

Fid. Well, sir! I could willingly wait upon you in the way of honour and reputation.

Car. No, no, you shall not need my *homo frugi*. Go about your business, and though men of my quality do seldom part with any thing for good uses, for gamesters and courtiers have but little charity, yet, for this once, I will trespass against custom, and here's something to put you into a fortune. I could wish it more, but you know how my man has used me, and my occasions.

Fid. I see yet in his good nature a reluctancy against ill courses, he has not quite shak'd off his humanity, there are hopes to reclaim him; if not, sir gallant, when all is spent, the return of this money will be grateful; and so, farewell!

[*Exit Fido.*

Car. Adieu, and commend me to my uncle! tell the mechanics without that I vouchsafe them admittance. I will not spend all in whoring and sack. I will have some clothes of value, though they be but to pawn in a vacation. For this purpose, I have sent this morning to consult with the authentical judgements of my tailor, sempster, and haberdasher; and now am I studying with what state I shall use them.

Actus I. Scena IV.

Careless, Tailor, Sempster, Haberdasher.

Car. Come in, fellows! I sent for you together, because you should receive your instructions: I am to make me a suit, and I would have you determine about the form and the accoutrements, for the fitting of the points and the garters, and the roses, and the colours of them. Nature is much beholding to you, though there be a difference in the accidents yet you can reconcile them, and make them suit handsomely together. I am a gentleman, and would not be disgrac'd for my irregularity.

Tai. You say well, sir.

Car. I tell you my disposition, I am wholly addicted to rarities, things that are new take me; new plays, new mistresses, new servants, new toys, new fangles, new friends, and new fashions, and these I deal with, as in a quarrel I would not be behind hand with any of them.

Semp. Sir, you shall command our endeavours.

Car. I thought fit to take your advice, and you are beholding to me; you are the only man in the world that can rule me.

Hab. Sir, for curiosity we have the maidenheads of all the wits in Europe, and to your service we will employ both our art and our industry.

Car. I am informed of your qualities, I hear you are men of intelligence. By this light, I wonder the state is not afraid of you.

Tai. We hope they have no reason for that, sir.

Car. Yes, you are dangerous fellows, and have plots and devices upon men's bodies, and are suspected to be sorcerers, that can transform a man into what shape you list.

Tai. It pleases you to be merry, sir.

Car. Nay, by this hand, 'tis given out, that you are great scholars, and are skill'd in all the habitual arts, and know their coherences, and that you are a kind of astrologers, observers of times and seasons, and for making of matches, beyond all the gallants in the Kingdom.

Tai. We would match things as near as we could, sir.

Car. And besides that, you are proud of your knowledge, for when you have once got a man's good name, you make what account you list of it.

Hab. Not so, sir.

Car. Yes, and presume upon't, and think whatever injury you do a man you can be saved by your book. This is true, and care not a pin of the law, for you hold good custom to be far beyond it.

Semp. We would be loth to give any gentleman distaste, sir.

Car. I must commend you, in that you are not partial, for you make the like reckoning of every man. Well, to the purpose!

Tai. You'll have your suit of the Spanish fashion?

Car. What, with two wallets behind me, to put up faults and abuses, or else I'll cashier my men, and they shall serve me for attendants, hangers on, ha? No, by this air, I am too good a gentleman to have my arms trickt up with such gewgaws.

Tai. Sir, you must be conformable.

Car. Well, I am content to be persuaded. When shall I have them?

Tai. You shall not miss within these three days, and what else is requisite, trust to my care to apply it.

Car. Well, I am satisfied, and hereafter believe me, as I believe thee.

Enter BOY.

Boy. Sir, Master Spruse is come to visit you.

Car. Master Spruse? prithee bid him come up! Well, there's a gentleman, of all I know, can justly claim admiration, for his compliment, his discourse, his habit, his acquaintance, and then for proffering of courtesies, and never doing any; I may give away all I have, before I shall arrive at the grace of it.

Hab. Pray, sir, when did you see the noble captain?

Car. Who, Captain Whibble? Mass! now I think on't thou shalt go seek him out, and entreat him to meet me at the Horse-shoe Tavern at dinner. I love that house for the sign's sake, 'tis the very print of the shoe that Pegasus wore, when he broke up Helicon with his hoof! and now, in relation of that, your poets and players still haunt about the brinks of it. Sirrah, tell him withall, that Master Lackwit the citizen's son will be there, and other good company, and we will have music and wenches. Go thy ways! and you Master Snip, meet me about three a clock to take up these commodities, so now I have done with you.

Actus I. Scena V.

CARELESS, SPRUSE, *with one garter untied, and a black box at his girdle.*

Spru. Save you, Master Careless!

Car. Master Spruse you have much honour'd me with your presence.

Spru. I met with a disaster coming up. Something has ravisht the tassel of my garter, and discompos'd the whole fabric, 'twill cost me an hour's patience to reform it; I had rather have seen the Commonwealth out of order.

Car. Sure, it was not fast tied to your leg.

Spru. As fast together, as the fashion is for friends now a-days to be tied, with certain knots of compliment, which the least occasion dis-joins. I'll only tuck it up, and, when my better leisure permits, reduce it to perfection.

Car. What box have you there?

Spru. A conceit, a conceit! a rare invention, one of the happiest that ever my wit teem'd withall.

Car. Bless me with the discovery.

Spru. You shall swear to be silent then?

Car. As close as that covering.

Spru. Then, look you! I will participate the mystery; this pettyfogging box promises that I have great suits in law, this is to delude the world now. But I must tell you I am a kind of a solicitor, an earnest suitor to every wench I see.

Car. Very pretty! proceed.

Spru. What do you think I have in this box then?

Car. I know not.

Spru. A bundle of blank love letters, ready penned with as much vehemency of affection, as I could get for money, only wanting the superscription of their names, to whom they shall be directed, which I can instantly and with ease indorse upon acquaintance.

Car. And so send them to your mistress?

Spru. You understand me. I no sooner fall into discourse with any lady, but I profess myself ardently in love with her, and, being departed, return my boy with one of these letters, to second it as I said, passionately deciphering how much I languish for her, which she cannot but deeply apprehend, together with the quickness and promptitude of my ingenuity in the dispatch of it.

Car. I'll practise this device. Prithee let me see one of them! What's here? "To the fair hands of —"

Spru. Ay, there wants a name: they fit any degree or person whatsoever.

Car. Let me see this then! "To the lady and mistress of his thoughts, and service."

Spru. There wants a name too. They are general things.

Car. I'll open it, by your favour, sir. What's here? "Most resplendent lady, that may justly be styled the accomplishment of beauty, the seat and mansion of all delight and virtue, in whom meet the joy and desires of the happy. Some man here perhaps might fear, in praising your worth, to heighten your disdain, but I am forc'd, though to the peril of my neglect, to acknowledge it; for to this hour my curious thoughts, and wandering, in the sphere of feminine perfection, could never yet find out a subject like your self, that could so detain and command my affection."

Spru. And so it goes on. How do you like it?

Car. Admirable good! put them up again.

Spru. Nay, I have so strange a wit, few men do jump with it.
All my delights are steept in elegancy,
And censur'd by an arbitration,
Before I do approve them; I have searcht
The dust of antiquity to find out
The rare inventions that I am verst in,
My several garbs and postures of the body,
My rules for banqueting, and entertainment:
And for the titillation of my laughter
Buffoons and parasites, for I must tell you
I still affect a learned luxury.

Car. You have a very complete suit on too, methinks.

Spru. 'Tis as fresh as the morning, and that's the grace on't. A new play, and a gentleman in a new suit, claim the same privilege; at their first presentment their estimation is double.

Car. And whither now do your employments direct you?

Spru. I took your lodging by the way. I am going to dazzle the eyes of the ladies with my apparition.

Car. I am not so conformable as I could wish, or else I would attend you. I took up a new man, for pity's sake, some three days since, to wait upon me, which foolish sin I will abandon whilst I live, for it. He ran away with two hundred pounds, the remnant of a mortgage, and since that I was put to a new perplexity to supply me.

Spru. By this hand, if you had spoke but yesterday I could have furnisht you.

Car. Why, what a rare way is here now, to engage a man for nothing! I must study it.

Spru. How does your brother digest the loss of his inheritance?

Car. Very well sure, for sometimes he has nothing else to digest; and he has enough of that too; it sticks in his stomach worse than a surfeit. Alas, we landed men are but fools to him, it makes him sober, and wise, very temperate.

Spru. There's Valeria! a foolish peevish thing that he calls mistress, good for nothing but to whet a man's wit, and make a whore on. I can't believe there's any real love between them.

Car. Has she received any of your letters?

Spru. Yes, twenty, and nothing will prevail. I have sought to corrupt her any time this twelve month, and can do no good on her; her father gives me opportunity out of pretence of good will, but I use it clean contrary; for alas, I cannot love any wench farther than to lye with her. I cannot fashion my tongue to speak in any other character. I would not willingly lose all this time and labour. I'll make short of it, either work her to obedience, or do her a mischief.

Car. 'Tis well resolved, and there's her sister Æmilia; she will glance sometimes affectionately upon me. Were it not a mad thing, when I have sold all my land to her father to get her into advantage? I think that will be the end of it.

Spru. Methinks Lackwit, her brother, might stand thee in some stead for the conveyance.

Car. Well, 'tis the truest spaniel that! I put a hundred jeers upon him, and yet he loves me the better. I can pawn him as familiarly as my cloak.

Spru. The time calls upon me,

Car. I'll dismiss you! will you present my service to the ladies and excuse me?

Spru. I shall be proud to make my tongue the organ of your commands, sir.

Car. I will hold you no longer from your happiness, but I shall envy the intercourse of your mirth. [*Exeunt.*

Actus I. Scena VI.

Dotario, Fido.

Dot. Then he is past hope?

Fid. He has no sense of his misery; a strong stupidity, a lethargy has possest him. His disease is infectious, it has caught hold of his estate, and brought that into a consumption.

Dot. No means to reclaim him?

Fid. I know not what to apply. When remedies are hurtful, give him good counsel, and you poison him.

Dot. I would my brother had been better advised, than to give his land to a prodigal.

Fid. Fitter indeed the right heir should have had it. You might do well to turn your compassion upon him; a poor injured gentleman, and stands equal in your blood.

Dot. No, I'll marry a wife, and get an heir of mine own. I have made a motion to Master Littlegood, the usurer, about one of his daughters, and we are partly agreed; I am going to ask her good will in it.

Fid. Look you, sir. Pray, stand by! here he comes with his train.

Enter Careless, Captain, Lieutenant.

Car. Is it not well resolv'd, Captain?

Cap. Yes, by the soul of Hercules! tis a good foresight, to sell all and prevent misfortunes. The world's full of uncertainties: Land may be barren, servants deceitful, make money I say, and what a man spends with his friends shall ne'er perish.

Lieu. I say, by the heart of valour! that man lives best at ease that has no money at all.

Car. What shall he do then, Lieutenant?

Lieu. By the faith of a soldier! for the exercise of his wits he may do any thing: if all trades fail he may turn pimp, 'tis a noble profession to live by. If he can perform that office well, he need ask no more of his *Genius.*

Capt. Body of me! nor no better preferment.

Lieu. As I am a sinner! 'tis a good science, a mathematical mystery of undermining holds, and, when the breach is open, be the first man that shall enter.

Car. But I think there be so many of them, they can hardly live one for another.

Lieu. As I am virtuous! 'tis grown into credit, and you have very good men that study it. Good knights and squires that have thriv'd by it.

Capt. Stab me! what sullen Saturn is that, looks so oblique upon us? as I am martial I will confront his aspect.

Car. Good Captain, be appeas'd! it is my uncle, I cannot avoid him; let me entreat your absence for a while! meet me at the Horse-shoe.

Capt. Fire of my blood! you shall rule me. Come, Lieutenant! [*Exeunt Captain and Lieutenant.*

ACTUS I. SCENA VII.

DOTARIO, CARELESS, FIDO.

Dot. Shall I speak or hold my peace?

Car. E'en which you please, good uncle.

Dot. Ay, 'tis all one to you, for any impression I shall make. Would I could refrain to take notice of you, but still nature oversways me, and affection breaks out into counsel, but to no purpose.

Car. Troth, uncle, youth will have his swing.

Dot. Ay, upon a gallows! if you hold on, that will

be the end of you. That I should live to see my brother's goods so misspent, the life of his labours suckt out by such horseleeches!

Car. Horseleeches! do you know what you say? No, you do not apprehend the worth that dwells in these men. To see how a man may be mistaken in the distinction of virtue!

Fid. Nay, sir,'tis as I told you :—you may as soon recall an arrow when 'tis flying, or a stone from præcipice, as reclaim him.

Car. Oh uncle, that you should thus carp at my happiness, and traduce my comradoes, men of such spirit and valour.

Dot. Yes, Captain and Lieutenant! how a vengence came they by these titles? fellows that have been only flesht in the ruin of black pots, and glass windows, the very scum of all rudeness.

Car. Have you any money about you?

Dot. What to do?

Car. Bribe me to keep counsel. You are but a dead man if they know on't: you have puft out your soul in their calumnies.

Fid. Hang them! fellows so sordid that no disgrace can stick upon them; they are choice company, for there's hardly the like of them. A man cannot discern the ground of their discourse for oaths. Unless you were divorced from all reason, you would not be wedded to such acquaintance.

Car. Why, how now, mongrel, are you barking? By this air! 'tis an indignity to my discretion, that is so happy in the election of their virtues: the only prime wits in town, things come so rarely from them, a man is kept in a perpetual appetite. I would not let them stay to offend you, neither can I endure their reproach. Farewell, uncle.

[*Exit Careless.*

Dot. Well, I will not trouble myself any more to look after him. I'll marry and thrust him out of all. That's the conclusion.

Desinit actus primus.

ACTUS II. SCENA I.

SPRUSE, LITTLEGOOD, VALERIA.

Spr. But are you certain of it?
Lit.   I o'erheard it,
When she did plot her own destruction,
And seal'd it with her hand, and kist upon't.
You know Aurelio?
Spr.   Yes, sir! was it he?
Lit. That beggar, that undone thnig!
Spr.   Let me alone
To fetch her off the quick-sands, and then I'll board her,
And steer her myself.
Lit.   That I were so happy
To know she lov'd you. Huswife, do you hear?
Here is a gentleman has land and means,
And wit, and beauty, more I wis than tother:
Make much of him, and what he says be ruled by him.
Spr. Let me alone, I warrant you.
Lit. I leave you.   [*Exit Littlegood.*
Spr. Now all the powers of love assist me in it,
To counterfeit a passion and dissemble.
All my delight's to fool them, and, then leave them.
I serve your women as the Hollanders
Do by some towns they get; when they have won them

They slight them straight. Now I address myself.
Lady, how fare you? You are melancholy.
 Val. If you do know't so well, why do you ask
  me?
 Spr. 'Tis from the tender care I have of you:
But an ill fate pursues my true endeavours,
To have them still misconstrued. 'Tis not well
  done,
To lay the burthen of your cruelty
On my affection, and to make that faith,
The passive subject of your dire disdain,
That is so active in obedience.
 Val. Pray, let me counsel you.
 Spr. Counsel! what's that?
Not Phœbus with his art, or all the drugs
Of Thessaly can ease my grief; the sea
Knows no such strait as I now labour in.
 Val. Why! what's the matter?
 Spr. Oh, my heart, my heart!
Would you would rip it up, that you might see
Yourself enthron'd, and all my faculties
Paying their homage to your memory.
I think I do it indifferently.
 Val. All this and more, lovers can speak at
  pleasure.
 Spr. Propose a course how I might win belief:
Were there a way to it, as deep with danger
As to the centre, I will search it out—
When I have nothing else to do.
 Val. Your thoughts have found such easy utter-
  ance,
That I suspect their truth; they seem to savour
Of art, more than of passion. I have heard
Great griefs are silent, neither do I find
Those symptoms of affection in your looks.
You change no colour, and your joints are steady,
Your eyes appear too full of petulancy,

As if they did reflect with inward scorn,
T' upbraid your falsehood.
   Spr. Now, by all my hopes,
By all the rites that crown a happy union,
And by the rosy tincture of your cheeks,
And by your all subduing eyes, more bright
Than heaven—
   Val.   Hold there!
   Spr. I prize you 'bove the world.
What should I say, when vows cannot prevail:
If you persist, and still so cruel be,
I'll swear there's no plague like love's tyranny.
And all this while I do not care a pin for her.
                                                     [*Aside.*
   Val. I have engaged it to your friend already.
   Spr. But love makes no distinction.
   Val.   If you say so,
I must debar my heart the knowledge of you.
   Spr. This will not do, I must be more lascivious.
Come, my fair Venus, sit by thy Adonis.
What, do you start? are you afraid of love,
That is all fair, and from whose brightest heaven
Are blown away all swol'n clouds of despair?
His brow is smooth, and all his face beset
With banks full of delight, a golden chain
Of wanton smiles hangs round about his neck;
And all his way before him strew'd with roses.
Come let us sit and dally, taste those pleasures.
Love is no niggard, we may eat and surfeit,
And yet our dainties still remain as fresh,
As they were never toucht.
   Val.   Is't come to that?
I thought whither you tended. I am unskillful:
Untaught in those deep, but ill mysteries.
   Spr. I'll teach you all, and lead your wand'ring
     steps

Through all those ways, where to find the way
Will be to lose it.
  Val.   I am very sorry,
The time's disease has so prevailed upon you.
'Tis the perfection now of compliment,
The only end to corrupt honesty.
To prostitute your oaths, and win our hearts
To your belief, is the Court eloquence.
  Spr. These are harsh tunes, and ill become your
    beauty,
Whose proper passion should be wantonness.
Why should you lose the benefit of youth,
And the delights ? give freedom to your will !
When age and weakness mortify your thoughts,
You may correct this looseness.
  Val.   Sir, I cannot
Hear you with safety.
  Spr. I must die then. I am slain, unless
Those words, and smiles, that wounded me, do
    heal me.
  Val. Had I known that, I'd have condemned
    them both
To silence and obscurity.
  Spr.   You had then
Robb'd nature of her best perfection,
And that had been a sacriledge. Nay, sweet,
Your beauty is a thing communicable,
And though you do impart, you may retain it.
  Val. Sir, I have summ'd th' accounts of all your
    cares,
And I do find their number more than weight.
Things but of custom with you, and your vows
Are but a cloud of wind, and emptiness ;
Forc'd by the storm of lust. When it is over,
And your thoughts calm'd, then you will love that
    virtue,
Which as a tie and anchor did withhold you

From driving to destruction. So I leave you.
                                                [*Exit Valeria.*

Spr. That ever any woman should be virtuous!
I have enclos'd a fire within my breast,
Will burn this frame of nature into cinders.
Her beauty has surpris'd me, I am caught
In love; by this light! 'twere a mad jest now
If I should turn honest, and woo her so:
If she persists, I must do so believ't,
And hate myself, as long as I live for it.
Well, I have played so long about the candle,
That my wings are sing'd with it; she is honest!
I see it, and that's something in this age.
Out of these doubts some strange thing will arise,
A strong disease must have strong remedies.

ACTUS II. SCENE II.

LITTLEGOOD, CROCHET.

Lit. Crochet, where are you?

Cro. I am here, sir!

Lit. Crochet, you know, that I am determined to marry my other daughter Æmilia to old Dotario the citizen?

Cro. Yes, sir! and then she and I shall be both in one predicament.

Lit. How so, man?

Cro. Why sir, for aught that I can perceive, she is like to have but a cold reversion, and that's the ordinary allowance for men of my function. There's not so much left of him, as will satisfy a lady's appetite for once; he is pickt to the very bones with age and diseases.

Lit. 'Tis no matter so long as his purse is well cram'd.

Cro. His purse that she looks after is lank enough, I warrant it. It grieves me to the heart, that such

I

a young beginner as my mistress should have no better hopes of trading.

Lit. Belike thou think'st that nature is uncharitable in him? no, he has benevolence in store for her. What because he is old, I am old myself, man.

Cro. And if he were older 'twere no great matter.

Lit. If I were older, knave?

Cro. No, sir, if he were older.

Lit. Why? what then?

Cro. His death would the sooner make her honourable: for having one foot in the bed, and the other in the grave, if she be rul'd by me, 'tis but her giving him a lift, and the next turn marry with a Lord.

Lit. Sayst thou me so?

Cro. Yes, sir, a citizen's wife no sooner casts her rider, but one of your Court gallants mounts her presently.

Lit. The knave is very pleasant.

Cro. Why, sir, your citizen's widows are the only rubbish of the Kingdom, to fill up the breaches of decayed houses.

Lit. What's her preferment, then, Crochet?

Cro. Why then, sir, she shall be made a Lady at the least, and take the place of her mother. She shall have clients wait at her gates with presents, and yet have their servile offices pass unregarded, she shall manage her husband's estate, and advise him in his office.

Lit. Is that all?

Cro. No, sir, she shall have more privileges than that: to be as proud as she list, and have new ways to express it; she shall ride up and down in her litter, and have a coach and four horses to follow after, full of gentlemen ushers and waiting women.

Lit. And yet the foolish girl will not perceive it?

Cro. Alas, sir, though you and I have so much

wit to look into these things, how should my young mistress be capable of it, when her husband that shall be is not able to put the case to her?

Lit. Go! fetch her hither; I'll advise myself. (*Exit Crochet.*) O, these perverse girls, that are led with nothing, but fancy foolish things, and yet have wit to be obstinate. If they set upon a toy, they must have it because they are willful, then they are as changeable in love as a cameleon, and think they can live by the air of it. They will venture to sell their fathers' fortunes and their own, for a night's lodging.

Actus II. Scena III.

Enter Littlegood, Æmilia, *and* Crochet.

Lit. Come, Æmilia! these showers are unseasonable. They will extinguish the torch, that should burn bright before thy nuptial; be not dismay'd, you are young and so is Aurora: she looks fresh every morning, yet disdains not to kiss her old Tithon, and lyes all night with him, and, when she rises, betrays with her blushes the wanton heat of her paramour.

Æmi. Good sir, think your power may command my duty, but not my affection.

Lit. Tempt not my patience! I would not willingly use the authority of a father to command, what I had rather win by entreaty.

Æmi. You know, sir, the inconvenience still happens to these forc'd matches: they never come to good, and, if you compel me to like of him, you must expect the same issue; you shall never make me any other president.

Lit. Not when I entreat you?

Æmi. I shall never love him.

Cro. And you know, sir, what an ominous thing

it is, when a woman does not love her husband;
she will either cuckold him, or poison him, and so
be burnt for a martyr in wedlock.

Lit. She must fashion herself to love him; I have
undertook it.

Cro. And then I'll undertake for the tother.

Lit. Will she have her liberty restrain'd? will
she renounce my protection? shall not I dispose of
her? if not, let her use her pleasure, betray herself
like her other sister to beggary, be like Scylla, cut
the purple hair of my life, and then turn monster,
let her!

Æmi. Oh! me, what shall I do? Would my
life were a sacrifice!

Lit. I'll tell you what you shall do, be advis'd;
refuse not a good offer, think of old Dotario, think
how to love him, think of his wealth, think of his
honour, think of me, think of yourself, think of
what will come after, if you be stubborn.

Cro. And whate'er you think to do, say nothing,
Mistress.

Lit. Well Crochet, I'll leave thee to persuade her
whilst I fetch the old man to confirm it.

[*Exit Littlegood.*

Æmi. O my distracted thoughts, and the rash
    counsel
Of love and hatred, when they are oppos'd
By avarice of parents, that confine
Their children's fancies to their sordid mind.
Were the bright sun their offspring, they would
    join him
Unto the earth, if gold might be engend'red.
We in ourselves have no part if debarred
The election of our love, and our condition
Is worse than beasts, whose will acknowledgeth
No check in that; the turtle takes her mate
Without compulsion, and, in summer's prime,

Each bird will choose out her own valentine.

Cro. Well, mistress! you do not apprehend the good you may have by marrying of an old man.

Æmi. Prithee, what good?

Cro. First, besides the honour he shall confer upon you by his age, you shall not find him so fiery and unruly as commonly your youths are, and thereupon, being cold of his tempter, you may the easier manage him.

Æmi. Thy mirth comes importunely on my grief.

Cro. Then you shall be his darling, and he shall dote upon you, and, though he strives to please you never so much, he shall lament that he can do it no better, and acknowledge his weakness, that he comes short of your desert, and what he desires, and be sorry that all he has is too little for you.

Æmi. I perceive it well enough, Crochet.

Cro. The only thing that you need fear him for is his tongue, for they say old men are great talkers, but you'll match that member well enough, and for any other part about him, you'll have but little to do withal.

Actus II. Scena IV.

Enter to them LITTLEGOOD, DOTARIO.

Lit. Look you, here comes the old lecher! he looks as fresh as an old play new vampt. Pray see how trim he is, and how the authors have corrected him; how his tailor and his barber have set him forth; sure he has received an other impression.

Æmi. I think the fool will be tedious.

Lit. Well, now I have brought you together, here I'll leave you. When lovers parley, parents are no fit auditors; see that you use the gentleman respectively, and though, sir, she seem coy and deny you, impute it not to perverseness but modesty. Maids in their first assault consult with shame, in the next with weakness. So I leave you. [*Exit Lit.*

Dot. Fair mistress, I would ask you a question, if you please to answer me.

Æmi. No mistress of yours, sir; yet, if you ask nothing but what I please to answer, you may.

Dot. I would first demand your opinion of me.

Æmi. Truly I have no skill to make any objection by the outward appearance, but, by the title page of your face, I should judge you to be somewhat ancient.

Dot. Take my word for it the index is false printed; if you please to turn to the book, you shall find no such thing written.

Æmi. O, 'tis worm eaten! time has cankered it; besides, there be so many dashes, my understanding will not serve me to read it, and a woman has no use of her clergy.

Dot. But love has renew'd it, sweet lady, and this is another edition.

Æmi. How long is it since the copy has been alter'd?

Dot. Let it not seem strange to you that I have felt this transformation. Your form has wrought a miracle upon me; the pulchritude of your feature, that is able to extract youth out of age, and could make Æson young again, without the help of Medea, it has put a fire into me, and I must impute it neither to herbs nor philtrums, but to the influence and power of your beauty.

Æmi. A fire? 'tis a foolish one that leads you without the precinct of your gravity. Ay, strange a man of your judgement should talk so preposterously.

Dot. Why, sweet lady?

Æmi. Sweet lady? what a petulant word is there, for a man of your beard? a boy of fifteen would not have spoke it without blushing, and there's a smile able to turn my stomach! I wonder you will make yourself so ridiculous.

Cro. If this be the best language she can afford him, 'twere safe for me not to hear it. I may be call'd for a witness.

Dot. Stay, Crochet, whither goest thou?

Cro. I'll come presently, sir! I'll come presently.
[*Exit Crochet.*

Æmi. Now you are alone, I'll tell you what I think of you. You are an old doting fool, one that twenty years since has drunk the Lethe of humanity and forgot of what sex thou wert, worn out of all remembrance of thyself; thou hast a body that a fever cannot heat, nor poison work upon, a face more rugged than winter, thy beard is moss, and thy skin so hard, that the perpetual dropping of thy nose cannot soften it.

Dot. These indignities are not to be endur'd; her abuses are more monstrous than the prodigy she would make of me.

Æmi. And yet you would be in love, forsooth, whom Cupid with all his strength is not able to pierce: you have not one pore open to let in an arrow. More need have a cordial to comfort you.

Dot. Rank injuries mock me to my teeth.

Æmi. If you had any.

Dot. I would your father heard you: he left no such thing in your commission. How dare you do it?

Æmi. Yes, and if I marry you, I'll use you accordingly: I'll have no mercy on your age. I tell you beforehand, that, when it happens, it may not seem strange to you.

Dot. Well, she may play with the line, I'll give her scope enough, but, when I have her fast, I'll twitch her, and draw her as I list to me. [*Aside.*

Æmi. Do but hear what I say to you, and it shall fall out ; no prognostication like it.

Dot. Sure 'tis some fury ! it cannot be a woman, she is so impudent.

Æmi. When I am your wife, if you are so hardy to venture on me, your whole study shall be to please me, and yet I will not grace it with acceptance. I will live as your Empress, lye a-bed, and command you and your servants, and you shall not dare to anger me.

Dot. Not dare to anger you ?

Æmi. No, if you do, I will fill the house with noise, and deaf thee with clamours.

Dot. Sweet heart, you shall have all content, I love [such] a life. These spirited wenches that are all fire and motion, they stir a quickness in a man, infuse an activity.

Æmi. He will not be put off, I must terrify him further. And, for your estate, you shall not meddle with it. I'll take up your rents for you, and dispose of them as I think fit ; only I'll allow you to carry some farthings in your pouch to give to beggars.

Dot. And what will you do with the rest, sweeting ?

Æmi. For the rest, I'll spend it upon myself in bravery : there shall not be a new fashion, but I'll have it. I'll look after nothing else ; your house shall be a mart for all trades. I'll keep twenty continually at work for me ; as tailors, perfumers, painters, apothecaries, coach-makers, sempsters, and tire-women. Besides embroiderers, and pensions for intelligencers.

Dot. She'll waste all I have in a month : the expenses of an army will not maintain her.

Æmi. Besides, I will have acquaintance with all the Ladies in Court, and entertain them with ban-

quets, yet for all that I will make my complaint of
you to them, traduce your infirmities, and they
shall conspire against you, and pity me.

Dot. I had rather be under twenty executions
than the lash of their tongues.

Æmi. Then you shall kiss me very seldom, and
when I vouchsafe you the favour : and you shall
do it not as a husband but as a father, not a smack
of lasciviousness.

Dot. What a sanctified creature shall I enjoy !

Æmi. I will lye with you the first year once a-
month, as a parson uses to instruct his Cure, and
yet not be question'd for neglect, or non-residence:
marry the next year, if you live so long, once a
quarter shall suffice you.

Dot. The next year if I live so long ? she thinks
of my death already.

Æmi. These are the least of your evils. I will
have one to cuckold you, and you shall take it for
a courtesy, and use him the kindlier for it.

Dot. Oh, me ! I can endure it no longer, that
word strikes cold to my heart. Were I an enemy,
and she had vanquisht me, I would not yield to
such articles. I'll propose these conditions to her
father, and see if he will allow them in all conscience to be reasonable. [*Exit Dotario.*

Æmi. Master Careless promised to be here instantly. I'll tell him what a fine youth he has to
his uncle.

Enter CARELESS, *drunk.*

Car. Here is the gulph that swallows all my
  land :
And to this desperate whirlpit am I reeling.
And there's the smooth stream that must guide me
  to it.
Were I as provident, as was Ulysses,

That Syren there might sing me to my ruin.
Save you, fair lady.
   Æmi. Save you, Master Careless.
   Car. Will you hear me speak any wise sentences?
I am now as discreet in my conceit
As the seven Sophics of Greece, I am full
Of oracles, I am come from Apollo;
Would he had lent me his tripos to stand upon,
For my two legs can hardly carry me.
   Æmi. Whence come you? from Apollo?
   Car. From the heaven
Of my delight, where the boon Delphic god
Drinks sack, and keeps his Bacchanalias,
And has his incense, and his altars smoking,
And speaks in sparkling prophecies; thence do I
    come!
My brains perfum'd with the rich Indian vapour,
And height'ned with conceits, from tempting
    beauties,
From dainty music and poetic strains,
From bowls of nectar, and ambrosiac dishes:
From witty varlets, fine companions,
And from a mighty continent of pleasure,
Sails thy brave Careless. Where's your father,
    lady?
   Æmi. I thought I had been worthy salutation.
   Car. These ceremonies are abolisht with me.
I kiss none but my punk, but, in this humour,
I'll kiss any body. I'll marry thee;
But not a penny jointure.
   Æmi.   Where I love,
I will not stand upon conditions.
   Car. I would accept this invitation,
But thy father is a usurer, a Jew;
And if I marry in his tribe, I shall thrive,
And I hate thriving. I am come to mortgage,
To pawn or sell, lady.

Æmi.   Do you want money?
Car.   Do I want money? let me consider this.
'Tis a good promising question, and requires
A sober and politic answer.   Yes, I want money.
   Æmi.   I have not ready coin; but there's a jewel
Will fetch you twenty pound.
   Car.   But do you dare trust me?
   Æmi.   I give it freely.
   Car.   Then, I say, thy father,
In getting thee has redeemed all his sin.
She has confirm'd my love, and I will marry her.
Let me survey it well, 'tis an amethyst.
   Æmi.   Why do you ask?
   Car.   Because they say that stone
Has secret virtue in it to recover
A man that's intoxicated, and I do find
That I am not so drunk, as I was.
   Æmi.   O, Master Careless, here has been your uncle
A-wooing to me.
   Car.   What! that piece of stockfish,
That has kept Lent thus long, would have young flesh now?
   Æmi.   If he could get it.
   Car.   'Tis such a rank goat.
   Æmi.   I made such sport with him, and terrified him,
How I would use him if I were his wife,
That he is frighted hence.
   Car. 'Tis well done of you! he upbraided me too
That he would marry, but I'll cross his worship.
We'll vex him ten times worse yet, I have plots
Maturing in my head shall crown thy wit,
And make him desperate, that he shall die
And leave us nothing.   I would not be troubled

With any of his wealth, no not so much
As to mourn for him, but I cannot stand
Now to relate it. Come, Æmilia!
I have declar'd my mind, but when I'll do it,
I'll in, and sleep, and dream upon't, and tell thee.

Actus II. Scene V.

Enter Littlegood, Mistress Fondling.

Fond. Bring me to that, and I'll yield to anything.

Lit. Nay, good wife, hear me!

Fond. You shall pardon me. He is my son, I hope, as well as yours, and he shall be fashion'd after my humour. Why should you think to hinder my prospect from looking to him? I say he shall rank with the best, spend his money and learn breeding.

Lit. Do, make a gallant of him or a gull, either will serve; he may ride up and down, and have his coach wait for him at the plays and taverns, take up upon trust, consort with wits and swordmen, be afraid of sergeants, and spend more for his protection than would pay the debt. He may be a stickler for quarrels, and compound them at his own charge; reel every night to his lodging, and be visited in the morning with borrowing letters, dice at ordinaries, and lend on all hands: seal at all hours, or be beaten to it. These are gifts in a son, beyond art or nature, for a father to be proud of; or else he may run away with all he can get, and, when 'tis gone, lye at a neighbour's house till his peace be made.

Fond. No, you shall keep him still at home with you; he shall not dare to enlarge his charter, to have any more wit than his father, let him sit in the shop with ne'er a pair of cuffs on his hands, and play at fox and geese with the foreman, entertain customers with a discourse as moth-eaten as your cloth, and not be able to look upon a lady, but court some silly creature of his own tribe, with speeches out of books, ten times worse than any remnant; and after supper steal abroad and be drunk in fear, this you can be content with. Well, when he was a child, it was the prettiest talking thing, and the wittiest withal, the neighbours took such delight to hear it. There was a good knight lay in my house then was so kind to him, but you ne'er knew the reason, since you have clean marr'd him, that's apparent.

Lit. I'll do anything, wife, that you will have me.

Fond. Yes, when 'tis too late, and the custom of rusticity is grown into another nature with him, when his mind is settled upon the lees of it, and the edge of his humour quite taken off, when learning has brought down his spirit, then you'll repent his restraint; has he not a pretty ingenuity?

Lit. So much the worse, when 'tis corrupted: mark me what I say, give him the reins, and if fiddlers sleep in a week, taverns keep their doors shut, the constable sit on a stall in peace, or wenches walk the streets for him (if he be like his father) ne'er credit me again.

Fond. So much the better, I would have it so, give him means to perform it, shew yourself a loving father, and be true in your prophecy.

Lit. I must yield to her for my quietness' sake. Was ever man thus tied to a chymera, thus vext with that should be his happiness? I have married with tumult, and begot my affliction, not one of my generation will be rul'd; and for my wife, she has a tongue will run post sixteen stages together, and ne'er tire of it; with that she can work me to any agreement. Well, take your son to your charge, do what you list with him: but for the wenches, I'll either chuse them husbands, or else they shall trudge without any other dowry than what nature has bestowed on them, that's certain.

Fond. Within there! call your young master hither, Crochet! he has been all this day at his study, makes the boy mopish with his scholarship, for want of better exercise; as revelling, courting, feasting, and the like, he stands plodding and musing as if his eyes turn'd with a wire, it has poison'd his very complexion, he is grown sallow with it. I know not what would become of him if I did not sometimes put money in his purse, and send him abroad, to sin for his recreation.

Lit. Sweet wife, be pacified.

Fond. No, I'll teach you what 'tis to anger a woman that brought a dowry with her.

Enter CROCHET *and* LACKWIT.

See what a picture of formality you have made of him! come hither, son Lackwit, what book have you there?

Lack. This is a book of Heraldry, forsooth, and I do find by this book that the Lackwits are a very ancient name, and of large extent, and come of as good a pedigree as any is in the city; besides they have often matcht themselves into very great families, and can quarter their arms, I will not say with Lords, but with squires, knights, aldermen, and the like, and can boast their descent to be as generous as any of the Lafools, or the John Daws whatsoever.

Fond. What be the Arms, son?

Lack. The Lackwits' Arms? why, they are three asses rampant, with their ears prickant, in a field or, and a ram's head for their crest, that's the Arms.

Fond. Well said, son, stand for the credit of the house.

Luck. Nay, I will uphold it besides! though my father be a citizen, yet I am a gentleman's son by the mother's side.

Fond. Ay, that he is, I'll be sworn, the Fondlings are as good gentlemen as any be in the city, the boy has a parlous head, how should he find out this, I marvail?

Luck. Find it out! as if I were such a fool I did know my own coat.

Fond. Yet husband, I never saw you wear one in my life.

Lit. Not a fool's coat, but, I shall have one of your spinning very shortly.

Luck. I'll tell you, father, if I list now; I can go twenty degrees back like a crab, to find out the track of our gentility.

Fond. Lo, you there! can you be content, thou man perverse to all reason, having a son of so large and prosperous hopes, that might stand up for the glory of his kindred, of such pregnancy of wit and understanding, so rich in the qualities that can bear up a gentleman, to let him sink and not cherish him with those helps that might advance his gallantry? You have had your flourishing season, and are now withered, your blossoms of beauty are blown off, and therefore must be content out of that dry stalk to afford some sap to maintain his succession; pray, how many young gentlemen have you in this town, that go in plush and their fathers to plough in the country? Shall we have worse presidents in the city? Impart I say, and give him twenty pieces, and when they are gone give him twenty more.

Lit. What to do?

Fond. Will you disparage him, as if he knew not what to do with it? Do you think that fencers, dancers, horse-matches—I'll have him versed in all these, and omit nothing that may demonstrate his breeding;—besides mistresses, and implements that belong to them require nothing?

Lit. Was ever any mother in this humour? that should reclaim her son from his ill courses, to animate him, and supply his riot: let her enjoy her follies, smart for them, and then repent. Here, hold: there's twenty pieces, I am sure all are thrown away; they are in a consumption already, and will be dead, and drawn out by to-morrow. What thinkest thou, Crochet?

Cro. Nay, sir, they are condemn'd, that's certain; you have past your judgement upon them, and my young master must execute it.

Lit. I give it lost, Crotchet, I give it lost; but stay, my daughters! I had need have Argus' eyes to look about me, or the dragons that watcht the Hesperides. I am beset on all hands; my daughters are wily, my wife wilful, my son I know not what, with the fear of my money, do so distract me that my wits are disjointed amongst them, all the remainder of my hopes is, if Valeria have proved tractable to Mr Spruse, and that Dotario has received comfort in his Æmilia. I labour with expectation till I go in and be delivered.

[*Exit Littlegood.*

Fond. Stay, husband, I'll go with you! but, hark you, son Lackwit, do you know to what purpose this gold was given you?

Lack. To no purpose at all, but I know what I purpose to do with it.

Fond. What is't?

Lack. I purpose to make a medicine of it.

Fond. A medicine!

Lack. Yes, I will dissolve it into *Aurum potabile*, and drink nothing but healths with it.

Fond. Then you are right.

Lack. Nay, I will domineer, and have my humours about me too.

Fond. Do anything for the improvement of your discipline. Come, Crochet. [*Exit Fondling.*

Lack. Stay, Crochet, do you perceive nothing? you dull animal, look here!

Cro. Ay, sir, I hope you mean to give me one or two of them.

Lack. No, I will not give, nor lend a friend a penny, there's no such confutation of a man's being a gentleman; but when I am drunk, and have my wine and my whores about me, I'll spend twenty or thirty shillings upon you, but I will not give you a penny, Crochet.

Cro. Then, farewell, sir!

Lack. You know where to come to me, you shall find me in my pontificalibus.

Desinit actus secundus.

Actus III. Scena I.

Enter Æmilia, and Valeria.

Æmi. Come sister, though our liberty be straightened,
Our mind stands free without compulsion,
There's none can make a rape upon our will.
Well if they understood a woman truly,
They would not seek to curb so, whose nature
Rejoices like a torrent, to make way
Spite of impediments. Now, if their wisdom
Should let us alone, we might perhaps ourselves
Find out the inconvenience and prevent it,

Which they like a false perspective would seek
To multiply upon us.
  Val.   I shall never
Recall that faith, which I have plighted once
To my Aurelio. I'll run all hazards
And violent attempts to throw myself
Into his arms.
  Æmi. I would not have you leave him,
Nor yet turn desperate. Now would I rather
Get him by some device, I love a witty
And an ingenuous trick above my life :
And should take more delight to over-reach them,
Than to enjoy my purpose.
  Val.   But I dare not
Play with my fortune so, nor trust adventures,
If fate would be so gracious to present
An opportunity.
  Æmi.   Come, fear it not !
You see what a man they would put upon me,
Might be my father. H' has less vigour in him
Than any Catamite.* There's not reserv'd
So much as one masculine grain in him.
A fellow that's as bald as a looking-glass,
And whose diseases are beyond arithmetic :
Not a joint of him free. A gouty numbness
Has seiz'd his feet and fingers, and there's all
The stiffness he has left : and, were I married,
I must spend all my life in rubbing of him
With hot woollen cloths, applying plaisters,
And cataplasms, and trenchers to his belly ;
Must undergo the person of a surgeon,
Not of a wife ; and yet I am not terrified :
It moves me not, I make a jest of it ;
Because I mean t'abuse them all, and chuse

 * A boy hired to be abused, contrary to nature. A Ganymede.—*Blount.*

Where I like best.
Val.   It is a happy spirit
That rules in you, I would I had one like it.
Æmi. Like me? thou hast not studied thyself so well,
Nor hast that season of thy mother in thee.
Observe her fashions, take example by them:
Although her husband be penurious,
Hard as the metal that he dotes upon,
Yet she can make him malleable,* and work him,
And turn, and hammer him, and wire-draw him,
And rule him with as much correction
As one would wish to govern. For my part,
When I have stretcht my brains, made all the shifts
The wit of woman can be pregnant of,
And shew'd my love by such experience
As shall outstrip belief, all for his sake
That shall enjoy me, which is Master Careless;
And when he has me, if he shall presume
On former passages of my affection
To oversway me in the least desire,
To contradict, and tempt my patience,
I'll shake off all obedience, and forget it.
I'll slight him, yet prevail.
Val.   Alas, my heart is
Tender and violable with the least weapon
Sorrow can dart at me.
Æmi.   You are a fool!
And every one that will can make you so:
When was your sweetheart, Master Spruse, here with you?
Val. But lately, and presented such a scene
Of protestations, and then varied it
So cunningly, that love and lust together
Were interwoven with such subtle threads

* In the original, "Mallemable."

That I could scarce distinguish them.
 Æmi. Take heed!
Whate'er he speaks it tends but to corrupt you!
I'd join commerce of language with a sphinx
Ere I'd deign to answer him. Master Careless
Told me his humours, seems he boasted of it,
He gave his character, the most perfidious
And love abusing creature in the world;—
That all his vows were treacherous, his smiles,
His words and actions, like small rivulets,
Through twenty turnings of loose passions,
At last would run to the dead sea of sin.
 Val. Whate'er he says I resolve ne'er to trust him.
 Æmi. Be wise, and constant, and then govern fate.
And in the interim, howe'er matters fall,
We'll find a trick, wench, how to cheat them all.

Actus III. Scena II.

Valeria, Æmilia, Spruse.

Val. See, here he comes again!
Spr. I come, sweet lady,
To rear the trophies of your conquest up,
And yield myself the greatest.
 Val. What's the matter?
 Spr. Your looks have tane me prisoner. I am captiv'd,
Bound with the golden chain of your loose hair,
And on your frowns depends my destiny.
 Val. 'Tis about the old matter; you may save
This labour, or go seek some new device.
In faith, these stale exordiums cannot take me.
 Æmi. Indeed, my sister and I know you well enough.

Spr. But, lady, since my change you do not
    know me.
I am now metamorphos'd, and that fancy
That roved, and was rebellious, by her power
Is brought within command.
    Val.   Ay, so you told me.
    Spr. Here I present a sad oblation,
A heart that bringeth its own fire with it,
And burns before your beauty's deity,
Offer'd up with as much devotion
As ever true love sacrificed any.
    Val. Well, you may jest with mortals, but I am
    not
So blind but I can see through all your mists:
Were I a goddess, as you term me one.
Sister to Phœbus, or armed like Minerva,
I would transform you straight; and fix you up
A monument for your hypocrisy.
    Spr. Now, by that sacred shrine, brighter than
    Venus,
To whom I pay my orizons, that form,
That fair Idea, that rules all my thoughts,
Thyself I mean, that spotless seat of pleasure—
The continent of all perfection,—
This spring of love, that issues from my soul,
Runs in a stream as pure as are your virtues,
Full fraught with zeal, immaculate and free
From all adulterate mixtures.
    Val.   On my life!
I can not frame me to believe one word.
    Æmi. Hold thy own there, wench, and I war-
    rant thee.
    Spr. Phœbus, how have I anger'd thee to lay
Cassandra's curse on me that was not trusted,
When she spake true and most prophetically?
    Æmi. Sir, he that is accustom'd to deceive
Gains this reward by it when he speaks truth,

Not to be credited.
  Spr.   Observe me, lady,
And mark the harmony; does it not sound
Upon the string, as if my heart kept touch ?
  Val. And so it sounded first to the same tune.
  Spr. That was ill-set; this is a different passion.
  Val. But 'tis all shew; and nothing serious.
  Spr. You cannot judge by former evidence:
It is no fit proof to confirm this motion,
This is a true text, that a false gloss of it.
  Val. But I shall never so interpret it.
  Spr. What can I say more, than to swear I love
    you ?
  Val. But should you now dissolve your eyes to
    tears,
Were every accent in your speech a sigh,
And every gesture, every motion in you,
An hieroglyphic to commend that love :
Had you the spells of it, and magic charms,
Set round about the circle of your arms,
To draw me to you, I would seal my ears,
Deaf as the sea, to shipwreck'd mariners.
And so I leave you to your better fortunes.
         [*Exeunt Valeria, Æmilia. Valeria loses her
           ring in a paper.*
  Spr. Am I despised and slighted ? Foolish girl,
Th' hast lost thyself; that which is best in nature
Turns to the worst corruption, my scorn'd love
Shall now convert to hatred. 'Tis decreed,
Fraud and revenge shall be my counsellors;
What's here ! a ring ? She lost it now, I know it,
The same Aurelio wont to wear on's finger;
He sent it as a gift ? 'tis so, the poesy :
          In love I write
          All my grief, all my delight.
The very same. Were I best to poison it,
And send it back to her ? No, it shall serve

T' poison her good name; there's no foul fact,
That love, when it is injur'd, dares not act. [*Exit.*

Actus III. Scena III.

Aurelio, Fido.

Aur. Come, honest Fido, thy best love supplies
Part of my hoped fortunes. That's true friendship,
Misery cannot shake, which crowns thy merit.

Fid. Sir, could my power produce forth anything
Worthy your acceptation, or my service,
I would with hazard of my life perform it.
So much I owe your virtues, so much pity
Your injuries; but this poor task so easy,
Consisting more of policy than danger,
Gives not my love an equal testimony.

Aur. You could not do an office more deserving,
Or grateful to my soul, than to bring tidings
How my love fares, each syllable she spake,
Though by an echo I receive the voice,
Is able to inspire new life into me.
How does she? is she well and mindful of us?
Speak it a thousand times; never did sound
Touch a more gladsome ear.

Fid.   By all circumstance
I could conjecture, I read in her looks
A strange disturbance. When I gave the ring,
A letter to her, as if joy and fear
Had run on several errands, and return'd,
Swift as her thoughts, and spoke her love in silence.

Aur. Th' hast seen the treasury of my happiness.
Speak! am I rich or no?

Fid.   She is a mine,
A store-house of all beauty, all content:
Her brow a bank of pleasure; her bright eyes,

The chief and only mover of your love,
So multiplied their flames, that they appear'd
To me most like a firmament of fires,
Yet chaster than the vestal; and below,
Clouded with sorrow, which dropt pearls for you,
And does enclose a soul richer than it,
Wherein is lockt the wardrobe of all virtues;
Yet sure that soul had left her mansion,
But that she stays to bid you welcome thither.
 Aru. And why should I be stay'd from going to her?
Why should a covetous eye watch o'er that wealth
That is my right? I will go claim my due,
And justify the seizure. Why should parents,
That can give to their children neither minds
Nor yet affections, strive to govern both?
'Tis not justice: yet where should I complain?
Love has no bar to plead at, nor no laws
To rule us by, nor Court to judge our cause.

Actus III. Scena IV.

Enter Captain Whibble.

What's he that interrupts our quiet sorrow?
 Fid. Sir, this is Captain Whibble, the town stale,
For all cheating employments: a parasite
Of a new sect; none of your soothing varlets,
But a swearing sycophant that frights a man
Into a belief of his worth; his dialect
Is worse than the report of a cannon,
And deafs a stranger with tales of his valour,
Till his conclusion be to borrow money.
His company is a cipher in the reckoning,
That helps to multiply it: your dear brother
Admires his discipline, and will swear to it,
 Aur. Is this one of his comrades?

Fid.   Sir, this is
His prime associate. I'll lay a hundred pound,
I guess by his physiognomy his business;
He is either trudging now unto a broker,
Or to invite some new heir unto a breakfast,
To seal for the commodity; or else
Wandering abroad to skelder* for a shilling
Amongst your bowling alleys; most commonly
There lies his scene: or perhaps man some whore,
A province that he usually adorns.
   Aur. Prithee, good Fido, go and baffle him!
Put an affront upon him. If his valour
Prompt him to make resistance I'll step out
And second thee.
   Fid. His valour? 'Tis the least
Thing to be fear'd, he has not one spark in him
To kindle a true anger.   [*Fido justles him.*
   Cap.   Sulphur of Styx!
Can you not see? death! where be your eyes?
You'd have me wash them in the channel, would
     you?
   Fid. Yes, very fain, sir, if you durst attempt it.
   Cap. Heart! do you stem me? and he had a beak
He might have split me: body of Jupiter!
He ran me athwart the midships: spirit of fury!
I think that he has sprung a plank in me.
   Fid. Then you may lye by the lee, and mend it.
   Cap. Horror of man! lay a captain aboard?
A man of war, and not cry amain to him?
   Fid. How! you a captain? I rather believe
That you are one of those that upon service
Were seen to carry tomkins in your guns,
And made a shift to discharge a league off:
Was it not so? that might take up your bullet,
And shoot again and do no hurt with it.
You a man of war?

                   * Swindle.

Cap. 'Slife! do you question it?
I'll tell the slave, to thy astonishment,
I have been styl'd "the rock of pirates," I;
I have plough'd up the sea, till Bosphorus
Has worship'd me; I have shot all the gulphs,
And seen the navel of the world, you stinkard!

Fid. How? slave! and stinkard! since you are so stout,
I will see your commission ere I part.

Cap. Strength of my brains! see my commission?
I'll blow thee up like a deck. Son of Neptune!
Off, or I'll fire thee.

Fid. I am grappled with you,
And will hang by your side till you be calmer,
And be so, or I'll lay my trident on you.
Come, to your tacklings!

Cap. 'Tis a bold active boy!
I see there's nothing to be got but knocks by him.
Give me thy hand, old Rover, hoist up thy top-sail,
And go in peace!

Fid. Sir, this will not appease me;
I must have satisfaction.

Cap. Reach me thy fist,
And be reconcil'd. What, thou dost not know me?
Though I am valiant, yet 'tis out of the road
Of my humour to disgrace any man.

Fid. This will not satisfy me.

Cap. I say again
Give me thy wrist! Know me and my lodging;
I'll give thee a supper: there's a good plump wench,
My hostess, a waterman's widow at the sign
Of the Red Lettuce in Southwark, shall bid thee welcome.

Fid. But I must have you leave your swearing first,
And be temperate.

Cap.   Hear me, honest Trojan!
As I am virtuous, as I love my friends,
That I may swear.
  Fid.   No, not as you are virtuous.
  Cap. Why, then, on my word, I'll give thee a
    supper.
What? I will not offend thee, my good drumstick;
I'll conform myself, come to me at night,
And I'll be as good as my word, old Bracer.
  Fid. But if I come, and lose my labour, what
    follows?
  Cap. Then, Teucer, in pure zeal and verity—
  Fid. I'll belabour you the next time I meet you.
  Cap. What, Scuffler! dost thou think I'll fail my
    friends?
No, Hector! I scorn it. I'll pawn my cloak first.
Farewell, Actorides.   [*Exit Captain.*

Enter AURELIO.

  Aur.   What, is he gone?
  Fid. Ay, and as glad he has escap'd from me,
As from the Syrtes.*
  Aur.   How! he bore it out
With impudence?
  Fid.   Yes, did you observe him?
There's nothing can discountenance him, still
This is his posture: he were excellent
To venture at a lottery.
  Aur.   Why, Mischief?
  Fid. I do not think he would ever draw a
    blank.

---

* Two sandbanks in the Mediterranean, on the coast of Africa—one near Leptis, the other near Carthage, most dangerous in navigation, from their often changing places. " From this circumstance," observes Lempriere, quoting from the best Latin authorities, " that word has been used to denote any part of the sea, if the navigation was attended with danger, either from whirlpool, or from hidden rocks."

Aur. We must pursue the project. Sup with him At any hand.

Fid. The jest is behind to see, In what a miserable perplexity, He will be put to entertain us.

Aur. Come! [*Exeunt.*

Actus III. Scena V.

Enter DOTARIO, LITTLEGOOD, ÆMILIA.

Dot. You know, father, for I must still call you so, how you charg'd your daughter to use me respectively.

Lit. Yes, marry, did I! and to show a double duty, as might suit with the reverence of your age, and honour of her husband.

Dot. Well, and as soon as you were gone, she had no more regard to me, than if I had been an old horse, or an old servingman.

Lit. Why, 'tis impossible she should transgress in such a high point of humanity.

Dot. Else there was some fury in her shape that did so. I am sure she shap'd me out to be the ridiculousest old ass in Europe.

Lit. Her modesty would not permit it in her.

Dot. If my words have any weight in them, she set as light by me, as by the least feather in her fan.

Lit. Why, is this true, Æmilia?

Æmi. No, indeed, sir.

Dot. How, no indeed? do you deny it? O palpable, she reckon'd up a whole catalogue of abuses and malicious practises that she would assault me with, if I were her husband; the least of which were above all patience.

Æmi. Do you think, sir, if I intended any such thing, I would have forewarned you?

Lit. No, 'tis not likely.

Dot. That you had but heard the disgrace she put upon me, in calumniating the vigour and ability of my person.

Lit. I cannot believe it.

Dot. And then terrified me, that the wind of her humour should be still against me, to cross me in everything I desired, yet the course of my destiny should be more impetuous than before.

Æmi. The old gentleman did but dream so.

Dot. Nay, more! she said I was an old, dry stump, that had not the least drop of moisture in me, yet, by the virtue of her humidity, she would make my temples so supple that they should sprout and bud a-fresh.

Lit. Come! she would not say so?

Dot. Yes, and that all my estate should be too little to maintain her in prodigality, and invite acquaintance.

Æmi. Alas, good gentleman! I told him how other women used their husbands, but I would conform myself to obedience.

Lit. Ay, that you might know what a blessing you had in her.

Dot. Oh! was it so? I cry you mercy, I mistook you. Here take this pearl for amends; I am sorry I have sinned against so sweet a simplicity.

Lit. Come, I knew you were in an error.

Dot. Then to avoid all cavillation hereafter, see what I have provided!

Lit. What have you there?

Dot. I have a Syngraphus, a writing with articles, that must be drawn between us before there can be any copulation.

Lit. Wherefore did you so?

Dot. Look you, sir, I was in a little suspense

of her behaviour, and therefore in relation of that, which I thought she objected, yet has since proved otherwise—notwithstanding these rules, which may so much conduce to my happiness, and have been so much advis'd upon with deliberation, I would have establish'd.

Lit. Pray, let's hear them!

Dot They are only some few propositions, and exceptions to be observ'd on her behalf, for the better security of my quiet, when I shall be married to her.

Lit. Now, I conceive you. Read them out!

Dot. First, that after Hymen has once joined us together, she shall admit of no man whatsoever, to entitle him with any suspicious name of friend, or servant. Do you mark me?

Lit. Well, proceed!

Dot. Next, if any of her old acquaintance come to visit her, as nurses, midwives, and the like, creatures of secrecy, she shall return them word she is not within, or otherwise accommodated.

Lit. Very good!

Dot. I'll have it written so upon the doors.

Lit. You may perceive by her silence, she will consent to anything.

Dot. Then, to avoid all occasions of writing epistles, she shall receive none, nor have any paper, pen, ink, or wax in her closet.

Lit. That's somewhat hard.

Dot. She shall not have any masculine bawdy-picture hang in her chamber, but shall take it down, and sell it away as a thing unprofitable, and an enticement of phantasy.

Lit. That, in my conceit, is very reasonable.

Dot. She shall bid no man to dinner, but I will invite them, and, when they are set, she shall not cast amorous glances upon them, nor drink to them, nor lick her lips at them, nor shew her teeth when she laughs, nor her tongue when she sneezes.

Lit. For all these, I'll engage myself.

Dot. Besides, she shall not take upon her to contrary me in anything, nor seem more or less wise than myself.

Lit. That's not much amiss neither.

Dot. She shall send no Hieroglyphics, nor meat cut in characters, nor tread upon any man's foot under the table, nor, when they are risen, give them her hand to kiss, or open her palm to have her fortune told her, nor yet shew them her ring, or receive any of theirs, and read the poesies.

Lit. Is this all?

Dot. She shall know no language but her own, nor speak any equivocating word.

Lit. In my mind now, these laws are very consonant to a good disposition, and, if I were to marry myself, I'd propose the like.

Dot. And, for her religion, she may pray to any innocent goddess, as Diana and the Graces, but if she have anything to say to Mars, Mercury, or Apollo, she shall acquaint me with it, and I will present her devotions.

Lit. Have you done now?

Dot. Last of all, when she is ready to go to bed, she shall not put out the candle to walk up and down in her smock, and shake her body in the dark; and if she be content, I take her as my own.

Lit. All these she shall subscribe to, if she be my daughter.

Dot. Why then, we'll proceed to the church.

Lit. Are you agreed or no?

Æmi. Pray let me speak one word with him in private.

Dot. Yes, what you please, sweet lady, it is

granted, were it a hundred pound to buy pins and
petticoats.

   Æmi. 'Tis not a thing, sir, of that dear expense,
Though you were pleas'd to tax me for that crime;
'Tis only this, time was I could not love you,
Though reason since has rectified my judgment,
And clear'd my eyes, that I can see my good.
Then, I confess, I made a solemn oath,
None should enjoy my love, but he that durst
Attempt to steal me; this is not intended,
For any peril to you, but for a safeguard
Of my first vow, which I must needs perform.
Now, if you please to come at a set hour,
None but yourself, and fetch me, I will yield
To go with you whither you shall command.

   Dot. 'Tis done, bright Helen! I will be thy Paris,
And fetch thee, though thou wer't at Lacedemon,
And care not a pin for all the power of Greece.

   Lit. What, are you agreed?

   Dot. Yes, we are both agreed.
Some few ceremonies, and then we have finish'd.
                                                   [*Exeunt.*

Act III. Scena VI.

Aurelio, Fido.

   Aur. Fido, I am now advised upon a plot,
If it succeed shall crown my invention.

   Fid. Something about the captain?

   Aur. Hang him, Kastrill!
I scorn to loose a thought on him; my brains
Repine at his memory. 'Tis a new device,
The issue of extremity. 'Tis thus,
I will turn a desperate gamester in love,
And venture all upon one cast.

   Fid. Take heed, sir!
There may be plots, but little policy;

Fortune and love are insolent, and ticklish.

Aur. Come, I'll do it! I'll send thee with a letter
Unto my mistress, that shall make her mad.

Fid. How! make her mad? what do you expect
from that? what can you gain by the loss of her
wits?

Aur. I shall gain my desire.

Fid. And do you prize
The satisfying of a lewd desire
So much, to rob your mistress of her senses?
Can you accuse her of inconstancy,
Or tax her of dishonesty? or will you
Prove false to her? What mischief do you intend?
What hopes can you conceive, that may secure
So great a sin from Heaven's just punishment?
Have you a drug or incantation,
And think to make her senseless of her grief,
With the privation of her understanding?

Aur. Not any of these.

Fid. If you do, you must employ
Some other messenger. Let me advise you
Keep her in her right mind while you have her:
Love of itself is an illusive spirit,
And will enough distract her without help.

Aur. She shall seem mad but in appearance,
  Fido,
And with that feigned frenzy move a pity
From all that must impute it to her sufferings.

Fid. 'Twere a mad jest! but is this all your
  plot?

Aur. No, this is not the main one! there's another
Of greater consequence and secrecy,
For a sound mind to bear, and 'tis a burthen
Worthy thy care and honesty. Think not
I am so desperate and heady, to launch forth
Into those dangerous seas without a pilot,

L

And I have chose thee for my Palinurus.
  Fid. You never knew a man of less experience.
I do not ken one rock, or shelf, and love
Has many.
  Aur. 'Tis no matter! thou and I
Will sing a Pæan to love's victory.
  Desinit actus tertius.

Actus IV.   Scena I.

Enter Careless, Captain, Lieutenant, Lackwit,
  four Wenches.

  Car. Come, my voluptuaries, my sons of comfort,
That know no sorrow, sing like grass-hoppers,
And fear no winter nor no poverty;
Lead on, my moving pillars of delight!
My Alchymists of pleasure, that convert
All like yourselves; can make old Cato dance,
And turn Fabricius to an epicure,
Should he behold you.
  Cap. Thou say'st right, Telemachus;
'Tis wine and mirth that breed these raptures in
    thee.
Body of Jove! there's nothing but a rabble
Of lean and starv'd imaginations
Accompany sobriety.   Some wine there!
That I may court my cockatrice.
  Car.   Good Captain,
Bid our noble friend welcome.
  Cap. You know my humour,
To men of ordinary pretence I seldom
Use to debase myself below the nod
Of salutation, but for your sake
I receive him as a man deserving.
Give me thy hand, Cadmus!

Lack. I desire, sir, to incorporate myself into your acquaintance.

Car. 'Tis well said! do the like noble office to our friend, here, sweet Lieutenant.

Lieu. Sir, he shall command my heart and hand on his occasions; I'll as soon draw in his quarrel as to piss against a wall.

Car. These are the mirrors of the time, old boy, that shall show you how to adorn your behaviour, that you may pass in all company with confidence of approbation.

Cap. And not err the breadth of a nail.

Lieu. He shall be able to pass through the needles of all occurrences.

Lack. An they would but learn me to swear and take tobacco! 'tis all I desire.

Car. Come, they shall do it! and I must tell you these suggestions in you are arguments of a generous disposition. Whence do they flow, I wonder?

Lack. That mother-wit that put them in my head has put money in my purse, and as far as that money will lead me I will be bold and wise. I have my humours, and I scorn the pollution of the mechanics.

Car. How do you like these replies, Captain.

Cap. Very well, by the faith of a soldier, excellent well! they are good relishing answers, and express an ebullition in his nature, swelling to conformity.

Lack. What, I will bear myself like a gentleman?

Cap. Ay, and the way to bear yourself like a gentleman is sometimes not to be able to bear yourself at all. Lieutenant, what say you?

Lieu. I say, by Hermes! he that has a fortune
And power to acquaint the world with his perfec-
    tions,
And seeks to smother them, let him die wretched.

Car. You have no other way than this, to render you worthy of society.

Cap. What! he may turn stinkard, and live in the country with roots and bacon, and not drink a cup of good wine in a twelve-month, nor know how the year goes about, but by observation of husbandry. He may keep two couple of dogs and a sparrow-hawk, and level his discourse by them. He may be styl'd a civil gentleman, ten spheres below a fool. He may marry a knight's daughter, a creature out of fashion, that has not one commendable quality more than to make a corner pie and a salad, no manner of courtship but two or three dances, as old as Monsieur, and can play a few lessons on the Virginalls that she learnt of her grandam: besides she is simple, and dull in her dalliance.

Car. He tells thee right, my brave frisker! they are lumpish girls, heavy in their sport, and cannot move with art.

Cap. There's a wench has her suburb tricks about her, I warrant you. Hold there Bellerophon! take thy Ocyrois, and mount her like Phlegon.

Lack. Now, do I want some two or three good oaths, to express my meaning withall.

Lieu. Captain, what think you, shall he be a brother?

Car. Yes, he deserves it; let him be a brother. Give him the principles of the brotherhood.

Cap. Are you resolved to be a brother, sir?

Lack. Anything I; you shall make a blowing horn, or what you list of me.

Cap. Nothing can be suddenly perfect, but must aspire by progression: he must be practised in certain duties before he can be an ingrafted member of the fraternity.

Car. He shall do anything that is requisite.

Cap. Well then, for the first two months we must dine every day at a tavern, where it shall be lawful for any brother to bring his shadow with him; and, besides the full income of wine and provision, to bespeak any superfluous dish that he affects; but that which shall most commend the discretion of your worth, is, that after the dissolution of the feast, no man besides yourself must know what's to pay or take notice of the reckoning.

Lack. I must pay all, must I?

Cap. You understand me rightly, and I applaud your capacity; from thence, we must have a coach attend at the door, to carry us to a play, and at night to a bawdy-house.

Lack. And all at my charges?

Cap. What else? And if any brother need a cloak or a suit, or so, you must not stay till he publish, or intimate his wants; but presently, by the strength of your own Minerva, pick out the meaning, and take order to supply him. Have you any credit with the tradesmen?

Lack. Yes, I have a tailor that will trust me for anything that I'll have him.

Cap. That tailor shall have custom, tell him so. And one thing more; now brother, for so I must call you, we must have all things in common, no difference in the possession of anything.

Lack. Pray explain that rule to me, I do not understand you.

Cap. Why thus; this hat is mine, and that yours, as you conceive now, but they are neither mine nor yours upon the premises; but may be transferr'd upon occasion to either, as thus, do you conceive me? 'Tis usual amongst us.

Lack. 'Tis very well! is this all?

Cap. I'll make but one experiment more of your apprehension, and have done. Look you!

[*They shift cloaks.*

Lack. O I shall do this to a hair, and, by the same consequence, I shall be a Captain sometimes; shall I not?

Cap. Yes, when the date of your task is accomplisht, you shall be anything.

Car. 'Tis enough! this once a week will render him exact. Shall's have a song and a dance, Captain?

Cap. Hang a song! you see what little room we have for our mirth, and you would fill it up with air, would you?

Car. Nay, but, by that air! I hold a song very delightsome, the very place, as a man would say, and superficies of pleasure.

Cap. Prithee let it alone! by that element it charms me into melancholy.

Lack. Then, good Captain, let's have a dance, for these gentlewomen's sakes; besides there be many that come to see nothing else.

Cap. Why, can you dance?

Lack. What a question is there to a man of quality? Yes, I can dance, and that some that are here shall see and feel before we part; for I mean to shake my heels with that fervour, that it shall strike them into a fit of my love, shall be worse than any ague to them.

Cap. Say you so? We'll try that, i'faith. Come on squeakers! rack up your feet and ears to your instruments.

Lack. What tune, Captain?

Cap. Play us "The Fine Companion."

The Dance.

Well said, my effeminate varlets! this was auspiciously performed.

Lack. I am afraid this dancing will breed spavins in my legs, this caper has put me in remembrance of a crick in my back I got at my last vaulting.

Cap. No, thou art deceiv'd, my noble Hyacinth! 'tis a mystery will exalt thee, Hylas; 'twill make thee rise I say, and put gold in thy purse. Thou shalt follow the court like a baboon, when a thousand proper fellows shall shirk for their ordinary; 'twill make thee conversant with ladies, and they shall give thee diamonds to pawn, and thou shalt ride up and down in thy foot-cloth, my little dolphin. Some wine there, Tony! I called for wine an hour ago, and could get none.

Enter DRAWER.

Fill out, sirrah! What's here, the epitome of a glass? By the womb of Bacchus! a score of them are too little for a draught.

Lack. O Lord, Captain! nine such hornets are able to sting a man to death.

Lieu. By Saint George! he that dies so, dies valiantly.

Cap. What, my bold bravo? be not afraid, and thou wert dead 'twere nothing. I'll come but with a troop of wenches, and a noise of fiddlers, and play thee back like Orpheus. What's to pay, Drawer?

Draw. Sir, you have built a sconce, since you came in, of thirty pounds, and before you have any more my master intends to be satisfied.

Cap. What money have you, brother?

Lack. Who, I? O Lord, brother Captain, I have not the third part of it.

Cap. No matter, I ne'er think upon such transitory reckonings. Come, let's have a health, and my brother Lackwit shall begin it. Reach three joint stools hither, Drawer.

Lack. What to do, Captain?

Cap. I'll shew you: you shall ascend here, and be Captain of this fort. I'll insconce you; come, intrench yourself, and play from your battery, and so every man round; there take your lintstock in your hand, and give fire! now every man as far off as he can from the command of his ordinance. Farewell, brother! [*Exeunt.*

Lack. Why, gentlemen, I hope you will not use me so. I am your brother! why gentlemen—

Cap. There, Drawer, take him for a pawn; tell him when he has no money he must be serv'd so: 'tis one of his chief articles.

Enter CROCHET.

Cro. How now! What, are you preaching o'er your cups? Now you are in your pontificalibus, indeed.

Lack. Good Crochet, help me down! I shall break my neck else.

Cro. How came you there?

Lack. I know not; an ill hour of the brotherhood. I'll after them with a vengeance.

Draw. You must stay and pay the reckoning first, besides the musicians expect something.

Lack. Who! I pay the reckoning? 'Slight! I came but now in.

Draw. That's all one; you were all of a nest, they are flown away, and there's none left but yourself.

Lack. 'Sdeath! the Captain is gone away with my hat, and my cloak too. I tell thee I'll pay no reckoning.

Draw. 'Tis all one to me, if you can satisfy my master so.

Lack. What shall I do, Crochet?

Cro. Give him what you have, and, if he will take your word for the rest, I'll excuse your hat and cloak, and say you lost them in a skirmish.

You must scratch your hands in half-a-dozen places with a pin.

Lack. Ay, so I will. Come, sir, I'll go in and talk with your master.

Cro. Besides, I have another business I came to tell you of, that you and I must do together. You shall reap the whole credit on't yourself, if you can manage it handsomely, 'twill gain you that reputation with your father that you shall never lose yourself while you live again.

Lack. What is't, Crochet?

Cro. Go in! and I'll tell you. [*Exeunt.*

Actus IV. Scena II.
Aurelio, Spruse.

Aur. You much amaze me!

Spr. Sir, perhaps I might,
With better judgment and more thanks, conceal
So great a wickedness, but my true love to you
Could not withhold it. You have read some stories,
And these are things in nature not unheard of.
No newness at all, the self-same lust and pride
As well rules her that treads upon the flint,
As her that rides upon the necks of slaves.

Aur. Stay, let me pause a-while! she is a woman
Whose age and form might tempt me to distrust her,
But yet her manners forbid me to believe it.

Spr. Believe't? She is a close adult'ress,
Of most strange exercise, a fricatrice
Insatiable : and has she none but you,
That she can find, to bait with her allurements,
To cover her lewd projects? This moved me,
I'd not have meddled else.

Aur. O, do not wrong her!
Good sir, do not wrong her! it cannot be.

Spr. You have been still kept ignorant. For my part,
I never yet expected better from them;
I count them but as ordinary chances,
Trivial, and drawn out from the lap of fortune.
Believe me, sir, there is no day so holy
That ceases to betray a woman's falsehood.
My medicine works, I shall be even with her

   Aur. I sought at first to make her mad in jest,
But now I'll make her mad in earnest: yet
'Tis not good to be too credulous. A word, sir.
I must have better proofs than your bare word,
To justify this accusation;
Her virtue must not stumble at a straw.

   Spr. Sir, 'tis not threats that can extort from me
More than I list to speak. I see you troubled,
And therefore will not leave you in suspense:
Know that I made myself experiment.
                                  [*He shews the ring.*
For all, let this confirm you: this she gave me
Upon the premises.

   Aur.   O, I shall burst!
Here is a sight to make the sun run backward;
Good sir, forgive me, that I prest you so,
Consider't as your own case. Were you he
That put your confidence, your happiness,
All in a woman's love and found her false?

   Spr. I must confess I think it would afflict me.
I'll leave you, sir, I have discharg'd my conscience,
But of more ill, than she has goodness in her.
                                        [*Exit Spruse.*

ACTUS IV. SCENA III.

FIDO, AURELIO.

   Fid. How now! what, planet-struck? How do you, sir?

This 'tis to be in love: what alterations
It breeds! it makes a man forget his friends.
Come, sir, be merry; your project has took.
She fell into her fit soon as she read it,
And tore the papers and talk'd idly, and shew'd
The symptoms of the prettiest lunacy.
What, have you lost your speech? those folded arms
And frowns express a sorrow, more than love.
His eyes, though fixt upon their object, shew
The wandering sphere of his disturbed mind
Is whirl'd about in error. Pray, look up, sir!

Aur. I am not dumb, I have a care within me
Speaks to my troubled soul.
  Fid.   Why, what's the matter?
 Aur. O hear it then, and witness it for ever.
Whene'er thou seest a woman in whose brow
Are writ the characters of honesty,
And calls the gods to justify her truth,
Swear she's a Syren and a crocodile.
Conclude her false, it is enough she vows,
And speaks thee fair; the winds wait on her lips,
Straight to disperse her oaths.*

 Fid. You do but jest, sure.
 Aur. There is not one of them that is the same
She would appear to be; they all are painted.
They have a fucus for their face, another
For their behaviour, their words, and actions.
 Fid. Come, come! these are but qualms of jealousy.
 Aur. Give no faith to their brow: for, in that green
And flourishing field of seeming virtue, lurks
A snake of lust, in whose voluminous wreaths
Are folded up a thousand treacheries,
Plots, mischiefs, and dissimulations,

---

* " Methinks the lady doth profess too much."—*Shakespeare.*]

That man ne'er thought of. For, in wickedness,
The wit of woman was ne'er yet found barren.
 Fid. I think he means to be mad himself too:
Your reprehensions are too general:
For, by these words, your own Valeria suffers.
 Aur. Why, there's the sum of all that I have spoke,
The abstract of all falsehood. 'Tis a name will
Blister the tongue of fame; in her report
Is drown'd the memory of all wicked women.
 Fid. Is your Valeria false?
 Aur. Once my Valeria, but now mine no more,—
For they have perish'd that have lost their shame—
Is fallen from virtue past recovery.
The golden organs of her innocence
Are broke, not to be solder'd.
 Fid.   In my conscience
You wrong her. This is nothing but th' abundance
Of love; will you go and sup with the Captain
And drive away melancholy?
 Aur.   O no! my heart
Is shut against all mirth.
 Fid.   Then I'll go seek
Your brother out, and he shall go along with me:
I'll shew him with a perspective, i'faith,
What a brave Captain he has; he shall be
In a disguise, as my companion,
Then if he will maintain a paradox,
That he is either valiant, or honest,
I'll be made the scorn of their company,
 Aur. But my fate guides me to the contrary;
For, if my mistress do not honest prove,
She's put a period to my life and love.

Actus IV. Scena IV.

Lackwit, Crochet.

Cro. Come, be not dismay'd! whate'er you say, I'll swear it: you must affirm you lost your hat And cloak in a skirmish.

Luck. So I will, Crochet. Mass! thou wert not with us at the first neither.

Cro. Why, what if I had, sir?

Lack. Thou might'st have carried Away two or three of the Captain's oaths with thee.

Cro. I can coin them myself without any treason, I warrant you.

Lack. Oh, Crochet, I am thinking now how bravely I'll live when my father is dead.

Cro. Yes, pray, let me hear you!

Lack. I have drawn the map of it already. I'll go every day in my cloak lin'd with plush, and my beaver hat; I'll keep my whores, and my running horses, and I'll maintain thee in as good a pyed livery, as the best footman of them all goes in.

Enter Littlegood.

Lit. You will, sir? What ungracious villain could have said this? Where's your cloak and hat? Yes, you shall have money to spend another time.

Enter Fondling.

Fond. How now, what's the matter?

Lit. Look you! do you know this gentleman?

Fond. How comes this about?

Cro. Nothing but the fortunes of the wars, forsooth: my young master has been in as stout a fray as ever the genius of Fleet Street trembled at.

Fond. How was it, son?

Lack. Let Crochet relate, I scorn to be the trumpet of mine own valour, I.

Fond. Do tell the story, Crochet.

Cro. Indeed, he made them all run away, that I am certain of.

Fond. Nay, but shew us the manner of it.

Cro. Why, forsooth, I came at the latter end of the feast and the beginning of the fray, and there my young master was got above them all, and stood upon his guard, and held his weapon in his hand so dreadfully, as if he would have poured down his fury upon any man that should come near him.

Fond. And will you be angry with him for this? 'twas well done, take no wrong of them: better lose all the clothes off from his back than to keep a cloak for his cowardice.

Cro. Now is the time to move the other business.

Lack. Well, mother, if you will give me twenty pound more, I'll do you such a piece of service, that you shall thank me for it as long as you live.

Fond. What is it, son?

Lack. Nay, you shall not know before it be done: the conclusion shall crown it.

Fond. Well, husband, give it this once, and I'll urge you no more. Let's see how the boy will employ it.

Lit. Yes, send one arrow after another, and lose both.

Fond. Nay, but give it him for my sake. I am confident he has a good project; you have example for it in your trade. How many have you, that break daily, and yet their friends set them up two or three times, one after the other?

Lit. Once more you shall prevail with me. Here, hold! but if this miscarry, ne'er ask me for a penny again.

Lack. I warrant you. Come, Crochet!
Fond. Must Crochet go with you?
Lack. Yes, 'tis a business that cannot be done by one alone.
Cro. Well, mistress, pray throw an old shoe after us!

Actus IV. Scena V.

FIDO, CARELESS (*disguised*), CAPTAIN.

Cap. Gentlemen, you are very welcome! What, hostess? come hither, good hostess!

Enter HOSTESS.

Fid. You have a good handsome Hostess, I perceive, Captain!

Cap. She is cleanly and good condition'd, that's my comfort; and, by the powers of beauty! if a man were combustible he might find in her eyes that would kindle a conflagration.

Host. What gentlemen be these, Captain?

Cap. Peace, good Hostess, I would not willingly proclaim their disgrace! one of them is a gentleman that I bastinadoed the other day; and now he is come to give me a supper, to be reconcil'd to me, but take you no notice.

Fid. Captain, here is a friend, that I would willingly commend to your acquaintance.

Cap. Sir, as I am a true soldier, I embrace your love in him, and that's as much as I can say. Hostess, these are not ordinary guests with you; therefore, you must be respectful: and, faith, if you say the word, gentlemen, one of these nights, we'll every man procure as many of our acquaintance as we can, and be merry here at supper for crowns a piece. What think you?

Fid. This is not the business we came about, sir.

Cap. I know it well enough. Hostess, pri'thee, good, sweet, honey, Hostess, step and buy us a joint or two of good meat, and a capon, and lay it to the fire presently.

Host. Where's the money?

Cap. Death to my honour! do not question it, but do as I bid you.

Host. I have not a sixpence in the world, the cobbler had all I had for mending of your boots.

Cap. Go! you must make shift, and get more then.

Host. Why, if these gentlemen come to bestow a supper on you, let them give me money beforehand.

Cap. Speak lower, woman! art mad?

Host. I tell you I have not a penny in the house.

Cap. Speak lower, I say. Go borrow it of thy neighbours, I'll see it paid.

Host. Yes, and turn me behind the door for my reckoning; You have serv'd me so I know not how often. No! I have trusted you too much already; you have not paid me a penny for your lodging since you came to my house, besides what I have lent you out of my purse.

Cap. Bane to my credit! you will exile me beyond the confines of reputation. Go pawn some pewter, or one of thy brass pots! 'Slight! do not disgrace me, do anything rather, take the sheets off from my bed.

Host. Yes, you care not what becomes of anything. Why can you not ask them for money?

Cap. 'Slife! a man may plot till his heart ache. An you still seek to cross me you will undo me in my designs.

Host. You have more signs in your head than hang at all the alehouses in town again.

Cap. Prithee, woman! hear me what I say. I

know they come to spend upon me, and will crouch, and do anything, yet when I, out of my nobleness, and beyond expectation, shall use them so courteously, 'twill be such an engagement, that I can borrow ten or twenty pieces of them at my pleasure.

Host. I tell you I cannot do it, nor I will not.
[*Exit Hostess.*

Cap. Faith, gentlemen! I must entreat you to excuse me. My Hostess is not very well, she tells me, and I think she is not so well stor'd with necessaries to entertain you as I could wish; and indeed she has ne'er a spit in the house, therefore we'll defer it till to-morrow night, when 'twill be more convenient at a tavern.

Fid. Well, sir! your excuse shall prevail. We are not inexorable upon extremity.

Cap. In this you have won me to your observance for ever.

Fid. Captain, I have another thing to propound to you. Here is a friend of mine has lately receiv'd injury from one Master Careless, and, upon debatement of the matter, this gentleman is so apprehensive of his disgrace, that he can not possible put it up with safety of his reputation, and therefore desires to have it determined in plain field. Now, as he is informed, his adversary accepts of it, and has chosen you for his patron in the quarrel.

Cap. By the shrine of Phœbus! I wonder what strange impudence has possest him. As I am a man of honour, I have brought him successively off from a hundred of these to the peril of my life, and yet am daily obnoxious to new assaults for him.

Fid. Then you disclaim to have any hand in the action?

Cap. By the passion of valour, gentlemen! I'll tell

M

you, I love a noble employment with my life, but, for such a pitiful, drunken, shallow coxcomb, I hate to be seen in such a business.

Fid. Do you think no better of him, Captain? If he be so unworthy, I would advise you not to meddle with him.

Cap. By the faith of a soldier! if he have any care of his credit, let him not deal with him; he will but defile himself with such an abject. I hold him to be so poor condition'd I would not enter a country gentleman upon him.

Fid. Yet you keep him company, Captain.

Cap. I confess I have done, and my intendments were good in it; I saw him so raw and young, I was induc'd to believe there might be some hopes of him, but, after much impulsion, when I found him so unapt, and indocile in his own nature, I gave him lost, and so I esteem of him, by my life!

[*Careless puts off his disguise.*

Car. Oh, thou treacherous villain! dost thou betray me to myself, and belie me to my face? How many quarrels have you brought me off from?

Cap. Never none, by Jove!

Car. I will not rail at you, but I will cudgel you, and kick you, you man of valour!

Cap. Hold! as thou art a man of renown, thou wilt strike thy foot into me else, my body is as tender as a bog.

Car. Thou cowardly perfidious rascal! have I, for this, made thee my associate, paid for thy swaggerings, and breaking of tapsters' and ostlers' pates, fed thee at a charge a man might have built an hospital; drench'd thee with sack and tobacco, as thy face can witness?

Cap. Oh, hold! as thou art worshipful.

Car. Come, sir! surrender your robes, that you have polluted with cosenage. Here, Fido! take this hat and cloak: I will not leave him a covering for his knavery; these are the trophies of your treachery, these.

Cap. Nay, good sir, do not pillage me of all; stay till I get my own again!

Car. If Lackwit will restore them he may, else you must resolve to go bare-headed before your right-worshipful fortune, with a truncheon in your hand like a verger, and so I leave you. Come, Fido! now for my mistress.

Cap. Well, those good qualities that are bred in a man will never out of him, that's my comfort.

And, since I am the scorn of Captains made,
I'll seek a better and more thriving trade.

Actus IV. Scena VI.

Aurelio, Spruse.

Aur. Come, sir! now I have found you, not the power,
And strength of fate, shall pull you from my vengeance.
And though I know my life too mean a ransom
For the redeeming of the priceless loss
Of her abused honour, yet, what Nature
Enables thee to pay, I'll take in part,
And leave the execution of the rest
Unto hell's justice.

Spr. What do you intend, sir?

Aur. Look you: t' unfold your heart, sir, with this sword,
And read the falsehood that is written in it.
Come, I must know the truth, and reason too,
If there be reason for a wicked act.

Spr. You mean about Valeria?

Aur.   The same.

Still an ill conscience will betray itself,
And sends forth many a scowling, fearful look,
To descry danger; if he stand confident,
And justify it to the face of terror,
Then she is false.

Spr.   I hear she is run mad.

Aur. Is, and the cause of her distemperature
Is the reproach you put upon her honour.

Spr. The wound then is too deep, and an ill fate
Has driven the shaft of my intended malice
Beyond the scope I aim'd at.

Aur.   Was it malice?
That word has strook me both with joy and anger,
Both in suspense, which should weigh down the scale
Of my deep burd'ned mind. What horrid baseness
Durst so attempt to profane innocence?

Spr. It was my love to her.

Aur.   What is his hate,
Whose love has proved so ominous?

Spr.   That love
Being wrong'd, begot that hate.

Aur.   Thou hast done ill,
And, like a foolish and young exorcist,
Hast conjur'd up a spirit of that fury,
Thy art cannot allay.

Spr.   Repentance may.
I only meant to give her name a gash,
That might be heal'd again without a scar
Or any spreading plaister of wide rumour,
With help of her compurgators, but only
To vex her.

Aur. What's the offence that did provoke
This imputation? Did she ever wrong you,
Malign your wit, disgrace you before your mistress?
Disparage your behaviour? Had she done so,

Yet this revenge were disproportionate.

Spr. Urge me no more! I cannot look on her
Without such a reflection of my crime
As must give shame a lustre; there's no man
But once in's life may sin besides his nature,
Nay, perhaps contrary: this is a deed
I must abhor to justify.

Aur. You have given
Almost a satisfaction.

Spr. 'Twas a scandal,
Arose from my repulse, and has no witness
Besides your ears; if it were silenc'd there
The world were ignorant of it. I hear
She is run mad upon the grief; I am sorry
Her punishment has outstript my desires.
I'll undertake whate'er you shall propose
For the recovery of her wits, or honour.

Aur. And I'll make use of your kind proffer, sir.

Spr. I will resign her where she most affects,
And give you all assistance to obtain her.

Aur. You speak honestly! I shall employ you;
I know you have that credit with her father,
You may advise him in a thing that reason
Shall seem to second: bring but this to pass,
You have made requital for all injuries.

Spr. Shew me the way, I'll do't! be you the mover,
I'll be the instrument.

Aur. You are my genius,
My hope, my opportunity, my fate;
And in effecting this you cannot err
To make me happy, and recover her.

Desinit actus quartus.

Actus V. Scena I.

Lackwit *with a head-piece and a long sword,* Crochet, Careless *disguised like* Dotario.

Lack. How do I look now, Crochet?

Cro. Very dreadfully! like a citizen in a fray, as fearful as Priapus in a garden.

Lack. Well, and thou art sure there is but one of them, and he comes disguised like Dotario, to steal away my sister?

Cro. Yes, sir! and this is the old gentleman himself, and somebody has stole away his habit to abuse him.

Lack. That man that has done so shall think of me and this place as long as he lives for it. Go and give warning, Crochet! that no man withstand me, unless he be weary of his life.

Cro. If any man be so hardy, let him take his chance.

Lack. Let him expect my fury, Crochet. I will batter any man that shall come near me, my fist is like a sling, my head like a ram, and my whole body an engine, and I will make any man toothless that shall offend me.

Cro. Then you will make his mouth as unserviceable as your father's gumm'd velvet.

Lack. I long to exercise my puissance! Thou art sure there is but one of them? stand by a little, and let me flourish with my sword to animate my spirits. Now, whatsoever he is that comes in my way, I pronounce him to be a miserable mortal.

[*Crochet pulls out three or four Napkins.*]
What hast thou there, Crochet?

Cro. I imagin'd there would be a great deal of blood spilt in the skirmish, and so I brought these to wipe the wounds, nothing else, sir. Look you! here they come.

Enter DOTARIO, ÆMILIA.

Lack. Give by, Crochet, till I question them: it behoves a wise man to deal with words, before he descend to blows. What errant knight are you, sir, and whither do you travel with that damoiselle?

Cro. Press that point home.

Dot. O, brother Lackwit! how came you so accoutred? or were you set here for a watchman to guard us?

Lack. No, sir, I do not guard, nor regard any man, and yet I'll stand upon my guard, and this is the point I'll maintain.

Dot. What do you mean, brother Lackwit?

Lack. How, I your brother? No, I scorn to have affiance with such a coney-catcher. You, sir Nessus, deliver up your theft, or I will play the Hercules with you.

Dot. I am going to marry her! my name is Dotario, and this is your sister Æmilia.

Lack. Ay, she is my sister, but you are a counterfeit, and have stolen her away.

Cro. Seize her for fellons' goods, she belongs to the Lord of the soil.

Lack. Thou villain! dost thou not know, if I were dead, and her other sister, she would be next heir and then thou mightst be hang'd for her?

Dot. But I had her consent, and her father's. My name is Dotario, your neighbour, that have fed you with custard and apple-pie a hundred times.

Lack. Ay, this gentleman has, but you have abus'd him, and took his wrong name upon you.

Dot. I am the same.

Cro. He lies! beat him for lying! What do you stay for?

Lack. I am considering with my eye, which part of him I shall first cut off.

Cro. Let's bind him fast, and then lay him upon his back, and geld him.

Lack. A match! Let's lay hold on him! What, is be gone? how finely might my father have been cheated, and all we now, if I had not been. That's some roguing servingman disguis'd, I'll lay my life on't. If I be not fit to be chronicled for this act of discretion, let the world judge of it. Well, Crochet, when I have married her to the right party, if my father does not give me forty pounds more, he shall marry the next daughter himself.

Cro. You must not be too sudden now in the opening of your plot, after you have married them.

Lack. Advise me, good Crochet.

Cro. Why, before you reveal your proceedings, you shall present yourself with a great deal of confidence, and promise of desert; walk up and down, with a joyful agony and a trembling joy, as if you had escap'd from a breach, or redeem'd your country! Then, when you see them sufficiently fill'd with expectation, you may draw the curtain of your valour, and stound them with admiration.

Lack. So I will, Crochet. Come, let us to the church! [*Exeunt.*

Actus V. Scena II.

Littlegood, Spruse, Fondling, Fido.

Spr. Come, master Littlegood, be comforted!
I have as great a share in the misfortunes
Of your distracted daughter as yourself.

Lit. O, do not say so! she was all my joy.

Fid. Then men begin to understand their
   good
When they have lost it, and an envious eye
Seeks after virtue when it is extinct,

That hated it alive.
    Lit.   You have reason
To pity me the more and lament for her,
Because I destin'd her in marriage to you.
    Spr. And I had well hoped to have been made happy
In her affection. A true lover's griefs
Transcend a parent's.
    Lit.   No, you are deceived!
A parent is confin'd, and his joys bounded,
And only limited to such a subject,
And, driven from thence, have nowhere else to rest on:
For, if his children be once taken from him,
Which are the cause, then his delight and comfort,
That are the effects, needs must vanish with them:
But in a lover it falls otherwise,
Such as yourself, whose passion, like a deaw,[*]
Can dry up with the beams of every beauty
That shall shine warm upon you, need not prize
The loss of any. You have no alliance,
Nor natural tie commands you to love any
More than your fancy guides you; and the winds
Have not so many turnings, nor the sands
So many shiftings, nor the moon changes.
    Fid. Sir, you speak truth, upon my knowledge that
He is as slippery as an eel, in love,
And wriggles in and out, sir, at his pleasure;
He can as easily dispense with vows
As swear them; and can, at a minute's warning,
If an occasion serve, supply himself
With a continual and fresh entertainment
Of a new mistress.
    Spr.   Troth! I must confess
I have been a little faulty in that way.

                 * Dough, paste.

Fond. And why would you, sir, knowing this be-
   fore,
Suffer your daughter to be abus'd by him?
Now, by my life! I think, an 'twere not for me,
You'd wind yourself into such labyrinths,
You'd not know how to extricate yourself.
   Lit. Peace, good wife! since there is no remedy.
   Spr. Do not despair! there is yet remedy.
I know a scholar, a great naturalist,
Whose wisdom does transcend all other artists,
A traveller besides, and though his body
Be distant from the heavens yet his mind
Has pierc'd unto the utmost of the orbs,
Can tell how first the chaos was distinguish'd,
And how the spheres are turn'd, and all their secrets,
The motion and influence of the stars,
The mixture of the elements, and all
The causes of the winds, and what moves the earth,
And then he has subjected to his knowledge
The virtues and the workings of all herbs,
And is an Æsculapius in Physic,
No grief above his art.
   Lit.   Can he heal mad folks?
   Spr. Were they as mad as Ajax Telamon,
That slew an ox instead of Agamemnon,
He'll warrant them.
   Fond. How should one speak with him?
   Spr. I brought him with me! he is at the door.
Prithee go call him, Fido! you shall hear him,
And, as you like his speech, so credit him.

     Enter AURELIO, *like a Doctor.*

   Lit. Is this the man?
   Spr.   This is the doctor, sir!
I am bold to make relation of your skill, here,
To this old gentleman, who has a daughter
That is suspected to be mad.

Aur. Suspected! is she no otherwise?
Lit. She is stark mad!
Aur. It came by love?
Lit. Yes sure, what think you on't?
Aur. An ordinary disease, and cure. In some things
I am of an opinion that Stertinius
The Stoic was, who held all the world mad.
Fond. As how, good Master Doctor?
Aur. Thus I prove it;
What is ambition and covetousness,
Or luxury or superstition,
But madness in men? and these reign generally.
Your lawyer trots, and writes, as he were mad,
His client is madder than he; your merchant that marries
A fair wife, and leaves her at home, is mad:
Your courtier is mad to take up silks and velvets
On ticket for his mistress; and your citizen
Is mad to trust him.
Fido. Nay, he is a rare man!
And has done many and strange cures, sir.
Aur. I have, indeed.
Fond. Pray, relate some of them.
Aur. To satisfy your ladyship, I will.
Fond. Yes, good sir, let us hear them.
Aur. Then, I'll tell you. There was once an astrologer brought mad before me, the circulations of the heavens had turn'd his brain round, he had very strange fits, he would ever be staring and gazing, and yet his eyes were so weak, they could not look up without a staff.
Spr. A Jacob's staff you mean?
Aur. Ay, and he would watch whole nights; there could not a star stir for him. He thought there was no hurt done but they did it, and that made him look so narrowly to them.

Fond. How did you heal him, sir?

Aur. Only with two or three sentences out of Picus Mirandula, in confutation of the act; and as many out of Cornelius Agrippa, for the vanity of it.

Fond. That was excellent!

Aur. The next was a soldier, and he was very furious; but I quieted him, by getting his arrearages paid, and a pension for his life.

Fond. You took a hard task in hand, Mr Doctor.

Aur. But the most dangerous of all was a Puritan chandler, and he run mad with illuminations. He was very strangely possest, and talk'd idly, as if he had had a noise of bells in his head; he thought a man in a surplice to be the ghost of heresy, and was out of love with his own members, because they were called organs.

Fond. O, monstrous!

Aur. Ay, and held very strange positions, for he counted Fathers to be as unlawful in the church, as Plato did poets in his commonwealth, and thereupon grounded his conclusion for the lawfulness of whoredom; for he said that marriage, as it is now used, was the only ringleader of all mischief.

Fond. How did you heal him, sir?

Aur. Why, lady, with certain pills of sound doctrine, and they purg'd his ill humours.

Lit. That was very speedy!

Aur. Then, there was a musician that run mad with crochets; the fit was so violent upon him, that he would nothing but sound perpetually.

Fond. How did you with him, sir?

Aur. I serv'd him as Hercules serv'd his master Linus: broke his fiddle about his pate, and sent him away without e'er a penny, and that brought his head in tune.

Fond. I'll remember this, i' faith!

Aur. Then there was a huntsman that was very wood;* he would do nothing but whoop and hollow, and was wonderfully in love with an echo.

Fond. How did you reclaim him?

Aur. Why, I serv'd him in his own kind. He had a very handsome wench to his wife, and, while he was playing the Cephalus abroad, and courting his Aurora, I turn'd him into an Actæon at home, set a fair pair of horns on his head, and made him a tame beast.

Fond. Husband, that was excellent! was it not?

Aur. I cured a poet too, and indeed they are a generation that are little better than mad at all times. I was fain to give him over, because himself and others took such delight in his fury. I could not tell what to make of him, his disease was so pretty and conceited, and he was no sooner well, but he would presently fall into a relapse. I could make relation of a thousand such, as painters, alchymists, and the like, but it would be tedious.

Lit. Nay, sir! we are confirmed of your skill. Will you have my daughter brought forth to you, sir, that you may see her in her fit?

Aur. No, by no means, 'twill spend her spirits too much. I'll take her home with me, and anoint her brows with a little Helleborum, and some other receipts that I'll give her, and, I'll warrant you, I'll bring her safe too in three hours, and well recovered.

Spr. Sir, you will do an office, that will not more deserve honour than reward.

Aur. Sir, I shall desire nothing but my pains for my satisfaction.

Fond. Good, sweet Fido, conduct him in, and go along with him! that if any hereafter shall be so

---

* Mad, furious.—"Clean red wud," is a common phrase in Scotland for one out of his wits,—"Red wud" means "wood in a blaze."

averse, in his ignorance to all goodness, as to question this miracle, you may be produc'd as a witness.

Lit. And what will you do, sweet wife?

Fond. Why, I'll stay here and expect my son, Lackwit, with his project. He sent me word he would come presently; and see, where he enters!

Enter LACKWIT, CROCHET.

Lack. Crochet, bid them stay without, till I call for them! Make room there, and let such produce their game, that have good cards to show.

Fond. How now, son Lackwit! whither away so furious?

Lack. I am sure all the wit and valour I had was at stake for it.

Lit. Why, what's the matter?

Lack There was old shuffling and cutting amongst them, an I had not spied their knavery they might have put a trick upon us, faith!

Fond. Why, were you at cards, son?

Lack. No, I was at dice. I came the caster with some of them I think, and I had like to have made their bones rattle for it. There was a rook would have gone at In and In with my sister; if I had not made a third man, he would have swept all away, and wiped our noses when he had done.

Fond. Tell us how was it, son?

Lack. No matter how; but if I have not play'd the wise man now, and done an act worthy of applause, let me be hist off for my labour.

Lit. Let's hear! what is it?

Lack. If it be no more thanks worthy I'll tell you at my leisure, when you have prepar'd your understanding.

Lit. What is it, Crochet?

Lack. Peace, Sirrah! I'll have no man tell it but myself, because the praise of it belongs wholly to me; an I could but effect half-a-dozen more such exploits, I'd write my own commentaries.

Fond. You put us too much into a longing, son.

Lack. Well, I am content to open the sluices of your happiness. Let them in, Crochet, but take heed you be not too greedy of it, lest the sudden joy overwhelm you.

Enter CARELESS, ÆMILIA, CROCHET.

Lit. What's here? Master Dotario, and my daughter Æmilia, hand in hand, and married together! Nay, then 'tis as I would have it. The boy has done well, and I must applaud him for it.

Lack. O, must you so, sir? Well, there they are bark and tree, but as I am a hairy beast, if I had not been, they had been as far asunder as Temple Bar and Aldgate.

Fond. How so, son?

Lack. Why, I'll shew you: there was another changling as like to him in shape as Jupiter to Amphitruo, nay, if I should say, as I am to, let me see what?

Cro. To a fool.

Lock. No, to thyself,

Cro. 'Tis all one.

Lack. That would have married her in his stead, and carried her away, if I had not prevented them.

Enter DOTARIO.

whether it be a shadow or a ghost, that haunts him in his own proper form, I know not, but there he comes again.

Lit. Why, how now, son Dotario? you have made haste to beget one so like you already.

Dot. O, sir, 'tis I am cheated, gull'd, and abus'd,

and, which is worse, by one that says he is myself too.

Lit. Why, what are you?

Dot. O, sir, I am that old gentleman, that should have married your daughter, and there's an Asmodeus, a devil in my habit, that has beguil'd me of her.

Cro. Come, sir, uncase yourself! 'tis no glory for you to lurk any longer under the person of such a wretch.

[*Careless puts off his disguise.*

Dot. Who is here! my nephew Careless? nay then 'tis ten times worse than I thought of: my disgrace will be as common as conduit water, the very tankard bearers will mock at me, I shall be made their laughter at taverns, the table talk at ordinaries.

Car. Nay, good Uncle, do not think so ill of me! a brace of thousands shall chain up my tongue, that you may live as conceal'd as you please.

Dot. O, sir, you have proved yourself to be a Fine Companion.

Lit. Nay, hold up your head, sir! this was your device, your master piece of wit, and valour? nay, you may brag of it, the credit belongs to you.

Lack. Crochet, I would thou wert a post, that I might beat out my brains against thee.

Enter FIDO, AURELIO, VALERIA.

Fid. Save you, gentlemen!

Spr. Look you, sir! here's the doctor, and your daughter already.

Lit. Well, there's some comfort yet to make amends for the rest.

Fid. Come, down on your knees, sir!

AURELIO *uncases.*

Lit. How now, what are you?

Aur. Lately the doctor, but now your son, Aurelio.

Lit. What, more gulleries yet? They have cosened me of my daughters, I hope they will cheat me of my wife too. Have you any more of these tricks to shew? ha!

Aur. No more, sir, if we may obtain your favour for these, and think, good sir, what love may do; you have been young yourself.

Lit. Troth, and so I have, and been as waggish as the best of you. Well, Master Doturio, what shall we do? The boys have out-stript us! there's now no remedy, and my affection relents.

Dot. So does mine too, and I would do anything if I might be freed of this ignominy, that it might not be known what a fool this love has made of me.

Fid. I'll undertake for that, sir, if you will yield to a motion.

Dot. Anything, upon these terms.

Fid. Then, thus: you are rich, and your nephew Aurelio here is poor, yet he was born to an inheritance; now, do you but confer something presently upon him, and assure him the rest after your death, and I'll promise they shall observe you with as much obsequiousness, as you desire.

Dot. And what shall my nephew Careless do?

Fid. Why, Master Littlegood shall give him his land again.

Det. If he will do one, I'll do the other!

Fond. That he shall. I'll see that done, upon my word.

Lit. I'll not stand against a good motion at any time.

Dot. Why, then, boys, be happy in your mistresses.

Car. Sir, this speech from you is more comfortable than if Hymen had spoke it; and, for my brother Lackwit, I'll take him to my protection and stand in his defence against all machinous engines that shall be planted for the battery of his wit and fortune.

Cro. Pray, sir, will you get him his cloak and hat, again, that he lost in the skirmish?

Car. Ay, so I will; Fido shall restore them to him.

Lack. Well, I would know, how all these things had come to so good perfection but for me now?

Cro. Nay, if fortune should not favour such as you and I are, she would leave her old wont.

Enter CAPTAIN *like a Host,* LIEUTENANT *with a jug and glass,* HOSTESS.

Car. What's my old reformado come again?

Cap. Nay, you need not fear me now. I am as mild as my beer: I am her husband and your host till death.

Car. What, turn'd host?

Cap. Yes, and I thought it my duty to present you with the first fruits of my profession. Fill out a glass, Tapster, that I may drink to this good company. Gentlemen, you are all welcome!

Fid. Is this your Tapster, Captain?

Cap. Yes, and does he not suit well with his function? he has learnt already to run upstairs and down stairs, as nimble as a squirel, and can answer to any man that shall call him, as loud and peremptorily as the best or them.

Car. That's a good entrance.

Cap. He is a little out of countenance at the first, but, when you come to my house, you shall hear him speak in a big accent, "what's to pay in the Lion?" "What's to pay in the Dragon?" be not dismay'd Tapster, be not dismay'd!

Car. Well, I perceive we must keep holiday:

there's nothing angers me now but Master Spruse is disappointed of his mistress.

Spr. Take no care of that! I have more mistresses than I can tell what to do with.

Car. Sir, I have a sister, though she had no part in this business yet, for her beauty, virtue, and dowry, may well deserve you: if you can like of her, I'll do what I can to obtain her for you.

Spr. Sir, you shall command me in what you please, and my thanks for your love; and here I vow never to dissemble any more in this kind, but to be truly and sincerely affectionated to whomsoever you shall commend me.

Car. Nay, if you would not do so, you were unworthy of her.

> To gain a woman's love thus all may strive,
> But wealth shall be put back, when wit shall thrive.

FINIS.

THE ANTIQUARY.

The Antiquary. A Comedy, acted by *Her Maiesties Servants at the Cock-Pit. Written by Shackerly Mermion, Gent. London*, Printed by F. K. for J. W. and F. E., and are to be sold at the *Crane, in S. Pauls Churchyard*. 1641. 4to.

THIS play, justly selected by the Editor of Dodsley's Old Plays as one of the best of our early dramatic poetry, has been reprinted in the several editions of that collection. It is also in Sir Walter Scott's Ancient British Drama. He thought very highly of it.

"It is," says Geneste, "a pretty good play. The nephew's imposing of false antiques on his uncle, in Modern Antiques [by John o' Keefe] is taken from this play, and perhaps a hint for the sham Duke in the 'Honeymoon.'" The remark as to "modern antiques" is evident enough, but that in reference to "the Honeymoon" is not so palpable.

Prefixed to the reprint of the play in Dodsley's collection is this note:—"Mr Samuel Gale told Dr Ducarrel that this comedy was acted two nights in 1718, immediately after the revival of the Society of Antiquaries; and that therein had been introduced a ticket of a turnpike (then new) which was called a *Tessera*. N."

Foote, in his Comedy of the Nabob, Act III., satirizes, in his usual clever style, the Society of Antiquaries of his period.

Langbaine, in noticing the 'Antiquary,' in a brief account of Marmyon, observes:—"Aurelio's declaring his marriage to the Duke and Leonardo, from Lucretia's lodging, where he got in by her maid's assistance, is an incident, as I have already shew'd, in several plays."

Durfey, in his Comedy of 'Madam Fickle; or, the Witty False one,' acted at the Duke of York's Theatre in 1677, introduces a character called 'Sir Arthur Old-Love,' which is a close copy of Veterano, the Antiquary.

Although the scene is stated as at Pisa, the mention of "the Rialto" in the first act, and of Venice in the third act, would appear to indicate that Venice and not Pisa was the *locale* intended by the author. This is, however, immaterial as regards the action of the piece.

THE ACTORS' NAMES.

THE DUKE OF PISA.
LEONARDO, } two Courtiers.
DONATO,
VETERANO, *the Antiquary.*
GASPARO, *a Magnifico of Pisa.*
LORENZO, *an old Gentleman.*
MOCCINIGO, *an old Gentleman that would appear young.*
LIONELL, *Nephew to the Antiquary.*
PETRUTIO, *a foolish Gentleman, son to Gasparo.*
AURELIO, *a young Gentleman.*
AURELIO'S *father, in the disguise of a Bravo.*
HIS BOY.
PETRO, *the Antiquary's boy.*

ÆMILIA, *wife to Lorenzo.*
LUCRETIA, *daughter to Lorenzo.**
ANGELIA, *sister to Lionell, in the disguise of a Page.*
JULIA, } *two Waiting-women.*
BACCHA,
A COOK.
Two SERVANTS.

The Scene, PISA.

---

* In the original edition, Æmelia, in error, is called "wife to Gasparo," and Lucretia "daughter to Gasparo."

THE ANTIQUARY.

Actus Primus.

Enter Lionell *and* Petrutio.

Lio. Now, sir, let me bid you welcome to your country, and the longing expectation of those friends, that have almost languish'd for the sight of you.—I must flatter him, and stroke him too, he will give no milk else. [*Aside.*

Pet. I have calculated, by all the rules of reason and art, that I shall be a great man: for, what singular quality concurs to perfection and advancement, that is defective in me? Take my feature and proportion; have they not a kind of sweetness and harmony to attract the eyes of the beholders? the confirmation of which, many authentical judgments of ladies have seal'd and subscrib'd to.

Lio. How do you, sir? are you not well?

Pet. Next, my behaviour and discourse, according to the Court-garb, ceremonious enough, more promising than substantial, able to keep pace with the best hunting wit of them all: besides, nature has bless'd me with boldness sufficient, and fortune with means. What then should hinder me? nothing but destiny, villanous destiny, that chains virtue to darkness and obscurity. Well, I will insinuate myself into the Court, and presence of the Duke: and if he have not the grace to distinguish of worth, his ignorance upon him.

Lio. What! in a muse, sir?

Pet. Cannot a gentleman ruminate over his good parts, but you must be troubling of him?

Lio. Wise men and fools are alike ambitious. This travelling motion has been abroad in quest of strange fashions, where his spungy brain has suck'd the dregs of all the folly he could possibly meet with, and is indeed more ass than he went forth. Had I an interest in his disgrace, I'd rail at him, and perhaps beat him for it; but he is as strange to me as to himself, therefore let him continue in his belov'd simplicity. [*Aside.*

Pet. Next, when he shall be instructed of my worth, and eminent sufficiencies, he cannot dignify me with less employment than the dignity of an embassador. How bravely shall I behave myself in that service! and what an ornament unto my country may I arrive to be, and to my kindred! But I will play the gentleman, and neglect them; that's the first thing I'll study.

Lio. Shall I be bold to interrupt you, sir?

Pet. Presently I'll be at leisure to talk with you. 'Tis no small point in State policy, still to pretend only to be thought a man of action, and, rather than want a colour, be busied with a man's own self.

Lio. Who does this ass speak to? surely to himself: and 'tis impossible he should ever be wise, that has always such a foolish auditory. [*Aside.*

Pet. Then, with what emulous courtship will they strive to entertain me in foreign parts! And what a spectacle of admiration shall I be made amongst those who have formerly known me! How dost thou like my carriage?

Lio. Most exquisite; believe me.

Pet. But is it adorn'd with that even mixture of fluency and grace, as are required both in a Statist and a Courtier?

Lio. So far as the divine prospect of my understanding guides me, 'tis without parallel most excellent; but I am no profess'd critic in the mystery.

Pet. Well, thou hast Linceus' eyes * for observation, or could'st ne'er have made such a cunning discovery of my practice; but will the ladies, think you, have that apprehension to discern and approve of me?

Lio. Without question; they cannot be so dull or stony-hearted, as not to be infinitely taken with your worth. Why, in a while, you shall have them so enamour'd, that they'll watch every opportunity to purchase your acquaintance; then again revive it with often banquetting and visits; nay, and perhaps invite others, by their foolish example, to do the like; and some that despair of so great happiness will enquire out your haunts, and walk there two or three hours together, to get but a sight of you.

Pet. Oh infinite! I am transported with the thought on't! It draws near noon, and I appointed certain gallants to meet me at the five-crown ordinary: after, we are to wait upon the like beauties you talk'd of, to the public theatre. I feel of late a strong and witty genius growing upon me, and I begin, I know not how, to be in love with this foolish sin of poetry.

Lio. Are you, sir? there's great hopes of you.

Pet. And the reason is, because they say 'tis both the cause and effect of a good wit, to which I can sufficiently pretend: for nature has not play'd the step-dame with me.

---

* Lynceus, son of Aphareus, was among the hunters of the Calydonian boar, and one of the Argonauts. He was so sharp-sighted that, as it is reported, he could see through the earth, and distinguish objects at the distance of above nine miles.

Lio. In good time, sir.

Pet. And now you talk of time, what time of day is it by your watch ?

Lio. I have none, sir.

Pet. How, ne'er a watch ? oh monstrous ! how do you consume your hours ? Ne'er a watch ? 'tis the greatest solecism in society that e'er I heard of : ne'er a watch ?

Lio. How deeply you conceive of it !

Pet. You have not a gentleman, that's a true gentleman, without one ; 'tis the main appendix to a plush lining : besides, it helps much to discourse ; for, while others confer notes together, we confer our watches, and spend good part of the day with talking of it.

Lio. Well, sir, because I'll be no longer destitute of such a necessary implement, I have a suit to you.

Pet. A suit to me ? Let it alone till I am a great man, and then I shall answer you with the greater promise, and less performance.

Lio. I hope, sir, you have that confidence I will ask nothing to your prejudice, but what shall some way recompense the deed.

Pet. What is't ? Be brief, I am in that point a Courtier.

Lio. Usurp then on the proffer'd means,
Shew yourself forward in an action
May speak you noble, and make me your friend.

Pet. A friend ! what's that ? I know no such thing.

Lio. A faithful, not a ceremonious friend ;
But one that will stick by you on occasions,
And vindicate your credit, were it sunk
Below all scorn, and interpose his life
Betwixt you and all dangers : such a friend,
That when he sees you carried by your passions

Headlong unto destruction, will so follow you,
That he will guide you from't, and with good
  counsel
Redeem you from ill courses: and, not flattering
Your idle humour to a vain expense,
Cares not to see you perish, so he may
Sustain himself a while, and raise a fortune,
Though mean, out of your ruins, and then laugh at
  you.
  Pet. Why, be there any such friends as these?
  Lio.   A word:
They walk like spirits, not to be discern'd;
Subtile and soft like air, an oily balm
Swimming o'er [all] their words and actions; but
Below it a flood of gall.
  Pet. Well, to the purpose! speak to the purpose.
  Lio. If I stand link'd unto you,
The Gordian knot were less dissoluble,
A rock less firm, or centre moveable.
  Pet. Speak your demand!
  Lio. Do it, and do it freely then! lend me a
hundred ducats.
  Pet. How is that? lend you a hundred ducats?
Not a—I'll never have a friend while I breathe.
First:—no, I'll stand upon my guard; I give all the
world leave to whet their wits against me, work
like moles to undermine me, yet I'll spurn all their
deceits like a hillock. I tell thee, I'll not buy the
small repentance of a friend or whore, at the rate
of a livre.
  Lio. What's this? I dare not
Trust my own ears, silence choke up my anger.
A friend, and whore! are they two parallels,
Or to be nam'd together? May he never
Have better friend, that knows no better how
To value them. Well, I was ever jealous
Of his baseness, and now my fears are ended.

Pox o' these travels! they do but corrupt
A good nature, and his was bad enough before.

Enter ANGELIA.

Pet. What pretty sparkle of humanity have we here? Whose attendant are you, my little knave?

Ang. I wait, sir, on Master Lionell.

Lio. 'Tis well you are come. What says the gentleman?

Ang. I deliver'd your letter to him. He is very sorry he can furnish you no better; he has sent you twenty crowns, he says, towards the large debt he owes you.

Pet. A fine child! and delivers his tale with good method. Where, in the name of Ganymede, had'st thou this epitome of a servitor?

Lio. You'd little think of what consequence and pregnancy this imp is: you may hereafter have both cause to know and love him.—What gentlemen are these?

Enter GASPARO *and* LORENZO.

Pet. One is my father.

Lor. I hear your son, sir, is return'd from travel,
Grown up a fine and stately gentleman,
Outstrips his compeers in each liberal science.

Gas. I thank my stars, he has improv'd his time
To the best use, can render an account
Of all his journal; how he has arriv'd.
Through strange discoveries and compendious ways,
To a most perfect knowledge of himself;
Can give a model of each Prince's Court,
And is become their fear. He has a mind
Equally pois'd, and virtue without sadness;
Hunts not for fame, through an ill path of life;

But is indeed, for all parts, so accomplish'd,
As I could wish or frame him.
 Lor.   These are joys,
In their relation to you, so transcendent,
As than yourself I know no man more happy.
May I not see your son?
 Gas.   See, where he stands,
Accompanied with young Lionell, the nephew
To Veterano the great antiquary.
 Lor. I'll be bold, by your favour, to endear
Myself in his acquaintance. Noble Petrutio,
Darling of Venus, minion of the Graces,
Let me adopt me heir unto your love:
That is, yours by descent, and which your father,
A grave wise man and a Magnifico,
Has not disdain'd.
 Pet. I am much bound to you for it.
 Lor. Is that all?
 Pet. See the abundant ignorance of this age! he cites my father for a precedent. Alas, he is a good old man, and no more; there he stands! he has not been abroad, nor known the world; therefore, I hope will not be so foolishly peremptory to compare with me for judgment, that have travell'd, seen fashions, and been a man of intelligence.
 Lor. Signior, your ear! pray let's counsel you.
 Pet. Counsel me? the like trespass again: sure the old man doats! Who counsell'd me abroad, when I had none but mine own natural wisdom for my protection? Yet, I dare say, I met with more perils, more variety of allurements, more Circes, more Calypsos, and the like, than e'er were fain'd upon Ulysses.
 Lor. It shew'd great wisdom, that you could avoid them.
Give o'er, and tempt your destiny no further!
'Tis time now to retire unto yourself:

Settle your mind upon some worthy beauty;
A wife will tame all wild affections.
I have a daughter, who, for youth and beauty,
Might be desir'd, were she ignobly born;
And for her dowry, that shall no way part you.
If you accept her, here before your friends,
I will betroth her to you.

Pet. I thank you, sir! you'd have me marry your daughter; is it so?

Lor. With your good liking, not otherwise.

Pet. You nourish too great an ambition. What do you see in me, to make such a motion? No, be wise and keep her; were I married to her I should not like her above a month at most.

Lor. How! not above a month?

Pet. I'll tell you, sir, I have made an experience that way on my nature: when I have hir'd a creature for my pleasure, as 'tis the fashion in many places, for the like time that I told you of, I have been so tired with her before 'twas out, as no horse like me; I could not spur my affection to go a jot further.

Gas. Well said, boy! thou art e'en mine own son; when I was young, 'twas just my humour.

Lio. You give yourself a plausible commends.

Pet. I can make a shift to love; but having enjoy'd, fruition kills my appetite: no, I must have several objects of beauty to keep my thoughts always in action, or I am nobody.

Gas. Still mine own flesh and blood!

Pet. Therefore I have chose Honour for my mistress, upon whose wings I will mount up to the Heavens: where I will fix myself a constellation for all this under-world of mortals to wonder at me.

Gas. Nay, he is a mad wag, I assure you, and knows how to put a price upon his desert.

Pet. I can no longer stay to dilate on these

vanities; therefore, gallants, I leave you. [*Exit.*

Lor. What, is he gone? Is your son gone?

Gas. So it seems. Well, gallants, where shall I see you anon?

Lor. You shall not part with us.

Gas. You shall pardon me; I must wait upon my son. [*Exit.*

Lor. Do you hear, signior? A pretty preferment!

Lio. Oh, sir, the lustre of good clothes, or breeding,
Bestow'd upon a son, will make a rustic,
Or a mechanic father, to commit
Idolatry, and adore his own issue.

Ang. They are so well match'd, 'twere pity to part them.

Lor. Well said, little-one! I think thou art wiser than both them.
But this same scorn I do not so well relish;
A whoreson humorous phantastic novice
To contemn my daughter? He is not worthy
To bear up her train.

Lio. Or kiss under it.
Will you revenge this injury upon him?

Lor. Revenge! Of all the passions of my blood,
'Tis the most sweet; I should grow fat to think on't,
Could you but promise.

Lio. Will you have patience?
Be rul'd by me, and I will compass it
To your full wish. We'll set a bait afore him,
That he shall seize as sharply as Jove's eagle
Did snatch up Ganymede.

Lor. Do but cast the plot,
I'll prosecute it with as much disgrace
As hatred can suggest.

Lio. Do you see this Page, then?

Lor. Ay! what of him?

Lio. That face of his shall do it.

o

Lor. What shall it do ? Methinks he has a pretty
innocent countenance.
   Lio. Oh! but beware of a smooth look at all
       times.
Observe what I say : he is a Siren above,
But below a very serpent. No female scorpion
Did ever carry such a sting, believe it.
   Lor. What should I do with him ?
   Lio.   Take him to your house !
There keep him privately, till I make all perfect.
If ever alchymist did more rejoice
In his projection, never credit me.
   Lor. You shall prevail upon my faith, beyond
My understanding. And, my dapper 'squire,
If you be such a precious wag, I'll cherish you.
Come, walk along with me. Farewell, sir !
   Lio. Adieu !   [*Exeunt Lorenzo and Angelia.*
Now I must travel, on a new exploit,
To an old Antiquary ; he is my uncle,
And I his heir. Would I could raise a fortune
Out of his ruins ! He is grown obsolete,
And 'tis time he were out of date. They say he sits
All day in contemplation of a statue
With ne'er a nose, and doats on the decays
With greater love than the self-lov'd Narcissus
Did on his beauty. How shall I approach him ?
Could I appear but like a Sibyl's son,
Or with a face rugged as father Nilus
Is pictur'd on the hangings, there were hope
He might look upon me. How to win his love
I know not. If I wist he were not precise,
I'd lay to purchase some stale interludes,
And give him them ; books that have not attain'd
To the Platonic year, but wait their course,
And happy hour, to be reviv'd again :
Then would I induce him to believe they were
Some of Terence's hundred and fifty comedies

That were lost in the Adriatic sea,
When he return'd from banishment. Some such
Gullery as this might be enforced upon him.
I'll first talk with his man, and then consider. [*Exit.*

Enter LORENZO, GASPARO, MOCCINIGO, *and*
ANGELIA.

Lor. How hapt you did return again so soon,
sir?

Gas. I'll tell you, sir. As I follow'd my son
From the Rialto, near unto the bridge
We were encount'red by a sort * of Gallants,
Sons of Clarissimos, and Procurators
That knew him in his travels: whereupon
He did insinuate with his eyes unto me,
I should depart and leave them.

Lor. 'Seems he was asham'd of your company?

Gas. Like will to like, sir.

Lor. What grave and youthful gentleman's that
with you?

Gas. Do you not know him?

Lor. No.

Gas. Not Signior Moccinigo?

Lor. You jest, I am sure.

Gas. Ay, and there hangs a jest:
For, going to a courtezan this morning,
In his own proper colour, his grey beard,
He had th' ill luck to be refus'd; on which,
He went and dy'd it, and came back again,
And was again, with the same scorn, rejected,
Telling him, that she had newly deny'd his father.

Lor. Was that her answer?

Gas. It has so troubled him,
That he intends to marry. What think you, sir,

---

* A number—a great body. "I speak it not gloriously, nor out of affectation, but there's he and the Count Frugale, Signior Illustre, Signior Luculento, and a sort of them."

Of his resolution?
  Lor.   By'r lady, it shows
Great haughtiness of courage : a man of his years
That dares to venture on a wife.
  Moc. A man of my years? I feel
My limbs as able as the best of them;
And in all places else, except my hair,
As green as a bay-tree : and for the whiteness
Upon my head, although it now lie hid,
What does it signify, but like a tree that blossoms
Before the fruit come forth? And, I hope a tree
That blossoms is neither dry nor wither'd.
  Lor. But pray, what piece of beauty's that you mean
To make the object of your love?
  Moc.   Ay, there
You 'pose me : for I have a curious eye,
And am as choice in that point to be pleased,
As the most youthful. Here one's beauty takes me;
And there her parentage or good behaviour;
Another's wealth or wit; but I'd have one
Where all these graces meet, as in a centre
  Gas. You are too ambitious. You'll hardly find
Woman or beast that trots sound of all four :
There will be some defect.
  Moc.   Yet this I resolve on,
To have a maid tender of age and fair.
Old fish and young flesh, that's still my diet.*
  Lor. What think you of a Widow?
  Moc.   By no means :
They are too politic a generation :
Prov'd so by similes. Many voyages
Make an experienc'd seaman ; many offices

---

* This, as the Editors of Dodsley's collection remark, is adapted from Chaucer in his Merchant's Tale. Pope, in January and May, seizes on the same idea.

A crafty knave; so, many marriages,
A subtile cunning widow. No, I'll have one
That I may mould, like wax, unto my humour.

   Lor. This doating ass is worth, at least, a million,
And, though he cannot propagate his stock,
Will be sure to multiply. I'll offer him my daughter.
By computation of age, he cannot
Live past ten years; by that time she'll get strength
To break this rotten hedge of matrimony,
And after have a fair green field to walk in,
And wanton where she please [*aside*]. Signior, a word!
And by this guess my love: I have a daughter,
Of beauty fresh, of her demeanour gentle,
And of a sober wisdom: you know my estate.
If you can fancy her seek no further.

   Moc. Thank you, signior: pray of what age
Is your daughter?

   Lor. But sixteen, at the most.

   Moc. But sixteen? is she no more? She is too young, then.

   Gas. You wish'd for a young one, did you not?

   Moc. Not that I would have her in years.

   Gas. I warrant you!

   Moc. Well, mark what I say: when I come to her,
She'll ne'er be able to endure me.

   Lor. I'll trust her.

   Gas. I think your choice, sir, cannot be amended,
She is so virtuous and so amiable.

   Moc. Is she so fair and amiable? I'll have her!
She may grow up to what she wants; and then
I shall enjoy such pleasure and delight,
Such infinite content in her embraces,

I may contend with Jove for happiness!
Yet one thing troubles me.
   Gas. What's that?
   Moc. I shall live so well on earth,
I ne'er shall think of any other joys.
   Gas. I wish all joy to you! but 'tis in th' power
Of fate to work a miracle upon you.
You may obtain the grace, with other men,
To repent your bargain before you have well seal'd
   it.
   Lor. Or she may prove his purgatory, and send
   him
To Heaven the sooner.
   Gas. Such like effects as these
Are not unheard of in nature.
   Moc. For all these scruples,
I am resolv'd. Bring me that I may see her!
Young handsome ladies are like prizes at a horse-
   race, where
Every well-breath'd gentleman may put in for his
   share.   *[Exeunt.*

            Enter DUKE *and* LEONARDO.

   Leo. But are you resolv'd of this course, sir?
   Du. Yes; we'll be once mad in our days, and do an exploit for posterity to talk of. Will you join with me?
   Leo. I am at your Grace's disposing.
   Du. No grace, nor no respect, I beseech you, more than ordinary friendship allows of: 'tis the only bar to hinder our designs.
   Leo. Then, sir, what fashion you are pleas'd to appoint me, I will be glad to put on.
   Luke. 'Tis well. For my part, I am determin'd to lay by all ensigns of my Royalty for awhile, and walk abroad under a mean coverture. Variety does well; and 'tis as great delight, sometimes, to

shroud one's head under a coarse roof, as a rich canopy of gold.

Leo. But what's your intent in this?

Duke. I have a longing desire to see the fashions of the vulgar; which, should I affect in mine own person, I might divert them from their humours. The face of greatness would affright them, as Cato did the Floralio from the theatre.*

Leo. Indeed, familiarity begets boldness.

Du. 'Tis true, indulgency and flattery take away the benefit of experience from Princes, which ennobles the fortunes of private men.

Leo. But you are a Duke, sir; and this descent from your honour will undervalue you.

Du. Not a whit. I am so toil'd out with grand affairs, and dispatching of embassages, that I am ready to sink under the burthen. Why may not an Atlas of State, such as myself, that bears up the weight of a commonwealth, now and then, for recreation's sake, be glad to ease his shoulders? Has not Jupiter thrown away his rays and his thunder to walk among mortals? Does not Apollo suffer himself to be depriv'd of his quiver, that he may waken up his Muse sometimes, and sing to his harp?

Leo. Nay, sir, to come to a more familiar example: I have heard of a Nobleman that has been drunk with a tinker, and of a Magnifico that has play'd at blow-point.†

---

* Games celebrated at Rome in honour of Flora. These began on the 28th April annually, and continued for several days, exhibiting scenes of the most unbounded licentiousness. Cato, it is said, had once signified his wish to be present at the celebration, but when he saw that the awe occasioned by his presence interrupted the festival, he retired, not choosing to be a spectator of the antics of nude women in a public theatre.

† A children's game, conjectured by Strutt to consist in blowing an arrow through a trunk at certain numbers by way of lottery. Nares thinks it was blowing small pins or points

Du. Very good then, take our degrees alike, and the act's as pardonable.

Leo. In a humour, sir, a man may do much. But how will you prevent their discovery of you?

Du. Very well; the alteration of our clothes will abolish suspicion.

Leo. And how for our faces?

Du. They shall pass without any seal of disguise. Who ne'er were thought on, will ne'er be mistrusted.

Leo. Come what will, greatness can justify any action whatsoever, and make it thought wisdom; but if we do walk undiscern'd, 'twill be the better. It tickles me to think what a mass of delight we shall possess, in being, as 'twere, the invisible spectators of their strange behaviours. I heard, sir, of an Antiquary, who, if he be as good at wine as at history, he is sure an excellent companion; and of one Petrutio, who plays the eagle in the clouds: and, indeed, divers others, who verify the proverb, *So many men, so many humours.*

Du. All these we'll visit in order: but how we shall comply with them, 'tis as occasion shall be offered, we will not now be so serious to consider.

Leo. Well, sir, I must trust to your wit to manage it. Lead on! I attend you. [*Exeunt.*

Finis Actus primi.

against each other.—See Apollo Shroving, 1627, p. 49; Hawkin's English Drama, iii. 243; Strutt's Sports, p. 403; Florio, ed. 1611, p. 506 "—*Halliwell.*

"My mistress upon good days puts on a piece of a parsonage;
And we pages play at blow-point for a piece of a parsonage."
The Return from Parnassus, a. 3. s. 1.

Actus Secundus.

Enter AURELIO *and* MUSICIANS.

Aur. This is the window! Now, my noble
   Orpheus,
As thou affect'st the name of rarity,
Strike with the soul of music, that the sound
May bear my love on his bedewed wing,
To charm her ear: as when a sacrifice,
With his perfumed steam flies up to Heaven,
Into Jove's nostrils, and there throws a mist
On his enraged brow. Oh how my fancy
Labours with the success!   [*Song above.*

Enter LUCRETIA.

Luc. Cease your fool's note there! I am not in
   tune
To dance after your fiddle. Who are you?
What saucy groom, that dares so near intrude,
And with offensive noise, grate on my ears?

Aur. What more than earthly light breaks
   through that window?
Brighter than all the glittering train of nymphs
That wait on Cynthia, when she takes her progress
In pursuit of the swift enchased deer
Over the Cretan or Athenian hills;
Or when, attended with those lesser stars,
She treads the azure circle of the Heavens.

Luc. Hey-dey, this is excellent! What voice is
   that?
Oh, is it you? I cry you mercy, sir:
I thought as much; these are your tricks still with
   me.
You have been sotting on't all night with wine,
And here you come to finish out your revels.
I shall be, one day, able to live private,—

I shall, and not be made the epilogue
Of all your drunken meetings. For shame, away!
The rosy morning blushes at thy baseness.
Julia, go throw the Music a reward,
And set them hence!
   Aur.   Divine Lucretia,
Do not receive with scorn my proffer'd service:
Oh turn again, though from your arched brow,
Stung with disdain, and bent down to your eye,
You shoot me through with darts of cruelty.
Ah, foolish man, to court the flame that burns him!
   Luc. What would this fellow have?
   Aur. Shine still, fair mistress!
And, though in silence, yet still look upon me;
Your eye discourses with more rhetoric
Than all the gilded tongues of orators.
   Luc. Out of my pity, not my love, I'll answer.
You come to woo me, and speak fair; 'tis well!
You think to win me too: you are deceiv'd;
For when I hate a person, all his actions,
Though ne'er so good, prove but his prejudice:
For flatteries are like sweet pills, though sweet,
Yet if they work not straight, invert to poison.
   Aur. Why, do you hate me, lady? Was there ever
Woman so cruel to hate him that lov'd her?
Oh, do not so degenerate from nature,
Which form'd you of a temper soft as silk:
And to the sweet composure of your body,
Took not a drop of gall or corrupt humour,
But all your blood was clear and purified.
Then as your limbs are fair, so be your mind;
Cast not a scandal on her curious hand,
To say, she made that crooked, or uneven;
For virtue is the best, which is deriv'd
From a sweet feature. Women crown their youth
With the chaste ornaments of love and truth.
   Luc. This is a language you are studied in,

And you have spoke it to a thousand.
    Aur.   Never,
Never to any! for my soul is cut so
To the proportion of what you are,
That all the other beauty in the world,
That is not found within your face, seems vile.
Oh! that I were a veil upon that face,
To hide it from the world! Methinks I could
Envy the very sun for gazing on you!
    Luc. I wonder, that a fellow of no worth
Should talk thus liberally : be so impudent,
After so many slightings and abuses
Extorted from me, beyond modesty,
To press upon me still. Have not I told you
My mind in words, plain to be understood,
How much I hate you? Can I not enjoy
The freedom of my chamber, but you must
Stand in my prospect? If you please, I will
Resign up all and leave you possession.
What can I suffer, or expect more grievous,
From the enforcement of an enemy?
    Aur. Do not insult upon my sufferings.
I had well hop'd I should receive some comfort
From the sweet influence of your words or looks ;
But now must fly, and vanish like a cloud,
Chas'd with the wind, into the colder regions
Where sad despair sits ever languishing ;
There will I calculate my injuries,
Summ'd up with my deserts : then shall I find
How you are wanting to all good and pity,
And that you do but juggle with our sense ;
That you appear gentle and smooth as water,
When no wind breathes upon it, but indeed,
Are far more hard than rocks of adamant.
That you are more inconstant than your mistress'
Fortune, that guides you ; that your promises
Are all deceitful ; and that wanton love,

Whom former ages, flattering their vice
And to procure more freedom for their sin,
Have term'd a god, laughs at your perjuries.
   Luc. You will do this? why do so, ease your mind,
So I be free from you. There's no such torment,
As to be troubled with an insolent lover
That will receive no answer: bonds and fetters,
Perpetual imprisonment, are not like it:
'Tis worse than to be seiz'd on with a fever,
A continual surfeit. For Heaven's sake, leave me!
And let me hear no more of you.
   Aur. Is this the best reward for all my hopes,
The dear expences of youth and service,
Spent in the execution of your follies?
When not a day or hour but witness'd with me,
With what great study and affected care,
More than of fame or honour, I invented
New ways to fit your humour? what observance,
As if you were the arbitress of courtship,
I sought to please you with? laid out for fashions,
And bought them for you? feasted you with banquets?
Read you asleep i' th' afternoon with pamphlets?
Sent you elixirs and preservatives,
Paintings and powders, that would have restor'd
Old Niobe to youth? the beauty you pretend to
Is all my gift. Besides, I was so simple,
To wear your foolish colours, cry your wit up
And judgment, when you had none, and swore to it;
Drank to your health, whole nights, in hippocras,*
Upon my knees, with more religion
Than e'er I said my prayers; which Heaven forgive me.

   * A compound wine mixed with several kinds of spices; (*Blount's Glassographia*) so called from Hippocrates, the Physician, whose invention it is alleged to have been.

Luc. Are these such miracles? 'Twas but your
    duty,
The tributary homage all men owe
Unto our sex. Should we enjoin you travel,
Or send you on an errand into France,
Only to fetch a basket of musk-melons,
It were a favour for you. Put the case
And that I were Hero and you were Leander:
If I should bid you swim the Hellespont,
Only to know my mind, methinks you might
Be proud of the employment. Were you a Puritan,
Did I command you wait me to a play,
Or to the church, though you had no religion,
You might not question it.
    Aur.   Pretty, very pretty!
    Luc. And then because I am familiar,
And deign, out of my nobleness and bounty,
To grace your weak endeavours with the title
Of courtesy, to wave my fan at you,
Or let you kiss my hand, must we straight marry?
I may esteem you in the rank of servants,
To cast off when I please, ne'er for a husband.
    Aur. If ever devil damn'd in a woman's tongue,
'Tis in thine. I am glad yet you tell me this,
I might have else proceeded, and gone on
In the lewd * way of loving you, and so
Have wander'd farther from myself: but now
I'll study to be wiser, and henceforth
Hate the whole gang of you; denounce a war,
Ne'er to be reconcil'd, and rejoice in it,
And count myself blessed for't, and wish all men
May do the like, to shun you. For my part,
If when my brains are troubled with late drinking,—
I shall have else the grace, sure, to forget you—
Then but my labouring fancy dream of you,
I'll start, affrighted at the vision.
               * Ignorant.

Luc. 'Las! how pitifully it takes it to heart!
It would be angry too, if it knew how.
  Aur. Come near me, none of you! if I hear
The sound of your approach I'll stop my ears;
Nay I'll be angry, if I shall imagine
That any of you think of me: and, for thy sake,
If I but see the picture of a woman,
I'll hide my face, and break it. So, farewell!
                              [*Exit Lucretia.*

Enter LORENZO, MOCCINIGO, *and* ANGELIA.

  Lor. What are you, friend, and what's your
        business?
  Aur. Whate'er it be, now 'tis dispatch'd.
  Lor. This is rudeness.
  Aur. The fitter for the place and persons then.
  Lor. How's that?
  Aur. You are a nest of savages, the house
Is more inhospitable than the quick sands.
Your daughter sits on that enchanted bay,
A Siren like, to entice passengers,
Who, viewing her through a false perspective,
Neglect the better traffic of their life;
But yet, the more they labour to come near her,
The further she flies back; until at last,
When she has brought them to some rock or shelf,
She proudly looks down on the wreck of lovers.
  Lor. Why, who has injur'd you?
  Aur.   No matter who:
I'll first talk with a Sphinx ere converse with you.
  Lor. A word. Expound your wrongs more to
        the full,
              If you expect a remedy.
  Aur. I'll rather
Seek out diseases, choose my death and pine,
Than stay to be cur'd by you.   [*Exit.*

Enter ÆMILIA *and* LUCRETIA.

Lor. If you be so obstinate,
Take your course—Why, wife Æmilia,
Daughter Lucretia—What's the matter here
With this same fellow? do you owe him money?
 Luc. Owe him money, sir? Does he look like one
That should lend money? He is a gentleman,
And they seldom credit any body.
 Lor.   Well, wife,
Where was your matron's wisdom, that should keep
A vigilant care upon your house and daughter,
And not have suffer'd her to be surpriz'd
With every loose aspect, and gazing eye,
That suck in hot and lustful motions?
You were best turn bawd, and prostitute her beauty.
 Æm. You were best turn an old ass,
And meddle with your bonds and brokage.
 Lor. What was his business?
 Luc. To tell you true, sir, he is one of those
Whom love and fortune have conspir'd to fool,
And make the subject of a woman's will.
His idle brain, being void of better reason,
Is fill'd with toys and humours; and, for want
Of other exercise, he takes great pains
For the expressing of his folly: sometimes
With starts and sighs, hung head and folded arms,
Sonnets and pitiful tunes, forgetting
All due respect unto himself and friends,
With doating on a mistress: she again,
As little pitying him, whose every frown
Strikes him as dead as fate, and makes him walk
The living monument of his own sorrow.
 Lor. I apprehend, he came a wooing to thee.

'Tis so? and thou did'st scorn him, girl; 'twas well
  done.
I'll ease thee of that care : see, I have brought
A husband to thy hand. Look on him well!
A worthy man and a Clarissimo.
  Luc. A husband, said you? Venus be propitious!
He looks more like the remedy of love,
A julep to cool it. She that could take fire
At such a dull flame as his eyes, I should
Believe her more than touchwood!
  Moc. A ravishing feature!
If her condition answer but her feature,
I am fitted. Her form answers my affection;
It arrides * me exceedingly; I'll speak to her.
Fair mistress, what your father has propos'd
In the fair way of contract, I stand ready
To ratify; and let me not seem less
In your esteem, because I am so easy
In my consent. Women love out of fancy,
Men from advise.†
  Luc. You do not mean in earnest?
Now, Cupid, deliver me!
  Moc. How! not in earnest?
As I am strong and mighty in desires,
You wrong me to question it.
  Luc. Good sir! consider
The infinite distance that is between us
In age and manners.
  Moc. No distance at all :
My age is youthful, and your youth is aged.
  Luc. But you are wise; and will you sell your
  freedom
Unto a female tyranny in despair?
Ere to be quit, you run a strange adventure,
Without perceiving what a certain hazard

* Looks pleasantly to me.
† "Such discourse bring on
As may advise him of his happy state;
Happiness in his power, made free to will."—*Paradise Lost.*

A creature of my inclination
Is apt to draw you to.
 Moc.   I cannot think it.
 Luc. 'Tis strange you'll not believe me, unless I lay
My imperfection open. I have a nature
Ambitious beyond thought, quite giv'n over
To entertainments and expense : No bravery
That's fashionable can escape me ; and then,
Unless you are of a most settled temper,
Quiet without passion, I shall make you
Horn-mad with jealousy.
 Moc. Come, come, I know
Thou'rt virtuous, and speakest this but to try me.
You will not be so adverse to your fortune,
And all obedience, to contradict
What your father has set down.
 Luc.   These are my faults
I cannot help, if you will be so good
As to dispense with them.
 Moc. With all my heart ! I forgive thee before thou offend'st.
 Luc. Then I am mighty stubborn and self-will'd,
And shall sometimes e'en long to abuse you :
And for my tongue, 'tis like a stone thrown down
Of an impetuous motion not to be still'd.
 Moc. All these cannot dismay me; for considering
How they are passions proper to your sex,
In a degree they are virtues.
 Luc.   Oh my fate !
He will not be terrified. Then, not to feed you
With further hopes, or pump for more excuses,
Take it in brief, though I am loth to speak,
But you compel me to it,—I cannot love you.
 Lor. How do you speed, sir ? Is she tractable ?
Do you approve of her replies ?
 Moc.   I know not ;

Guess you; she said she cannot love me? and 'tis
The least thing I should have mistrusted. I durst
Have sworn she would ne'er have made scruple
   on't.
   Lor. Not love you? Come she must and shall.
Do you hear, housewife?
No more of this, as you affect my friendship.
What, shall I bring here a right worshipful Prætor
Unto my house, in hope you will be rul'd,
And you prove recreant to my commands?
By my vex'd soul! thou hast done a deed were
   able
In the mere questioning of what I bid,
Were not I a pious and indulgent father,
To thrust thee, as a stranger, from my blood.
   Moc. Be not too rash, sir! women are not won
With force, but fair entreaty. Have I been vers'd
Thus long i' th' school of love; know all their arts,
Their practices, their ways, and subtleties,
In all my encounters still return'd a victor,
And have not left a stratagem at last
To work on her affection? let me suffer.
   Lor. Nay, and you have that confidence, I'll
   leave you.
   Moc. Lady, a word in private with you.
                                       [*Whisper.*
   Æm. Pray, sweetheart,
What pretty youth is that?
   Lor. Who, this same chicken?
He is the son of a great nobleman,
And my especial friend. His father's gone
Into the country to survey his lands,
And let new leases, and left him in charge
With me till his return.
   Æm. Now, as I live!
'Tis a well-favour'd lad, and his years promise
He should have an ability to do,

And wit to conceal. When I take him single,
I'll try his disposition. [*Aside.*
    Moc.   This, for your sake,
I'll undertake and execute.
    Luc.   For my sake?
You shall not draw me to the fellowship
Of such a sin.
    Moc. I know 'tis pleasing to thee,
And therefore am resolv'd.
    Luc. I may prevent you.
    Lor. What! are you resolv'd?
    Moc. We are e'en at a point, sir.
    Lor. What's more to be done, let's in and consider. [*Exeunt.*

Enter ANTIQUARY *and* PETRO.

Ant. Well, sirrah! But that I have brought you up, I would cashier you for these reproofs.

Pet. Good sir, consider, 'tis no benefit to me; he is your nephew that I speak for, and 'tis charity to relieve him.

Ant. He is a young knave, and that's crime enough: an he were old in any thing, though 'twere in iniquity, there were some reverence to be had of him.

Pet. Why, sir, though be a young knave, as you term him, yet he is your kinsman, and in distress too.

Ant. Why, sir, and you know again, that 'tis an old custom,—which thing I will no way transgress—for a rich man not to look upon any his kinsman in distress.

Pet. 'Tis an ill custom, sir, and 'twere good 'twere repeal'd.

Ant. I have something else to look after. Have you dispos'd of those relics, as I bade you?

Pet. Yes, sir.

Ant. Well, thou dost not know the estimation of

what thou hast in keeping. The whole Indies, seeing they are but newly discover'd, are not to be valued with them: the very dust that cleaves to one of those monuments, is more worth than the ore of twenty mines!

Pet. Yet, by your favour, sir, of what use can they be to you?

Ant. What use! Did not the Seigniory build a state-chamber for antiquities? and 'tis the best thing that e'er they did: they are the registers, the chronicles of the age they were made in, and speak the truth of history better than a hundred of your printed commentaries.

Pet. Yet few are of your belief.

Ant. There's a box of coins within, most of them brass, yet each of them a jewel, miraculously preserv'd in spite of time or envy; and are of that rarity and excellence, that saints may go a pilgrimage to them, and not be ashamed.

Pet. Yet, I say still, what good can they do to you, more than to look on?

Ant. What good, thou brute? An thou wer't not worth a penny, the very shewing of them were able to maintain thee. Let me see now, an you were put to it, how you could advance your voice in their commendation. Begin!

Pet. All you gentlemen, that are affected with rarities, such, the world cannot produce the like, snatch'd from the jaws of time, and wonderfully collected by a studious antiquary, come near and admire!

Ant. Thou say'st right: the limbs of Hippolitus were never so dispers'd.

Pet. First, those twelve pictures that you see there are the portraitures of the Sibyls, drawn five hundred years since, by Titianus of Padua, an excellent painter and statuary.

Ant. Very well.

Pet. Then here is Venus all naked, and Cupid by her, on a dolphin: both these were drawn by Apelles of Greece.

Ant. Proceed!

Ped. Then here is Hercules and Antæus; and that Pallas at length, in alabaster, with her helmet and feathers, and that's Jupiter, with an eagle at his back.

Ant. Exceeding well!

Pet. Then, there's the great silver box that Nero kept his beard in.

Ant. Good again!

Pet. And after decking it with precious stones did consecrate it to the Capitol.

Ant. That's right!

Pet. And there hangs the net that held Mars and his mistress, while the whole bench of bawdy deities stood spectators of their sport.

Ant. Admirable good!

Pet. Then, here is Marius to the middle, and there Cleopatra with a veil over her face; and next to her, Marcus Antonius, the Triumvir; then, he with half a nose is Corvinus, and he with ne'er a one is Galba.*

Ant. Very sufficient!

Pet. Then, here is Vitellius, and there Titus and Vespasian: these three were made by Jacobus Sansovinus, the Florentine.

Ant. 'Tis enough!

Pet. Last of all, this is the urn that did contain the ashes of the emperors.

Ant. And each of these worth a King's ransom——

---

* Et Curios jam dimidios, nasumque minorem corvini, et Galbam auriculis nasoque carentem?—*Juvenal Sat.* 8.

Enter DUKE *and* LEONARDO.

Duke. Save you, sir!

Ant. You are welcome, gentlemen.

Duke. I come, sir, a suitor to you. I hear you are possess'd of many various and excellent antiquities; and though I am a stranger, I would entreat your gentleness a favour.

Ant. What's that, sir?

Duke. Only that you would vouchsafe me to be a spectator of their curiosity and worth; which courtesy shall engage me yours for ever.

Ant. For their worth I will not promise: 'tis as you please to esteem of them.

Leo. No doubt, sir, we shall ascribe what dignity belongs to them, and to you their preserver.

Ant. You speak nobly! and thus much let me tell you, to your edifying: the foolish doating on these present novelties is the cause why so many rare inventions have already perish'd; and, which is pity, antiquity has not left so much as a footstep behind her, more than of her vices.

Leo. 'Tis the more pity, sir.

Ant. Then, what raises such vanities amongst us, and sets fantastical fancies a-work? What's the reason that so many fresh tricks and new inventions of fashions and diseases come daily over sea and land, upon a man that never durst adventure to taste salt water, but only the neglect of those useful instructions which antiquity has set down.

Duke. You speak oracles, sir.

Ant. Look farther, and tell me what you find better, or more honourable than age. Is not wisdom entail'd upon it? Take the pre-eminence of it in every thing; in an old friend, in old wine, in an old pedigree.

Leo. All this is certain.

Ant. I confess to you, gentlemen, I must reverence and prefer the precedent times before these, which consum'd their wits in experiments: and 'twas a virtuous emulation amongst them, that nothing which should profit posterity should perish.

Leo. It argued a good fatherly providence.

Ant. It did so. There was Lysippus, that spent his whole life in the lineaments of one picture, which I will shew you anon: then was there Eudoxus the philosopher, who grew old in the top of a mountain, to contemplate astronomy; whose manuscript I have also by me.

Duke. Have you so, sir?

Ant. I have that, and many more; yet see the preposterous desires of men in these days, that account better of a mass of gold than whatever Apelles or Phidias have invented!

Duke. That is their ignorance.

Ant. Well, gentlemen, because I perceive you are ingenious, I would entreat you to walk in, where I will demonstrate all, and proceed in my admonition. [*Exeunt.*

Enter AURELIO *and* LIONELL.

Lio. 'Tis well, sir: I am glad you are so soon got free from your bondage.

Aur. Yes, I thank my stars, I am now my own man again; I have slept out my drunken fit of love, and am recovered. You, that are my friends, rejoice at my liberty.

Lio. Why, was it painful to you?

Aur. More tedious than a siege. I wonder what black leaf in the book of fate has decreed that misery upon man, to be in love; it transforms him to a worse monster than e'er Calypso's cup did: a country gentleman among courtiers, or their wives among the ladies, a clown among citizens, nay an ass among apes, is not half so ridiculous as that makes us. Oh! that I could but come by it, how I would tear it, that never such a witched passion should arise in any human breast again.

Lio. You are too violent in your hate: you should never so fall out with a friend, as to admit no hope of reconcilement.

Aur. I'll first be at peace with a serpent. Mark me! if thou hast care of thy time, thy health, thy fame, or thy wits, avoid it.

Lio. I must confess, I have been a little vain that way, yet never so transported, but when I saw a handsomer in place I could leave the former, and cleave to the latter. I was ever constant to beauty.

Aur. Hold thee there still! and if there be a necessity at any time that thou must be mad, let it be a short fury and away: let not this paltry love hang too long upon the file, be not deluded with delays; for if these she-creatures have once the predominance, there shall be no way to torture thee, but they'll find it out and inflict it without mercy: they'll work on thy disposition, and if thou hast any good-nature they'll be sure to abuse thee extremely.

Lio. Speak you this in earnest?

Aur. I know not what you call earnest, but before I'll endure that life again, I'll bind myself to a carrier, look out any employment whatever, spend my hours in seeing motions and puppet-plays, rook at bowling-alleys, mould tales and vent them at ordinaries, carry begging epistles, walk upon projects, transcribe fiddlers' ditties.

Lio. Oh, monstrous!

Aur. But since I have tasted the sweetness of my freedom, thou dost not know what quickness and agility is infused into me. I feel not that weight was wont to clog me where'er I went; I am all fire and spirit, as if I had been stript of my mortality. I hear not my thoughts whisper to me, as they were wont—Such a man is your rival; There's an affront, call him to an account; Redeem your mistress' favour; Present her with such a gift; Wait her at such a place;—none of these vanities.

Lio. You are happy, sir.

Enter DUKE, PETRO, *and* LEONARDO.

Pet. Come, gentles, follow me, I'll bring you to them: look you where they are!

Duke. Signior Lionell, I have trac'd much ground to inquire for you.

Lio. I rest engag'd to you for your last night's love, sir.

Duke. And I for your good company. Did you ever see such a blind ruinous tippling-house, as we made shift to find out?

Leo. Ay, and the people were as wretched in it: what a mist of tobacco flew amongst them!

Lio. And what a deluge of rheum!

Pet. If the house be so old as you speak of, 'twere good you brought my master into it, and then throw 't a-top of him; he would never desire to be better buried.

Duke. Well said, Petro.

Lio. Sir, if it be no trouble to you, I would entreat you know my worthy friend here.

Duke. You shall make me happy in any worthy acquaintance.

Pet. Well, Signior Lionell, you are beholden to these gentlemen for their good words unto your uncle for you: they spoke in your behalf, as earnestly as e'er did lawyer for his client.

Lio. And what was the issue?

Pet. He is hide-bound, he will part with nothing. There is an old rivell'd* purse hangs at his side, has not been loos'd these twenty years, and, I think, will so continue.

Lio. Why, will his charity stretch to nothing, Petro?

Pet. Yes, he has sent you something.

Lio. What is't?

Pet. A piece of antiquity, sir; 'tis English coin; and if you will needs know, 'tis an old Harry groat.†

Lio. Thank him heartily.

Pet. And 'tis the first, he says, that e'er was made of them; and, in his esteem, is worth three double ducats newly stampt.

Lio. His folly may put what price he please upon it, but to me 'tis no more than the value, Petro.

Pet. He says, moreover, that it may stand you in some use and pleasure hereafter, when you grow ancient; for it is worn so thin with often handling, it may serve you for a spectacle.

Lio. Very well.

Duke. 'Twere a good deed to conspire against him; he has a humour easy to be wrought on, and, if you'll undertake him, we'll assist you in the performance.

Lio. With all my heart, gentlemen, and I thank you.

Duke. Let us defer it no longer then, but instantly about it.

Lio. A match! Lead on; good wit and fortune guide us. [*Exeunt.*

* Wrinkled.

† The groats coined in the reign of Henry the Eighth, are the old Harry groat, which bears the head of the King with a long face and long hair; the gun-hole groat; the first and second gun-stone groat, &c.—*Heuit's Treatise on Coins.*

Act III. Scene I.

Enter Bravo *and* Boy.

Bra. Boy, how sits my rapier?

Boy. Close, sir, like a friend that meant to stick to you.

Bra. He that will purchase honour, and the name of Bravo, must, by consequence, be a brave fellow; his title requires it.

Boy. But pray, sir, were you never put to the worst in your days?

Bra. Who, I worsted? no, boy; I do manage my rapier with as much steadiness and facility, as a vineor * does his antler.

Boy. Sure you must needs be very strong then.

Bra. Not so, neither; 'tis courage in me. I do it by a sleight, an activity, and by that I can controul any man's point whatsoever.

Boy. Is it possible?

Bra. I tell thee, boy, I do as much surpass Hercules at my rapier, as he did me in club-fighting.† Have you drawn a register of those men that have been forc'd by this weak instrument to lay down their lives? I think it has cut more lives than Atropos.

Boy. But pray, sir, were they all your own exploits?

Bra. Indeed, boy, thou may'st question it; for, an they were to perform again, they would hardly be done. What will this age come to? Where be those stirring humours that were wont to trouble the world? Peace, I think, will o'erspread them all like a gangrene, and men will die with a lethargy: there's no malice extant, no jealousies, no employ-

---

* Presumed to be "unicorn."

† "I do excel Sampson in my rapier, as much as he did me in carrying gates."—*Love's Labour Lost.*

ment to set wickedness a-work! 'tis never a dead time with me, but when there's nobody to kill.

Boy. That's a miserable extremity indeed, sir.

Bra. Leave me, boy, to my meditations!

[*Exit Boy.*

Enter MOCCINIGO.

Well go thy ways, old Nick Machivel, there will never be the peer of thee for wholesome policy and good counsel. Thou took'st pains to chalk men out the dark paths and hidden plots of murther and deceit, and no man has the grace to follow thee: the age is unthankful, thy principles are quite forsaken, and worn out of memory.

Moc. There's a fellow walks melancholy, and that's commonly a passion apt to entertain any mischief; discontent and honesty seldom harbour together. How scurvily he looks, like one of the devil's factors! I'll tempt him.—By your leave, sir.

Bra. Ha?

Moc. No hurt, good sir; be not so furious, I beseech you.

Bra. What are you?

Moc. I am bold to disturb you, and would fain communicate a business, if you had the patience to hear me.

Bra. Speak, what is't?

Moc. You seem a man upon whom fortune, perhaps, has not cast so favourable an aspect as you deserve.

Bra. Can you win her to look better?

Moc. Though not her, yet, perhaps a servant of hers, that shall be as gracious to you, and as profitable.

Bra. What's she?

Moc. It may be, you want money: there is a way to purchase it, if you have the heart.

Bra. The heart? Hast thou the heart to speak, nay to conceive what I dare not undertake?

Moc. A fit instrument for my purpose! How luckily has fortune brought me to him.—Do you hear, sir, 'tis but the slight killing of a man, or so; no more.

Bra. Is that all?

Moc. Is that nothing?

Bra. Some queasy stomach might turn, perhaps, at such a motion; but I am more resolv'd, better harden'd. What is he? For I have my several rates, salaries for blood: for a lord, so much; for a knight, so much; a gentleman, so much; a peasant, so much; a stranger, so much; and a native, so much.

Moc. Nay, he is a gentleman, and a citizen of Venice.

Bra. Let him be what he will, and we can agree: it has been a foolish ambition heretofore, to save them, and men were rewarded for it with garlands;* but I had rather destroy one or two of them, they multiply too fast.

Moc. Do you know one Signior Aurelio then? He is the man! he woo'd my mistress, and sought to win her from me.

Bra. A warrantable cause! shew me the man, and 'tis enough.

Moc. And what must I give you?

Bra. At a word, thirty livres; I'll not bate you a betso.†

Moc. I'll give you twenty.

---

* The Romans bestowed an oaken wreath on him who had preserved the life of a citizen. The mother of *Coriolanus*, in Shakespeare, boasts that he "return'd, his brows bound with oak."—S.

† A coin of the least value current in Venice, of the value of half a sol; that is, scarcely a farthing.—*See Coryat's Crudities*, 1611, p. 286.

Bra. You bid like a chapman. Well, 'tis a hard time; in hope of your custom hereafter, I'll take your money.

Moc. There 'tis. Now for the means; how can you compass it? Were you not best poison him, think you?

Bra. With a bullet or stiletto; poison him? I scorn to do things so poorly. No, I'll use valour in my villainy, or I'll do nothing.

Moc. You speak honourably; and, now I think on't, what if you beat him wellfavour'dly, and spared his life?

Bra. Beat him? stay there; I'll kill him for this sum, but I'll not beat him for thrice the value; so he might do as much for me: no, I'll leave him impotent for all thought of revenge.

Enter LUCRETIA.

Moc. Well, sir, use your pleasure. Look you, here's the gentlewoman for whose sake it is done.— Lady, you are come most opportunely, to be a witness of my love and zeal to you; he is the man that will do the feat.

Luc. What feat?

Moc. That you and I consulted of; kill the rascal Aurelio! take him out of the way. What should he live any longer for? I'll have no man breathe that you disgust.

Luc. Then ought you to go and hang yourself.

Moc. Who? I hang myself! for what? my good service, and respect to your quiet? If he have any mind to haunt your chamber hereafter, he shall do it as a ghost, without any substantial shape, I assure you.

Luc. I think the fool be in earnest: I must use policy, and not play away a man's life so.

[*Aside.*

Nay, prythee, sweatheart, be not angry, 'twas but
to try thee. This kiss, and my love
    Moc. Why, here's some amends yet! now 'tis
as it should be.
    Luc. I am as deep and eager in this purpose
As you are, therefore grant me leave, a little,
To talk with him. I have some private counsel
To give him, for the better execution.
    Moc. May I not hear?
    Luc. No, as you love me, go!
    Moc. Her humour must be law. We that are
      suitors
Must deal with women as with towns besieg'd;
Offer them fair conditions, till you get them,
And then we'll tyrannize. Yet there's a doubt
Is not resolv'd on.
    Luc. Good sir, begone!
    Moc. I vanish! Were I best trust this fellow
      with my mistress?
Temptations may rise: 'tis all one, I am
A right Italian, and the world shall see
That my revenge is above jealousy.   [*Exit.*
    Bra. Now, lady, your pleasure?
    Luc. I would not allow myself any conference
with you, did my reason persuade me that you
were as bad as you seem to be. Pray, what are
you?
    Bra. I am, sweet creature, a kind of lawless jus-
ticer, or usurping martialist of authority, that will
kill any man with my safety.
    Luc. And you purpose the death of this gentle-
man?
    Bra. I will do anything for hire.
    Luc. Have you no conscience?
    Bra. Conscience! I know not what it is. Why
should any man live, and I want money?
    Luc. Have you no regard then of innocence?

Bra. 'Tis crime enough he has a life.
Luc. How long have you been vers'd in this
   trade?
Bra. 'Tis my vocation,
Luc. Leave it! 'tis damnable;
And thou the worst and basest of all villains.
It had been better for the womb that bare thee,
If it had travail'd with a pestilence.
What seed of tigers could beget thee to
Such bold and rash attempts? for a small lucre,
Which will be straight as ill spent as 'twas got,
To destroy that, whose essence is divine;
Souls, in themselves more pure than are the
   heavens,
Or thy ill-boding stars; more worth than all
The treasure lock'd up in the heart of earth:
And yet do this unmov'd or unprovok'd.
   Bra. I have no other means, nor way of living.
   Luc. 'Twere better perish, than be so supported;
There are a thousand courses to subsist by.
   Bra. Ay, but a free and daring spirit scorns
To stoop to servile ways, but will choose rather
To purchase his revenue from his sword.
   Luc. I see you are growing obdurate in your
      crimes,
Founded to vice, lost to all piety;
Without the apprehension of what wrong
You do your country, in depriving her
Of those she now enjoys, as useful members;
And killing their posterity, who, perhaps,
Might, with their art or industry, advance her.
   Bra. What courteous itch, I wonder, has pos-
      sest
Your virtuous ladyship to give me advice?
Best keep your wits until you get a husband,
Who may, perhaps, require your learned counsel.
   Luc. 'Tis true, such as do act thy villanies

Hate to be told, or think of them; but hear me!
Hast thou no sense, nor no remorse of soul?
No thought of any Deity, who, though
It spare thee for a while, will send at last
A quick return of vengeance on thy head,
And dart thee down like Phaeton?
    Bra. Sweet virgin,
Faces about* to some other discourse,
I cannot relish this.
    Luc. So I believe; but yet
Compose your thoughts for speedy penitence,
Your life for an amendment, or, I vow
To lay your actions open to the Senate.
    Bra. Did not your sweetheart tempt me to this
        deed,
And will you now betray me?
    Luc. He, my sweetheart?
I hate you both alike: that very word
Is enough to divorce thee from my pity
Past hope of reconcilement; for what mercy
Is to be had of two such prodigies?
Will you recant yet? Speak! will you be honest?
    Bra. I think you'll force me to become your
        patient.
    Luc. It is the way to heal thee of a sore,
Whose cure is supernatural. What art,
What mirror is sufficient to demonstrate
The foulness of thy guilt, whose leprous mind
Is but one stain seas cannot cleanse? Why, murder!
'Tis of all vices the most contrary
To every virtue and humanity;
For they intend the pleasure and delight,
But this the dissolution, of nature.

    * "Double your files; as you were; faces about!"—*Beaumont and Fletcher*.
    " I have read divine Seneca; thou know'st nothing but the earthly part, and can'st cry to that, 'faces about.' "—*Parson's Wedding*.

Bra. She does begin to move me.

Luc. Think of thy sin!
It is the heir apparent unto hell;
And has so many, and so ugly shapes,
His father Pluto, and the Furies hate
To look on their own birth: yet thou dar'st act
What they fear to suggest, and sell thy soul
To quick perdition.

Bra. This has wak'd me more
Into a quicker insight of my evils,
That have impal'd me round with horrid shapes,
More various than the sev'ral forms of dreams
That wait on Morpheus in his sleepy den.

Luc. Then, 'tis a fearful sin, and always labours
With the new birth of damn'd inventions
And horrid practices; for 'tis so fearful,
It dares not walk alone, and, where it bides,
There is no rest, nor no security,
But a perpetual tempest of despair.

Bra. All this I feel by sad experience.
Where have I been, where have I liv'd a stranger,
Exil'd from all good thoughts? Never till now
Did any beam of grace or good shine on me.

Luc. Besides, 'tis so abhorr'd of all that's good,
That when this monster lifts his cursed head
Above the earth, and wraps it in the clouds,
The sun flies back, as loth to stain his rays
With such a foul pollution; and night,
In emulation of so black a deed,
Puts on her darkest robe to cover it.

Bra. Oh, do not grate too much upon my suff'rings!
You have won upon my conscience, and I feel
A sting within me tells my troubled soul,
That I have trod too long those bloody paths
That lead unto destruction.

Luc. Then be sorry,
And with repentance purge away thy sin.

Bra. Will all my days and hours consum'd in
  prayers,
My eyes dissolv'd to tears, wash off such crimes ?
  Luc. If they be serious, and continued.
  Bra. You are a virgin, and your vows are chaste,
Do you assist me.
  Luc.   So you'll do the like
For me in what I shall propose.
  Bra.   I will,
And joy to be employ'd : there's no thought,
Which can proceed from you, but which is
  virtuous ;
And 'tis a comfort, and a kind of goodness,
To mix with you in any action.
  Luc. Nay, more, in recompence of your fair proffer,
Because you say you are destitute of means,
I'll see that want supplied.
  Bra.   Divinest lady,
Command my service.
  Luc. Walk then in with me !
And then I will acquaint you with the project.
                                          [*Exeunt.*

Enter DUKE, LIONELL, *and* LEONARDO, PETRUTIO
                      following.

  Duke. I see him coming ! let's fall into admiration of his good parts, that he may over-hear his own praise.
  Lio. I have, methinks, a longing desire to meet with Signior Petrutio.
  Pet. I hear myself nam'd amongst them. 'Tis no point of civility to listen what opinion the world holds of me, I shall conceive it by their discourse : a man behind his back shall be sure to have nothing but truth spoke of him.
  Leo. Pray, sir, when saw you that thrice noble and accomplish'd gentleman, Petrutio ?

Pet. Thrice noble and accomplish'd! There's a new style thrust upon me.

Duke. It pleas'd the indulgency of my fate to bless me with his company this morning, where he himself was no less favourable to grace me with the perusal of a madrigal, or an essay of beauty, which he had then newly compos'd.

Lio. Well, gallants, either my understanding misinforms me, or he is one of the most rare and noble-qualified pieces of gentility, that ever did enrich our climate.

Leo. Believe it, sir, 'twere a kind of profanation to make doubt of the contrary.

Pet. How happy am I in such acquaintance! A man shall have his due, when your meaner society has neither judgment to discern worth, nor credit to commend it.

Duke. 'Twas my happiness, th' other day, to be in the presence with certain ladies, where I heard him the most extoll'd and approv'd: one of them was not asham'd to pronounce it openly, that she would never desire more of heaven than to enjoy such a man for her servant.

Pet. It shall be my next employment to enquire out for that lady.

Lio. 'Tis a miracle to me, how, in so small a competency of time, he should arrive to such an absolute plenitude of perfection.

Leo. No wonder at all; a man that has travell'd, and been careful of his time.

Lio. But, by your favour, sir, 'tis not every man's happiness to make so good use on't.

Duke. I'll resolve you something: there is as great a mystery in the acquisition of knowledge as of wealth. Have you not a citizen will grow rich in a moment, and why not be ingenious? Besides, who knows but he might have digg'd for it, and so found out some conceal'd treasure of understanding.

Pet. Now, as I am truly noble, 'tis a wrongful imputation upon me.

Leo. Well, if he had but bounty annex'd to his other sufficiencies, he were unparallel'd.

Duke. Nay, there's no man in the earth more liberal: take it upon my word, he has not that thing in the world so dear or precious in his esteem which he will not most willingly part with upon the least summons of his friend.

Pet. Now must I give away some two or three hundred pounds worth of toys, to maintain this assertion.

Lio. You spoke of verses e'en now; if you have the copy, pray vouchsafe us a sight of them.

Duke. I cannot suddenly resolve you. Yes, here they are!

Lio. What's this?

A Madrigal of Beauty.

If I should praise her virtue and her beauty.
    as 'tis my duty;
And tell how every grace doth her become:
    'tis ten to one
But I should fail in the expression.

Leo. Ay, marry, sir! this sounds something like excellent.

Lio.   Then, by your leave,
Although I cannot write what I conceive:
    'tis my desire,
That what I fail to speak you would admire.

Leo. Why, this has some taste in't: how should he arrive to this admirable invention?

Duke. Are you so preposterous in your opinion to think that wit and elegancy in writing are only confin'd to stagers and book-worms? 'Twere a solecism to imagine, that a young bravery, who lives in the perpetual sphere of humanity, where every waiting-woman speaks perfect Arcadia, and the ladies' lips distil with the very quintessence of conceit, should be so barren of apprehension as not to participate of their virtues.

Leo. Now, I consider, they are great helps to a man.

Duke. But when he has travell'd, and delibated * the French and the Spanish; can lie a-bed, and expound Astræa,† and digest him into compliments; and, when he is up, accost his mistress with what he had read in the morning; now if such a one should rack up his imagination, and give wings to his muse, 'tis credible he should more catch your delicate court-ear, than all your head-scratchers, thumb-biters, lamp-wasters of them all.

Leo. Well, I say the iniquity of fortune appears in nothing more than not advancing that man to some extraordinary honours.

Lio. But I never thought he had any genius that way.

Duke. What, because he has been backward to produce his good qualities? Believe it, poetry will out; it can no more be hid than fire or love.

Pet. I'll break them off, they have e'en spoken enough in my behalf for nothing, o'conscience.—Save you, Cavalieros!

Duke. My much honour'd Petrutio, you are welcome; we were now enter'd into a discourse of your worth. Whither do your occasions enforce you so fast?

Pet. Gentlemen, to tell you true, I am going upon some raptures.

Leo. Upon raptures, say you?

Pet. Yes, my employment is tripartite: I have

---
* Had a taste of.
† A French Romance, popular during the last century.

here an anagram to a lady I made of her name this morning; with a posy to another, that must be inserted into a ring; and here's a paper carries a secret word too that must be given and worn by a knight and tilter; and all my own imaginations, as I hope to be bless'd.

Lio. Is't possible? how, have you lately drunk of the horse-pond,* or stept on the forked Parnassus, that you start out so sudden a poet?

Pet. Tut! I leave your Helicons, and your pale Pirenes,† to such as will look after them; for my own part, I follow the instigation of my brain, and scorn other helps.

Lio. Do you so?

Pet. I'll justify it, the multiplicity of learning does but distract a man. I am all for your modern humours, and, when I list to express a passion, it flows from me with that spring of amorous conceits, that a true lover may hang his head over, and read in it the very phys'nomy of his affection.

Duke. Why, this is a rare mirror!

Leo. 'Tis so, indeed, and beyond all the art of optics.

Pet. And when my head labours with the pangs of delivery, by chance up comes a Countess's waiting-woman, at whose sight, as at the remembrance of a mistress, my pen falls out of my hand; and then do I read to her half a dozen lines, whereat we both sit together, and melt into tears.

Leo. Pitiful-hearted, carted creatures!

Pet. I am now about a device, that this gentleman has promis'd shall be presented before his Highness.

Duke. Yes, upon my word, sir, and yourself with it.

---

* Fonte labra prolui *Caballino. Perius.* S.

† Pallidamque Pyrenen. *Ib.* A fountain in Mount Helicon, made by the hoof of Pegasus.

Pet. Shall the Duke take notice of me too? Oh Heavens, how you transport me with the thought on't!

Duke. I'll bring you to him, believe me; and you know not what grace he may do you.

Pet. 'Tis a happiness beyond mortals! I cannot tell, it may be my good fortune to advance you all.

Lio. We shall be glad to have dependence on you.

Pet. Gentles, I would entreat you a courtesy.

Duke. What's that, signior?

Pet. That you would be all pleas'd to grace my lodging to-morrow at a banquet: there will be ladies and gallants; and, among the rest, I'll send to invite your uncle the Antiquary, and we'll be very merry, I assure you.

Leo. Well, sir, your bounty commands us not to fail you.

Pet. Bounty! there's a memorandum for me. In the meantime, pray accept these few favours at my hands, as assurances that you will not fail me; till when, I take my leave. [*Exit.*

Lio. Farewell, sir! Go thy ways; thou hast as dull a piece of scalp, as e'er covered the brain of any traveller.

Duke. For love's sake, Lionell, let's haste to thy uncle, before the coxcomb prevent us.

Lio. Why, sir, I stay for you.

Leo. Has Petro prepar'd him for your entrance? And is your disguise fit?

Lio. I have all in a readiness.

Duke. On then! and when you are warm in your discourse, we'll come with our advice to affright him: 'twill be an excellent scene of affliction.

Leo. Be sure you mark your cue, sir, and do not fail to approach.

Duke. Trust to my care! I warrant you. [*Exeunt.*

Enter AURELIO *and* SERVANT.

Aur. A gentlewoman without speak with me, say you ?

Ser. Yes, sir, and will by no means be put back.

Aur. I am no lawyer, nor no secretary. What business can she have here, I wonder ?

Ser. She is very importunate to enter.

Aur. I was once in the humour never to admit any of them to come near me again, but since she is so eager let her approach. I'll try my strength what proof 'tis against her enchantments: if ever Ulysses were more provident, or better arm'd to sail by the Sirens, I'll perish ; if she have the art to impose upon me, let her beg my wit for an anatomy, and dissect it———

Enter LUCRETIA.

Now, Lady Humour, what new emotion in the blood has turn'd the tide of your fancy to come hither ?

Luc. These words are but unkind salutes to a gentlewoman.

Aur. They are too good for you. With what face dare you approach hither, knowing how infinitely you have abus'd me ? You want matter to exercise your wits on, the world's too wise for you ; and ere you ensnare me again, you'll have good luck.

Luc. Pray, sir, do not reiterate those things which might better be forgotten. I confess I have done ill, because I am a woman, and young, and 'twill be nobleness in you not to remember it.

Aur. I'll sooner plough up shore and sow it, and live in expectation of a crop, before I'll think the least good from any of your sex while I breathe again.

Luc. I hope, sir, that time and experience will rectify your judgment to a better opinion of us.

Aur. I'll trust my ship to a storm, my substance to a broken citizen, ere I'll credit any of you.

Luc. Good sir, be entreated. I come a penitent lover, with a vow'd recantation to all former practices and malicious endeavours that I have wrought against you.

Aur. How can I think better of you, when I consider your nature, your pride, your treachery, your covetousness, your lust; and how you commit perjury easier than speak?

Luc. Sure, 'tis no desert in us, but your own misguided thoughts that move in you this passion.

Aur. Indeed, time was I thought you pretty foolish things to play withal; and was so blinded as to imagine that your hairs were golden threads,* that your eyes darted forth beams, that laughter sate smiling on your lips, and the coral itself look'd pale to them; that you mov'd like a goddess, and diffus'd your pleasures wide as the air: then could I prevent† the rising sun to wait on you, observ'd every nod you cast forth, had the patience to hear your discourse, and admir'd you when you talk'd of your visits, of the Court, of councils, of nobility, and of your ancestors.

Luc. And were not these pleasing to you?

Aur. Nothing but a heap of tortures: but since I have learn'd the Delphic Oracle, *to know myself*, and ponder what a deal of mischief you work, I am content to live private and solitary without any pensive thought what you do, or what shall become of you.

Luc. Sir, if you calculate all occasions, I have not merited this neglect from you.

* Her hairs like golden threads, play'd with her breath.—
Shakespeare's Rape of Lucretia.

† Anticipate.

Aur. Yes, and more. Do you not remember what tasks you were wont to put me to, and expenses? when I bestow'd on you gowns and petticoats, and you, in exchange, gave me bracelets and shoe-ties, how you fool'd me sometimes, and set me to pin plaits in your ruff two hours together, and made a waiting frippery of me? how you rack'd my brain to compose verses for you, a thing I could never abide? nay, in my conscience, an I had not took courage you had brought me to spin, and beat me with your slippers.

Luc. Well, sir, I perceive you are resolv'd to hear no reason; but, before my sorrowful departure, know, she that you slight is the preserver of your life; therefore, I dare be bold to call you ingrate, and in that I have spoke all that can be ill in man.

Aur. Pray, stay! come back a little.

Luc. Not till you are better temper'd. What I have reveal'd is true; and, though you prove unthankful, good deeds reward themselves: the conscience of the fact shall pay my virtue. So I leave you. [*Exit.*

Aur. That I should owe my life to her! which way I wonder? Something depends on this I must win out: well, I will not foreswear it, but the toy may take me in the head, and I may see her. [*Exit.*

Enter ANTIQUARY *and* PETRO.

Ant. Has he such rare things, say you?

Pet. Yes, sir! I believe you have not seen the like of them, they are a couple of old manuscripts, found in a wall, and stor'd up with the foundation; it may be they are the writings of some prophetess.

Ant. What moves you to think so, Petro?

Pet. Because, sir, the characters are so imperfect;

for time has eaten out the letters, and the dust makes a parenthesis betwixt every syllable.*

Ant. A shrewd convincing argument! This fellow has a notable reach with him. Go, bid him enter! A hundred to one some fool has them in possession, that knows not their value; it may be a man may purchase them for little or nothing—

Enter LIONELL, *like a scholar, with two books.*

Come near, friend, let me see what you have there! Umph, 'tis as I said, they are of the old Roman binding. What's the price of these?

Lio. I would be loath, sir, to sell them under rate only to merit laughter for my rashness: therefore I thought good to bestow them on you, and refer myself to your wisdom and free nature for my satisfaction.

Ant. You say well; then am I bound again in conscience to deal justly with you: will five hundred crowns content you?

Lio. I'll demand no more, sir.

Ant. Petro, see them deliver'd! Now, I need not fear to tell you what they are: this is a book *de Republica*, 'tis Marcus Tullius Cicero's own handwriting; I have some other books of his penning give me assurance of it.

Pet. And what's the other, sir?

Ant. This other is a book of mathematics that was long lost in darkness, and afterwards restored by Ptolemy.

Lio. I wonder, sir, unless you were Time's secretary, how you should arrive to this intelligence.

---

* Printed bookes he contemnes as a novelty of this latter age: but a manuscript he pours on everlastingly, especially if the cover be all moth-eaten, and the dust make a parenthesis betweene every syllable.—*Micro cosmographie, or a piece of the world discovered:*—*Antiquary.* 1628.

Ant. I know it by more than inspiration. You had them out of a wall, you say?

Lio. Yes, sir.

Ant. Well then, however you came by them, they were first brought to Venice by Cardinal Girmannus, a patriarch, and were digged out of the ruins of Aquileia, after it was sack'd by Attila king of the Huns.

Lio. This to me is wonderful.

Ant. Petro, I mean to retire, and give myself wholly to contemplation of these studies; and, because nothing shall hinder me, I mean to lease out my lands, and live confin'd. Enquire me out a chapman that will take them of me.

Lio. If you please to let them, sir, I will help you to a tenant.

Ant. Will you, sir? with all my heart, and I'll afford him the better bargain for your sake.

Pet. (*Aside.*) He may pay the rent with counters, and make him believe they are antiquities.

Ant. What's the yearly rent of them, Petro?

Pet. They have been rack'd, sir, to three thousand crowns; but the old rent was never above fifteen hundred.

Ant. Go to, you have said enough! I'll have no more than the old rent. Name your man, and the indenture shall be drawn.

Lio. Before I propose that, sir, I thought good to acquaint you with a specialty I found among other writings; which, having a seal to it, and a name subscrib'd, does most properly belong to you.

Ant. Let me see it. What's here? Signior Jovanno Veterano, de Monte Nigro! He was my great grandfather, and this is an old debt of his that remains yet uncancell'd. You could never have pleas'd me better to my cost: this ought in conscience to be discharg'd, and I'll see it satisfied the first thing I do. Come along!

Pet. Will you afford your nephew no exhibition out of your estate, sir?

Ant. Not a sol; not a gazet.* I have articles to propose before the Senate shall disinherit him.

Lio. Have you, sir? Not justly, I hope. Pray. what are they?

Ant. One of them is, he sent me letters beyond sea, dated *stilo novo*.

Lio. That was a great oversight.

Ant. Then you remember, Petro, he took up commodities, new-fashion'd stuffs, when he was under age too, that he might cozen his creditors.

Pet. Yes, sir.

Ant. And afterwards found out a new way to pay them too.

Lio. He serv'd them but in their kind, sir: perhaps they meant to have cheated him.

Ant. 'Tis all one; I'll have no such practices. But the worst of all, one time when I found him drunk and chid him for his vice, he had no way to excuse himself, but to say he would become a new man.

Lio. That was heinously spoken, indeed.

Ant. These are sufficient aggravations to any one that shall understand my humour.†

Enter DUKE *and* LEONARDO.

Duke. Save you, sir!

Ant. These gentlemen shall be witnesses to the bonds. You are very welcome!

Duke. I hardly believe it, when you hear our message.

Ant. Why, I beseech you?

* Almost a penny; whereof ten doe make a liver, that is, ninepence. *Coryat p.* 286. See note in Davenant's works. present series, vol. ii., p. 8.

† "Humour" *in original Ed.*

Duke. I am sorry to be made the unkind instrument to wrong you; but, since 'tis a task impos'd from so great a command, I hope you will the easier be induced to dispense with me.

Ant. Come nearer to your aim: I understand you not.

Duke. Then thus, sir: the Duke has been inform'd of your rarities; and, holding them an unfit treasure for a private man to possess, he hath sent his mandamus to take them from you. See, here's his hand for the delivery!

Ant. Oh, oh!

Leo. What ails you, sir?

Ant. I am struck with a sudden sickness: some good man help to keep my soul in, that is rushing from me, and will by no means be entreated to continue!

Leo. Pray sir, be comforted.

Ant. Comfort? no, I despise it: he has given me daggers to my heart!

Leo. Shew yourself a man, sir, and contemn the worst of fortune.

Ant. Good sir, could not you have invented a less studied way of torture to take away my life?

Duke. I hope 'twill not work so deeply with you.

Ant. Nay, and 'twould stop there, 'twere well: but 'tis a punishment will follow me after death, and afflict me worse than a fury.

Leo. I much pity the gentleman's case.

Ant. Think what 'tis to lose a son when you have brought him up, or, after a seven years' voyage, to see your ship sink in the harbour!

Duke. 'Twere a woeful spectacle indeed!

Ant. They are but ticklings to this: I have been all my life a-gathering what I must now lose in a moment. The sacking of a city is nothing to be compared with it.

Leo. And that's lamentable.

Ant. 'Twill but only give you a light to conceive of my misery.

Lio. Pray, sir, be not importunate to take them this time; but try rather, if by any means you can revoke the decree.

Duke. 'Twill be somewhat dangerous; but, for your sake, I'll try.

Ant. Shall I hope any comfort? Then, upon my credit, gentlemen, I'll appoint you all mine heirs so soon as I am dead.

Duke. You speak nobly.

Ant. Nay, and because you shall not long gape after it, I'll die within a month, and set you down all joint executors.

Lio. But when you are freed from the terror of his imposition, will you not recant?

Ant. Nay, an you doubt me, walk along, and I'll confirm't upon you instantly. [*Exeunt.*

Actus Quartus.

Enter ÆMILIA *and* ANGELIA.

Æm. Why, gentle boy, think what a happy bliss
Thou shalt enjoy, before thou know'st what 'tis!

Ang. 'Twill be a dear experiment, to waste
My prime and flower of youth, and suffer all
Those liquid sweets to be extracted from me
By the hot influence of consuming lust,
Only to find how well you can express
What skilful arts are hid in wickedness!

Æm. Thou dream'st, fond boy: those sweets of
   youth and beauty

Were lent, to be employ'd upon their like;
And when they both do meet, and are extinguish'd,
From their mixt heat a rich perfume shall rise,
And burn to love, a grateful sacrifice.
   Ang. But I'll not be so prodigal to lavish
Such gifts away that be irrevocable
And yet the first that leave us.
   Æm. 'Twill be ne'er exacted
How soon you have bestow'd them, but how well.
What good or profit can a hidden treasure
Do more than feed the miser's greedy eye,
When, if 'twere well bestow'd, it might enrich
The owner and the user of it? Such
Is youth, and nature's bounty, that receive
A gain from the expense; but, were there none
But a mere damage, yet the pleasure of it
And the delight would recompense the loss.
   Ang. Whate'er the pleasure be, or the delight.
I am too young, not plum'd for such a flight.
   Æm. Too young? a poor excuse! alas, your
     will
Is weaker than your power. No one can be
Too young to learn good arts; and, for my part.
I am not taken with a boisterous sinew,
A brawny limb, or back of Hercules,
But with a soft delicious beauty; such
As people, looking on his doubtful sex,
Might think him male or female.
   Ang. I cannot blame
These just Italians to lock up their wives,
That are so free and dissolute: they labour
Not with their country's heat more than their
     own.
Will you be satisfied I am too young?
   Æm. Too young? I like you the better. There
     is a price
Due to the early cherry: the first apples

Deserve more grace: the budding rose is set by;
But stale, and fully-blown, is left for vulgars
To rub their sweaty fingers on. Too young?
As well you may affirm the tender tree
Too young to graft upon; or you may say,
The rising sun's too young to court the day.
 Ang. But there are bonds Hymen has laid upon you,
Keep us asunder.
 Æm. Those are only toys,
Shadows, mere apparitions of doubt
To affright children. Do but yield unto me,
My arms shall be thy sphere to wander in,
Circled about with spells to charm these fears;
And, when thou sleep'st, Cupid shall crown thy slumbers
With thousand shapes of lustful dalliance:
Then will I bathe thee in ambrosia,
And from my lips distil such nectar on thee,
Shall make thy flesh immortal.

   Enter LORENZO.

 Lor. How now, wife, is this your exercise?
Wife, did I say? Stain of my blood and issue,
The great antipathy unto my nature,
Courting your paramour? Death to my honour!
What have I seen and heard? Curse of my fate!
Would I had first been deaf, or thou struck dumb,
Before this Gorgon, this damn'd vision,
Had numb'd my faculties.
 Æm. What have you seen
Or heard, more than a dialogue I read
This morning in a book?
 Lor. Would thou and that book
Were both burnt for heretics!—You genial powers,
Why did you send this serpent to my bosom,
To pierce me through with greater cruelty

Than Cleopatra felt from stings of adders?
Hence from my sight, thou venom to my eyes!
Would I could look thee dead, or with a frown
Dissect thee into atoms, and then hurl them
About the world to cast infection,
And blister all they light on!
   Æm. You are mad,
And rave without a cause!
   Lor. Oh, Heavens! she means
To justify her sin! Can'st thou redeem
Thy lost fame and my wrongs?
   Æm. No, sir, I'll leave you!
You are too passionate. [*Exit.*
   Ang. Pray, sir, be satisfied we meant no hurt.
   Lor. What charm held back my hand I did not let
Her foul blood out, then throw't into the air,
Whence it might mount up to the higher region,
And there convert into some fearful meteor,
To threaten all her kindred? Stay, sweet child,
For thou art virtuous:—yet go, however;
Thou put'st me in remembrance of some ill.
[*Exit Ang.*
Diana blush'd Actæon to a stag:
What shall lust do? Chastity made horns!
I shall be grafted with a horrid pair,
And between every branch a written scroll
Shall speak my shame, that foot-boys shall discern it,
And sailors read it as they pass along!
If I bear this I have no soul nor spleen.
I must invent some mischief. Smallest cares
Are talkative whil'st great ones silent are.* [*Exit.*

       Enter ÆMILIA.
   Æm. What have I done, that with a clue of lust

* Curæ leves loquuntur ingentes stupent. *Seneca.* S. P.

Have wrought myself in such a labyrinth,
Whence I shall ne'er get free ? There is no wrong
Like to the breach of wedlock : those injuries
Are writ in marble time shall ne'er rase out.
The hearts of such, if they be once divided,
Will ne'er grow one again : sooner you may
Call the spent day, or bid the stream return,
That long since slid beside you. I am lost ;
Quite forfeited to shame, which, till I felt,
I ne'er foresaw, so was the less prepared.
But yet, they say, a woman's wit is sudden,
And quick at an excuse. I was too foolish.
Had he confounded Heaven and earth with oaths,
I might have sworn him down, or wept so truly,
That he should sooner question his own eyes
Than my false tears : this had been worth the
    acting,
Or else I might have stood to the defence on't.
Been angry, and took a courage from my crimes ;
But I was tame and ignorant !

Enter LIONELL.

Lio. Save you, lady !
Æm. Oh Signior Lionell, you have undone me.
Lio. Who, I ! Which way ?
Æm. The boy you brought my husband.
Lor. Ay, what of him ?
Æm. He is a witch, a thief,
That has stol'n all my honours. His smooth
    visage
Seemed like to a sea becalm'd, or a safe harbour,
Where love might ride securely, but was found
A dangerous quicksand, wherein are perish'd
My hopes and fortunes, by no art or engine
To be weigh'd up again.
Lio. Instruct me how.
Æm. Teach me the way then, that I may relate

My own ill story with as great a boldness
As I did first conceive, and after act it.
What wicked error led my wand'ring thoughts
To gaze on his false beauty, that has prov'd
The fatal minute of my mind's first ruin?
Shall I be brief?
   Lio. What else?
   Æm. How can I speak,
Or plead with hope, that have so foul a cause!
   Lio. You torture me too much! the fear of evil
Is worse than the event.
   Æm. Then, though my heart
Abhor the memory, I'll tell it out.—
The boy I mentioned—whatever power
Did lay on me so sad a punishment—
I did behold him with a lustful eye,
And, which is the perfection of sin,
Did woo him to my will.
   Lio. Well, what of that?
You are not the first offender in that kind.
   Æm. My suit no sooner ended but came in
My jealous husband.
   Lio. That was something, indeed!
   Æm. Who overheard us all.
   Lio.   A shrewd mischance!
   Æm. Judge with what countenance he did be-
     hold me,
Or I view him, that had so great a guilt
Hang on my brow. My looks and hot desire
Both fell together; whilst he, big with anger
And swoll'n high with revenge, hastes from my
     presence,
Only to study how to inflict some torture,
Which I stay to expect: and here you see
The suffering object of his cruelty.
   Lio. Methinks it were an easy thing for one
That were ingenious, to retort all

On his own head, and make him ask forgiveness.
 Æm. That would be a scene indeed!
 Lio. I have been fortunate
In such turns in my days,
 Æm.   Could you do this,
I'd swear you had more wit than Mercury,
Or his son Autolycus, that was able
To change black into white.
 Lio.   Do not despair!
I have a genius was ne'er false to me;
If he should fail me now in these extremes,
I would not only wonder, but renounce him:
He tells me! something may be done. Be rul'd!
And if I plot not so to make all hit,
Then you shall take the mortgage of my wit.
 Æm. However, sir, you speak comfortably.
            [*Exeunt.*

 Enter AURELIO *above,* DUKE *and* LEONARDO
    over the stage.

 Aur. Good morrow, gentlemen. What! you are for the feast, I perceive.
 Duke. Master Aurelio, good morrow to you. Whose chamber's that, I pray?
 Aur. My own, sir, now: I thank ill fortune and a good wife.
 Duke. What! are you married, and your friends not pre-acquainted? This will be constru'd amongst them.
 Aur. A stol'n wedding, sir! I was glad to apprehend any occasion when I found her inclining.—We'll celebrate the solemnities hereafter, when there shall be nothing wanting to make our Hymen happy and flourishing.
 Leo. In good time, sir. Who is your spouse, I pray?
 Aur. Marry, sir, a creature, for whose sake I

have endured many a heat and cold, before I could vanquish her. She has prov'd one of Hercules' labours to me; but Time, that perfects all things, made my long toil and affection both successful: and, in brief, 'tis Mistress Lucretia, as very a haggard* as ever was brought to fist.

Du. Indeed! I have often heard you much complain of her coyness and disdain; what auspicious charm has now reconcil'd you together?

Aur. There is, sir, a critical minute in every man's wooing, when his mistress may be won, which, if he carelessly neglect to prosecute, he may wait long enough before he gain the like opportunity.

Leo. It seems, sir, you have lighted upon't.— We wish you much joy in your fair choice.

Aur. Thank you, gentlemen; and I to either of you no worse fortune. But that my wife is not yet risen, I would intreat you take the pains come up and visit her.

Du. No, sir, that would be uncivil; we'll wait some fitter occasion to gratulate your rites. Good-morrow to you! [*Exeunt.*

Aur. Your servant! Nay, lye you still, and dare not so much as proffer to mutter, for if you do I vanish. Now, if you will revolt, you may. I have laid a stain upon your honour, which you shall wash off as well as you can.

Enter LUCRETIA.

Luc. Was this done like a gentleman, or indeed like a true lover, to bring my name in question, and make me no less than your whore? Was I ever married to you? Speak!

Aur. No; but you may when you please.

* "A haggard faulcon—a faulcon that prayed for herself before she was taken." *Blount.*

Luc. Why were you then so impudent to proclaim such a falsehood, and say I was your wife, and that you had lain with me when 'twas no such matter.

Aur. Because I meant to make you so, and no man else should do it.

Luc. 'Slight, this is a device to over-reach a woman with? He has madded me and I would give a hundred crowns I could scold out my anger.

Aur. Come, there's no injury done to you, but what lyes in my power to make whole again.

Luc. Your power to make whole? I'll have no man command me so far. What can any lawful jury judge of my honesty, upon such proofs as these, when they shall see a gentleman making himself ready so early, and saluting them out of the chamber, whether—like a false man—thou hast stol'n in by the bribery of my servant? Is this no scandal?

Aur. 'Twas done on purpose and I am glad my inventions thrive so; therefore do not stand talking, but resolve.

Luc. What should I resolve?

Aur. To marry me for the safe-guard of your credit, and that suddenly; for I have made a vow that, unless you will do it without delay, I'll not have you at all.

Luc. Some politician counsel me! There's no such torment to a woman, though she affect a thing never so earnestly yet to be forc'd to it.

Aur. What, are you agreed?

Luc. Well, you are a tyrant, lead on! what must be must be; but, if there were any other way in the earth to save my reputation I'd never have thee.

Aur. Then I must do you a courtesy against your will. [*Exeunt.*

Enter PETRUTIO *and* COOK.

Pet. Come, honest cook, let me see how thy imagination has wrought as well as thy fingers, and what curiosity thou hast shewn in the preparation of this banquet; for gluttoning delights to be ingenious.

Cook. I have provided you a feast, sir, of twelve dishes, whereof each of them is an emblem of one of the twelve signs in the Zodiack.

Pet. Well said! Who will now deny that cookery is a mystery?

Cook. Look you, sir, there is the list of them.

Pet. Aries, Taurus, Gemini; good! for Aries, a dish of lamb-stones and sweet-breads; for Taurus, a sirloin of beef; for Gemini, a brace of pheasants; for Cancer, a butter'd crab; for Libra, a balance, in one scale a custard, in the other a tart—that's a dish for an alderman; for Virgo, a green salad; for Scorpio, a grand one; for Sagittarius, a pasty of venison; for Aquarius, a goose; for Pisces, two mullets. Is that all?

Cook. Read on, sir!

Pet. And in the middle of the table, to have an artificial hen made of puff-paste, with her wings display'd, sitting upon eggs compos'd of the same materials; where in each of them shall be enclosed a fat nightingale, well season'd with pepper and amber-greece.* So then will I add one

---

* "In pastry built, or from the spit, or boil'd,
Gris amber steam'd."—*Milton.*
"Be sure
The wines be lusty, high, and full of spirit,
And amber'd all."—*Beaumont and Fletcher.*

Peck, commenting on the above passage in Milton, states that "a curious lady" supplied him these particulars:—"Grey amber is the amber our author here speaks of, and melts like butter. It was formerly a main ingredient in every concert for a banquet,—viz., to fume the meat with, and that, whether

invention more of my own; for I will have all
these descend from the top of my roof, in a throne,
as you see Cupid or Mercury in a play.

Cook. That will be rare indeed, sir! [*Exit.*

Enter DUKE *and* LEONARDO.

Pet. See, the guests are come! go, and make all
ready. Gentles, you are welcome.

Du. Is the Antiquary arriv'd, or no? can you
tell, sir?

Pet. Not yet, but I expect him each minute—

Enter ANTIQUARY.

See, your word has charm'd him hither already!

Du. Signior, you are happily encounter'd, and
the rather, because I have good news to tell you:
the Duke has been so gracious as to release his
demand for your antiquities.

Ant. Has he? You have fill'd me all over with
spirit, with which I will mix sixteen glasses of wine,
to his health, the first thing I do. Would I knew
his Highness, or had a just occasion to present my
loyalty at his feet!

Du. For that, take no thought; it shall be my
care to bring you and signior Petrutio here, both
before him. I have already acquainted him with
both your worths, and, for aught I can gather by
his speech, he intends to do you some extraordinary
honours: it may be, he will make one a Senator,
because of his age; and, on the other, bestow his

boil'd, roasted, or baked; laid often on the top of a baked
pudding; which last I have eat of at an old courtier's table.
And, I remember, in our old chronicles there is much complaint of the nobilities being made sick at Cardinal Wolsey's
banquets with rich-scented cates and dishes most costly dressed
with ambergris. I also recollect I once saw a little book writ
by a gentlewoman of Queen Elizabeth's Court, where ambergris
is mentioned as the haut-gout of that age."

It was also esteemed a restorative. See *Marston's Fawne.*
In addition, see D'avenant's works in this series, vol. ii., p. 224.

daughter or niece in marriage. There's some such thing hatching, I assure you.

Pet. Very likely! I imagin'd as much. That last shall be my lot; I knew some such destiny would befall me. Shall we be jovial upon this news, and thrust all sadness out of doors?

Leo. For our parts, Vitellius was never so voluptuous: all our discourse shall run wit to the last.

Du. Our mirth shall be the quintessence of pleasure,
And our delight flow with that harmony;
Th' ambitious spheres shall to the centre shrink,
To hear our music; such ravishing accents,
As are from poets in their fury hurl'd,
When their outrageous raptures fill the world.

Pet. There spoke my genius!

Ant. Now you talk of music, have you e'er a one that can play us an old lesson, or sing us an old song?

Pet. An old lesson? yes, he shall play "the beginning of the world;"* and, for a song, he shall sing one that was made to the moving of the orbs, when they were first set in tune.

Ant. Such a one would I hear.

Pet. Walk in then! and it shall not be long before I satisfy your desire. [*Exeunt.*

Enter PETRO *and* JULIA, *with two bottles.*

Jul. Come, Master Petro, welcome heartily! while they are drinking within we'll be as merry as the maids. I stole these bottles from under the cupboard, a purpose, against your coming.

Pet. Courteous Mistress Julia, how shall I deserve this favour from you?

---

* "Sellinger's Round, or the beginning of the World," is to be found in Queen Elizabeth's and Lady Neville's Virginal Books, also in "the Dancing Mortar."—*Chappell's Ancient English Ballads.*

Jul. There is a way, Master Petro, if you could find it; but the tenderness of your youth keeps you in ignorance. 'Tis a great fault, I must tell you.

Pet. I shall strive to amend it, if you please to instruct me, Lady.

Jul. Alas, do not you know what maids love all this while? You must come oftener amongst us; want of company keeps the spring of your blood backward.

Pet. It does so, but you shall see, when we are private, I shall begin to practice with you better.

Enter BACCHA.

Bac. Master Petro, this was kindly done of you.

Pet. What's my master a doing, can you tell?

Bac. Why, they are as jovial as twenty beggars, drink their whole cups, six glasses at a health: your master's almost tipt already.

Pet. So much the better, his business is the sooner dispatch'd.

Jul. Well, let not us stand idle, but verify the proverb "Like master like man;" and it shall go hard, Master Petro, but we will put you in the same cue.

Pet. Let me have fair play! put nothing in my cup, and do your worst.

Bac. Unless the cup have that virtue to retain the print of a kiss or the glance of an eye to enamour you, nothing else, I assure you.

Pet. For that, I shall be more thirsty of than of the liquor.

Jul. Then, let's make no more words, but about it presently. Come, Master Petro, will you walk in?

Pet. I attend you.

Bac. It shall go hard but I'll drink him asleep, and then work some knavery upon him. [*Exeunt.*

Enter DUKE, LEONARDO, *and the* ANTIQUARY *drunk.*

Ant. I'll drink with all Xerxes' army now; a whole river at a draught.

Du. By'r lady, sir! that requires a large swallow.

Ant. 'Tis all one. To our noble Duke's health! I can drink no less, not a drop less; and you his servants will pledge me, I am sure.

Leo. Yes, sir, if you could shew us a way, when we had done, how to build water-mills in our bellies.

Ant. Do you what you will; for my part, I will begin it again and again till Bacchus himself shall stand amaz'd at me.

Leo. But should this quantity of drink come up, 'twere enough to breed a deluge and drown a whole country.

Ant. No matter! they can ne'er die better than to be drown'd in the Duke's health.

Du. Well, sir, I'll acquaint him how much he is beholden to you.

Ant. Will you believe me, gentlemen, upon my credit?

Leo. Yes, sir, any thing.

Ant. Do you see these breeches then?

Leo. Ay, what of them?

Ant. These were Pompey's breeches, I assure you.

Du. Is't possible?

Ant. He had his denomination from them: he was call'd Pompey the Great from wearing of these great breeches.

Leo. I never heard so much before.

Ant. And this was Julius Cæsar's hat when he was kill'd in the Capitol; and I am as great as either of them at this present.

Leo. Like enough so.

Ant. And, in my conceit, I am as honourable.
Du. If you are not you deserve to be.
Ant. Where's signior Petrutio?

Enter PETRUTIO *and* GASPARO.

Pet. Nay, good father, do not trouble me now; 'tis enough now, that I have promis'd you to go to the Duke with me. In the meantime let me work out matters; do not clog me in the way of my preferment. When I am a nobleman I will do by you as Jupiter did by the other deities; that is, I will let down my chair of honour, and pull you up after me.

Gas. Well, you shall rule me, son.   [*Exit.*
Du. Signior, where have you been?
Pet. I have been forcing my brain to the composition of a few verses in the behalf of your entertainment, and I never knew them flow so dully from me before; an exorcist would have conjured you up half a dozen spirits in the space.

Leo. Indeed I heard you make a fearful noise, as if you had been in travail with some strange monster.

Pet. But I have brought them out at last, I thank Minerva, and without the help of a midwife.

Ant. Reach me a chair! I'll sit down and read them for you.

Leo. You read them?
Ant. Yes, but I'll put on my optics first. Look you, these were Hannibal's spectacles.

Du. Why, did Hannibal wear spectacles?
Ant. Yes! after he grew dim with dust in following the camp he wore spectacles. Reach me the paper.

Leo. No, an author must recite his own works.
Ant. Then I'll sit and sleep.
Leo. Read on, signior!

Pet. They were made to shew how welcome you are to me.

Du. Read them out!

Pet. *As welcome as the gentry's to the town,*
After a long and hard vacation:
As welcome as a toss'd ship's to a harbour,
Health to the sick, or a cast suit to a barber,
Or as a good new play is to the times,
When they have long surfeited with base rhymes:
As welcome as the spring is to the year,
So are my friends to me, when I have good cheer.
           [*While he reads the Antiquary falls asleep.*

Du. Ay, marry, sir! we are doubly beholden to you. What! is Signior Veterano fall'n asleep, and at the recitation of such verses? A most inhuman disgrace, and not to be digested!

Pet. Has he wrong'd me so discourteously? I'll be reveng'd, by Phœbus!

Leo. But which way can you parallel so foul an injury?

Pet. I'll go in, and make some verses against him.

Du. That you shall not; 'tis not requital sufficient: I have a better trick than so. Come, bear him in, and you shall see what I will invent for you. This was a wrong and a half.   [*Exeunt.*

Enter ÆMILIA *and* LIONELL.

Æm. Now, Master Lionell, as you have been fortunate in the forecasting of this business so pray be studious in the executing, that we may both come off with honour.

Lio. Observe but my directions and say nothing.

Æm. The whole adventure of my credit depends upon your care and evidence.

Lio. Let no former passage discourage you; be but as peremptory as [your] cause is good.

Æm. Nay, if I but once apprehend a just occasion to usurp over him, let me alone to talk and look scurvily. Step aside, I hear him coming!

Enter LORENZO.

Lor. My wife? Some angel guard me! The looks of Medusa were not so ominous. I'll haste from the infection of her sight as from the appearance of a basilisk.

Æm. Nay, sir, you may tarry; and if virtue has not quite forsook you, or that your ears be not quite altogether obdurate to good counsel, consider what I say, and be asham'd of the injuries you have wrought against me.

Lor. What unheard-of evasion has the subtlety of woman's nature suggested to her thoughts to come off now?

Æm. Well, sir, however you carry it, 'tis I have reason to complain; but the mildness of my disposition, and enjoined obedience, will not permit me, though indeed your wantonness and ill carriage have sufficiently provoked me.

Lor. Provok'd you! I provok'd you? As if any fault in a husband should warrant the like in his wife! No, 'twas thy lust and mightiness of desire that is so strong within thee. Had'st thou no company, no masculine object to look upon, yet thy own fancy were able to create a creature, with whom thou might'st commit, though not an actual, yet a mental wickedness?

Æm. What recompense can you make me for those slanderous conceits, when they shall be prov'd false to you?

Lor. Hear me, thou base woman! thou that art the abstract of all ever yet was bad; with whom mischief is so incorporate, that you are both one piece together; and, but that you go still hand in hand, the devil were not sufficient to encounter with; for thou art, indeed, able to instruct him! Do not imagine, with this frontless impudence, to stand daring of me: I can be angry, and as quick in the execution of it, I can.

Æm. Be as angry as you please; truth and honesty will be confident, in despite of you: those are virtues that will look justice itself in the face.

Lor. Ay, but where are they? Not a-near you; thou would'st blast them to behold thee: scarce, I think, in the world, especially such worlds as you women are.

Æm. Umh! to see what an easy matter it is to let a jealous peevish husband go on, and rebuke him at pleasure!

Lor. So lewd and stubborn mads me. Speak briefly, what objection can you allege against me, or for yourself?

Æm. None, alas, against you! You are virtuous; but you think you can act the Jupiter, to blind me with your escapes and conceal'd trulls: yet I am not so simple, but I can play the Juno, and find out your exploits.

Lor. What exploits? What conceal'd trulls?

Æm. Why, the suppos'd boy you seem to be jealous of, 'tis your own leman, your own dear morsel: I have searched out the mystery. Husbands must do ill, and wives must bear the reproach! A fine inversion!

Lor. I am more in a maze, more involv'd in a labyrinth, than before.

Æm. You were best plead innocence too, 'tis your safest refuge: but I did not think a man of your age and beard had been so lascivious, to keep

a disguis'd callet * under my nose, a base cockatrice †
in page's apparel, to wait upon you, and rob me
of my due benevolence! There's no law nor
equity to warrant this.

Lor. Why, do I any such thing?

Em. Pray, what else is the boy, but your own
hermaphrodite? a female siren in a male outside!
Alas! had I intended what you suspect, and accuse me for, I had been more wary, more private
in the carriage, I assure you.

Lor. Why, is that boy otherwise than he appears to be?

Enter LIONELL.

Em. 'Tis a thing will be quickly search'd out
Your secret bawdry, and the murder of my good
name, will not long lye hid, I warrant you.

Lio. Now is my cue to second her.   [*Aside.*

Lor. Signior Lionell, most welcome! I would
entreat your advice here, to the clearing of a
doubt.

Lio. What's that, sir?

Lor. 'Tis concerning the boy you plac'd with
me.

Lio. Ay, what of him?

Lor. Whether it were an enchantment or no,
or an illusion of the sight, or if I could persuade
myself it was a dream, 'twere better; but my imagination so persuaded me, that I heard my wife
and him interchanging amorous discourse together.

* A trull.
  "He call'd her whore! a beggar, in his drink,
  Could not have laid such terms upon his callet."
                                       Shakespear.

† "Marry! to his cockatrice, or punquetto, half-a-dozen taffata gowns, or satin kirtles, in a pair or two of months: why,
they are nothing."   *Johnson's Cynthia's Revels.*

To what an extremity of passion the frailty of man's nature might induce me to!

Lio. Very good!

Lor. Not very good neither; but, after the expense of so much anger and distraction, my wife comes upon me again, and affirms that he is no boy, but a disguis'd mistress of my own; and, upon this, swells against me, as if she had lain all night in the leaven.

Æm. Have not I reason?

Lor. Pray, sir, will you inform us of the verity of his sex?

Lio. Then take it upon my word, 'tis a woman.

Æm. Now, sir, what have you to answer?

Lor. I am not yet thoroughly satisfied; but, if it be a woman, I must confess my error.

Æm. What satisfaction's that, after so great a wrong, and the taking away of my good name? You forget my deserts, and how I brought you a dowry of ten talents: besides, I find no such superfluity of courage in you to do this neither.

Lor. Well, were he a boy or no, 'tis more than I can affirm; yet this I'll swear, I entertain'd him for no mistress, and, I hope, you for no servant: therefore, good wife, be pacified.

Æm. No, sir, I'll call my kindred and my friends together, then present a joint complaint of you to the Senate, and, if they right me not, I'll protest there's no justice in their court or government.

Lor. If she have this plea against me, I must make my peace; she'll undo me else. Sweet wife, I'll ask thee forgiveness upon my knees, if thou wilt have me: I rejoice more that thou art clear, than I was angry for the suppos'd offence. Be but patient, and the liberty thou enjoyedst before, shall be thought thraldom hereafter. Sweet sir, will you mediate?

Lio. Come, sweet lady, upon my request you shall be made friends; 'twas but a mistake! conceive it so, and he shall study to redeem it.

Æm. Well, sir, upon this gentleman's entreaty, you have your pardon. You know the propensity of my disposition, and that makes you so bold with me.

Lor. Pray, Master Lionell, will you acquaint my wife with the purpose of this concealment, for I am utterly ignorant, and she has not the patience to hear me?

Lio. It requires more privacy than so, neither is it yet ripe for projection; but because the community of counsel is the only pledge of friendship, walk in, and I'll acquaint you.

Lor. Honest, sweet wife, I thank thee with all my heart! [*Exeunt.*

Enter DUKE, LEONARDO, *and* PETRUTIO, *bringing in the* ANTIQUARY, *in a Fool's coat.*

Du. So, set him down softly! then let us slip aside, and overhear him.

Ant. Where am I? What metamorphosis am I crept into? A fool's coat! what's the emblem of this, trow? Who has thus transform'd me, I wonder? I was awake, am I not asleep still? Why, Petro, you rogue, sure I have drank of Circe's cup, and that has turn'd me to this shape of a fool: an I had drank a little longer I had been chang'd into an ass. Why, Petro, I say! I will not rest calling, till thou com'st—

Enter PETRO *in woman's clothes.*

Hoyday! what, more transmigrations of forms?

I think Pythagoras has been amongst us. How came you thus accoutred, sirrah ?

Pet. Why, sir, the wenches made me drunk, and dress'd me as you see.

Ant. A merry world the while ! My boy and I make one hermaphrodite, and now, next Midsummer-ale,* I may serve for a fool, and he for a Maid-Marian.

Enter DUKE *and* LEONARDO.

Du. Who is this ? Signior Veterano ?

Ant. The same, sir ; I was not so when you left me. Do you know who has thus abus'd me ?

Du. Not I, sir.

Ant. You promis'd to do me a courtesy.

Du. Any thing lies in my power.

Ant. Then, pray, will you bring me immediately to the Duke ?

Du. Not as you are, I hope.

Ant. Yes, as I am ; he shall see how I am wrong'd amongst them. I know he loves me, and will right me. Pray, sir, forbear persuasion to the contrary, and lead on ! [*Exeunt.*

ACTUS QUINTUS.

Enter LORENZO, MOCCINIGO, ÆMILIA, *and* LUCRETIA.

Lor. Now, signior Moccinigo, what haste requires your presence !

* Rustic festivous meetings were called "ales," as at such meetings, ale, with provisions, for which subscriptions were levied on the parishioners by those whom they chose as wardens, were produced. These meetings were called "Church-ale, Whitsun-ale, Bride-ale, Midsummer ale," &c. For "Church-ale," see *Carew's Survey of Cornwall.* 1769. p. 68.

Moc. Marry, sir! this. You brought me once into a paradise of pleasure, and expectation of much comfort; my request therefore is, that you would no longer defer what then you so liberally promis'd.

Lor. How do you mean?

Moc. Why, sir, in joining that beauteous lady, your daughter, and myself in the firm bonds of matrimony; for I am somewhat impatient of delay in this kind, and indeed the height of my blood requires it.

Luc. Are you so hot? I shall give you a card to cool you,* presently.

Lor. 'Tis an honest and a virtuous demand, and on all sides an action of great consequence; and, for my part, there's not a thing in the world I could wish sooner accomplished.

Moc. Thank you, sir!

Lor. There's another branch of policy, besides the complying of you two together, which springs from the fruitfulness of my brain, that I as much labour to bring to perfection as the other.

Moc. What's that, sir?

Lor. A device upon the same occasion, but with a different respect; 'tis to be impos'd upon Petrutio. I hate to differ so much from the nature of an Italian, as not to be revengeful; and the occasion, at this time, was, he scorn'd the love of her that you now so studiously affect. But I'll fit him in his kind.

Moc. Did he so? He deserves to have both his eyes struck as blind as Cupid's, his master, that should have taught him better manners. But how will you do it?

* "Euphues, to the intent he might bridle the overlashing affections of Philautus, conveid into his studie a certeine pamphlet which he tearmed *A cooling card* for Philautus; yet generally to bee applyed to all lovers "—*Lyly's Euphues.*

Lor. There's one Lionell, an ingenious witty gentleman.

Æm. Ay, that he is, as ever breath'd, husband, upon my knowledge.

Lor. Well, he is so, and we two have cast to requite it upon him. The plot, as he informs me, is already in agitation, and afterwards, sans delay, I'll bestow her upon you.

Luc. But you may be deceiv'd. [*Aside.*

Moc. Still you engage me more and more your debtor.

Lor. If I can bring both these to success, as they are happily intended, I may sit down and with the poet, cry, *jamque opus eregi.*

Moc. Would I could say so too; I wish as much, but 'tis you must confirm it, fair mistress. One bare word of your consent, and 'tis done; the sweetness of your looks encourage me that you will join pity with your beauty. There shall be nothing wanting in me to demerit it: and then, I hope, although I am base,

> *Base in respect of you, divine and pure;*
> *Dutiful service may your love procure.*

Lor. How now, signior? What, love and poetry! have they two found you out? Nay, then you must conquer. Consider this, daughter; shew thy obedience to Phœbus and god Cupid: make an humble proffer of thyself! 'twill be the more acceptable and advance thy deserts.

Æm. Do, chicken, speak the word, and make him happy in a minute!

Lor. Well said, wife, solicit in his behalf! 'tis well done—I am loth to importune her too much, for fear of a repulse.

Æm. Marry come up, sir! you are still usurping in my company. Is this according to the articles propos'd between us, that I should bear rule and you obey with silence? I had thought to have endeavour'd for persuasion; but, because you exhort me to it, I'll desist from what I intended. I'll do nothing but of my own accord, I.

Lor. Mum, wife! I have done. Thus we that are married must be subject to.

Moc. You give an ill example, Mistress Æmilia; you give an example—

Æm. What old fellow is this that talks so? Do you know him, daughter?

Moc. Have you so soon forgot me, lady?

Æm. Where has he had his breeding, I wonder? He is the offspring of some peasant, sure! Can he shew any pedigree?

Lor. Let her alone, there's no dealing with her. Come, daughter! let me hear you answer to this gentleman.

Luc. Truly, sir, I have endeavour'd all means possible, and in a manner enforc'd myself to love him.

Lor. Well said, girl.

Luc. But could never effect it.

Lor. How?

Luc. I have examined whatever might commend a gentleman, both for his exterior and inward abilities; yet, amongst all that may speak him worthy, I could never discern one good part or quality to invite affection.

Lor. This is it I fear'd. Now should I break out into rage, but my wife and a foolish nature withhold my passion.

Moc. I am undone, unspirited! my hopes vain, and my labours nullities!

Lor. Where be your large vaunts now, signior? What strange tricks and devices you had to win a woman!

Moc. Such assurance I conceiv'd of myself; but, when they affect wilful stubbornness, lock up their ears, and will hearken to no manner of persuasion, what shall a man do?

Lor. You hear what taxes are laid upon you, daughter: these are stains to your other virtues.

Luc. Pray, sir, hear my defence! What sympathy can there be between our two ages, or agreement in our conditions? But you'll object he has means. 'Tis confess'd; but what assurance has he to keep it? Will it continue longer than the law permits him possession, which will come like a torrent and sweep away all? He has made a forfeiture of his whole estate.

Lor. What, are you become a Statist's daughter, or a prophetess? Whence have you this intelligence?

Moc. I hope she will not betray me.

Luc. If murder can exact it, 'tis absolutely lost.

Lor. How, murder?

Luc. Yes, he conspir'd the other day with a bravo, a cut-throat, to take away the life of a noble innocent gentleman, which is since discover'd by miracle: the same that came with music to my window.

Moc. All's out; I'm ruin'd in her confession! That man that trusts woman with a privacy, and hopes for silence, he may as well expect it at the fall of a bridge.* A secret with them is like a viper; 'twill make way, though it eat through the bowels of them.

Lor. Take heed how you traduce a person of his rank and eminency! a scar in a mean man becomes a wound in a greater.

* *i.e.* At the fall of water through a bridge. The idea seems to be taken from the noisy situation of the houses formerly standing on London Bridge. S.

Luc. There he is, question him! and, if he deny it, get him examined.

Lor. Why, signior, is this true?

Æm. His silence bewrays him: 'tis so.

Moc. 'Tis so, that all women thirst man's overthrow; that's a principle as demonstrative as truth: 'tis the only end they were made for; and when they have once insinuated themselves into our counsels, and gain'd the power of our life, the fire is more merciful; it burns within them till it get forth.

Lor. I commend her for the discovery: 'twas not fit her weak thoughts should be clogg'd with so foul a matter. It had been to her like forc'd meat to a surfeited stomach, that would have bred nothing but crudities in her conscience.

Moc. Oh, my cursed fate! shame and punishment attend me! they are the fruits of lust. Sir, all that I did was for her ease and liberty.

Luc. Nay, sir, he was so impudent to be an accessary. Who knows but he might as privately have plotted to have sent me after him; for how should I have been secure of my life, when he made no scruple to kill another upon so small an inducement?

Æm. Thou say'st right, daughter! thou shalt utterly disclaim him. The cast of his eye shews he was ever a knave.

Moc. How the scabs * descant upon me!

Lor. What was the motive to this foul attempt?

Luc. Why, sir, because he was an affectionate lover of mine, and for no other vile reason in the earth.

Æm. Oh mandrake! was that all? He thought,

---

* Scab :—A paltry fellow. "One of the usurers, a head man of the city, took it in dudgeon to be ranked cheek by jowl, with a scab of a carrier."—*L'Estrange.*

belike, he should not have enough. Thou covetous ingrosser of venery! Why, one wife is able to content two husbands.

Moc. Sir, I am at your mercy; bid them not insult upon me. I beseech you let me go as I came!

Lor. Stay there! I know not how I shall censure your escape, so I may be thought a party in the business.

Luc. Besides, I hear since, that the mercenary varlet that did it, though he be otherwise most desperate and hardened in such exploits, yet, out of the apprehension of so unjust an act, and mov'd in conscience for so foul a guilt, is grown distracted, raves out of measure, confesses the deed, accuses himself and the procurer, curses both, and will by no means be quieted.

Lor. Where is that fellow?

Luc. Sir, if you please to accompany me, I will bring you to him, where your own eye and ear shall witness the certainty; and then, I hope, you will repent that ever you sought to tie me to such a monster as this, who preferr'd the heat of his desires before all laws of nature or humanity.

Lor. Yes, that I will, and gratulate the subtlety of thy will, and goodness of fate, that protected thee from him.

Æm. Away with him, husband! and be sure to beg his lands betimes, before your Court-vultures scent his carcase.

Lor. Well said, wife! I should never have thought on this now, an thou had'st not put me in mind of it. Women, I see, have the only masculine policy, and are the best solicitors and politicians of a State. But I'll first go see him my daughter tells me of, that, when I am truly inform'd of all, I may the better proceed in my accusation against them. Come along, sir!

Moc. Well, if you are so violent, I'm as resolute : 'tis but a hanging matter, and do your worst.
[Exeunt.

Enter BRAVO *and* BOY.

Bra. What news, boy ?

Boy. Sir, Mistress Lucretia commends her to you, and desires, as ever her persuasion wrought upon you, or, as you affect her good, and would add credit and belief to what she has reported. that you would now strain your utmost to the expression of what she and you consulted of.

Bra. I apprehend her : where is she ?

Boy. Hard by, sir. Her father and the old fornicator Moccinigo, and I think her mother, are all coming to be spectators of your strange behaviour.
[Exit.

Bra. Go wait them in ! let me alone to personate an ecstasy ;* I am near mad already, an I do not fool myself quite into't, I care not. I'll withdraw till they come. *[Exit.*

Enter LORENZO, MOCCINIGO, ÆMILIA, LUCRETIA, *and* BOY.

Lor. Is this the place ?

Luc. Yes, sir. Where's your master, boy ? how does he ?

Boy. Oh, sweet mistress, quite distemper'd ! his brains turn round like the needle of a dial, six men's strength is not able to hold him ; he was bound with I know not how many cords this morning, and broke them all.—See where he enters !

* " Now, see that noble and most sovereign reason,
  Like sweet bells jangled out of tune and harsh,
  That unmatch'd form, and feature of blown youth,
  Blasted with ecstasy."—*Shakspeare.*

Enter BRAVO.

Bra. Why, if I kill'd him, what is that to thee ?
Was I not hir'd unto it ? 'twas not I,
But the base gold, that slew Sir Polydore :*
Then damn the money.

Lor. He begins to peach.

Em. Will he do us no mischief, think you ?

Boy. Oh no, he is the best for that in his fits, that e'er you knew. He hurts nobody.

Moc. But I am vilely afraid of him.

Boy. If you are a vile person, or have done any great wickedness, you were best look to yourself ; for those he knows by instinct, and assaults them with as much violence as may be.

Moc. Then am I perish'd. Good sir, I had rather answer the law than be terrified with his looks.

Lor. Nay, you shall tarry, and take part with us, by your favour.

Em. How his eyes sparkle !

Bra. Look where the ghost appears, his wounds
    fresh bleeding !
He frowns, and threatens me ; could the substance
Do nothing, and will shadows revenge ?

Lor.   'Tis strange !
This was a fearful murder.

Bra.   Do not stare so,
I can look big too ; all I did unto thee,
'Twas by an instigation :

---

* Polydorus, a son of Priam, who sent him, at the commencement of the siege of Troy, to the Court of Polymnestor, King of Thrace, with a large sum of money and the greater part of the treasures of Troy. When Priam's death became known in Thrace, Polymnestor took possession of these riches, which had been entrusted to his care, after having assassinated Polydorus, and thrown his body into the sea.

There be some that are as deep in as myself;
Go, and fright them too!
  Moc. Beshrew him for his counsel!
  Lor. What a just judgment's here! 'Tis an old
    saying
Murder will out; and, 'fore it shall lye hid,
The authors will accuse themselves.
  Bra.   Now he vanishes!
Dost thou steal from me, fearful spirit? See
The print of his footsteps!
  Moc. That ever my lust should be the parent to
    so foul a sin!
  Bra. He told me, that his horrid tragedy
Was acted over every night in hell,
Where sad Erinnys, with her venom'd face,
Black with the curls of snakes, sits a spectatrix.
That lift their speckled heads above their shoulders,
And thrusting forth their stings, hiss at their entrance;
And that serves for an applause.
  Moc. How can you have the heart to look upon
    him?
Pray, let me go! I feel a looseness in my belly.
  Lor. Nay, you shall hear all out first.
  Moc.   I confess it!
What would you have more of me?
  Bra. Then fierce Enyo holds a torch, Megæra
Another; I'll down and play my part amongst
    them,
For I can do't to th' life.
  Lor.   Rather to the death.
  Bra. I'll trace th' infernal theatre, and view
Those squalid actors, and the tragic pomp
Of hell and night.
  Moc. How ghastly his words sound! pray keep
    him off from me.

Lor. The guilt of conscience makes you fearful, signior!

Bra. When I come there, I'll chain up Cerberus, Nay, I'll muzzle him; I'll pull down Æacus
And Minos by the beard: then with my foot
I'll tumble Rhadamanthus from his chair,
And for the Furies, I'll not suffer them;
I'll be myself a Fury.

Moc. To vex me, I warrant you.

Bra. Next will I post unto the destinies,
Shiver their wheel and distaff 'gainst the wall,
And spoil their housewifery; I'll take their spindle,
Where hang the threads of human life like beams
Drawn from the sun, and mix them altogether;
Kings with the beggars.

Moc. Good sir, he comes towards me!

Bra. That I could see that old fox, Moccinigo,
The villain that did tempt me to this deed!

Moc. He names me too; pray sir, stand between us!
Ladies, do you speak to him, I have not the faith.

Em. What would you do with him, if you had him?

Bra. I'd serve him worse than Hercules did Lychas,
When he presented him the poison'd shirt,
Which when he had put on, and felt the smart,
He snatch'd him by the heels into the air,
Swung him some once or twice about his head,
Then shot him like a stone out of an engine,
Three furlongs length into the Euboic sea.

Lor. What a huge progress is that, for an old lover to be carried!

Bra. What's he that seeks to hide himself?
Come forth,
Thou mortal, thou art a traitor or a murderer
Oh, is it you?

Moc. What will become of me ? pray help me! I shall be torn in pieces else.

Bra. You and I must walk together : come into the middle ! yet further.

Enter AURELIO *as an Officer, and two* SERVANTS.

Aur. Where be these fellows here that murder men ? Serjeants, apprehend them, and convey them straight before the Duke.

Bra. Who are you ?

Aur. We are the Duke's officers.

Bra. The Duke's officers must be obey'd, take heed of displeasing them. How majestically they look !

Lor. You see, wife, the charm of authority ! an a man be ne'er so wild it tames him presently.

Æm. Ay, husband, I know what will tame a man besides authority.

Aur. Come, gentles, since you are altogether, I must entreat your company along with us, to witness what you know in his behalf.

Lor. Sir, you have prevented us, for we intended to have brought him ourselves before his Highness.

Aur. Then I hope your resolution will make it the easier to you. What, sir, will you go willingly?

Bra. Without all contradiction ; lead on !

[*Exeunt—flourish.*

Enter LIONELL *as the* DUKE : DUKE, PETRUTIO, GASPARO, ANGELIA *as a woman.*

Du. Come, signior !
This is the morning must shine bright upon you,
Wherein preferment, that has slept obscure,
And all this while linger'd behind your wishes,
Shall overtake you in her greatest glories :
Ambition shall be weak to think the honours
Shall crown your worth.

Pet. Father, you hear all this?
Gas. I do with joy, son, and am ravish'd at it;
Therefore I have resign'd m' estate unto thee—
Only reserving some few crowns to live on—
Because I'd have thee to maintain thy part.
Pet. You did as you ought.
Gas. 'Tis enough for me
To be the parent of so blest an issue.
Pet. Nay, if you are so apprehensive, I am satisfied.
Lio. Is this the gentleman you so commended?
Du. It is the same, my liege, whose royal virtues
Fitting a Prince's Court, are the large field
For fame to triumph in.
Lio. So you inform'd me:
His face and carriage do import no less.
Du. Report abroad speaks him as liberally;
And in my thoughts fortune deserves but ill
That she detain'd thus long her favours from him.
Lio. That will I make amends for.
Gas. Happy hour,
And happy me to see it! Now, I perceive
He has more wit than myself.
Pet. What must I do?
Du. What must you do? Go straight and kneel before him,
And thank his Highness for his love.
Pet. I can't speak,
I am so overcome with sudden gladness;
Yet I'll endeavour it. Most mighty Sovereign,
Thus low I bow in humble reverence,
To kiss the basis of your regal throne.
Lio. Rise up!
Pet. Your Grace's servant.
Lio. We admit you
Our nearest favourite in place and council.

Du. Go to, you are made for ever!
Pet. I'll find some office
To gratulate thy pains.
Lio. What was the cause
That you presented him no sooner to us?
We might have bred him up in our affairs,
And he have learnt the fashions of our Court,
Which might have rend'red him more active.
Du. Doubt not
His ingenuity will soon instruct him.
Lio. Then, to confirm him deeper in our friendship,
We here assign our sister for his wife.
What! is he bashful?
Pet. Speaks your Grace in earnest?
Lio. What else? I'll have it so.
Du. Why do you not step and take her?
Pet. Is't not a kind of treason?
Du. Not if he bid you.
Pet. Divinest lady, are you so content?
Ang. What my brother commands I must obey.
Lio. Join hands together! be wise, and use
Your dignities with a due reverence.
Tiberius Cæsar joy'd not in the birth
Of great Sejanus' fortunes with that zeal
As I shall to have rais'd you; though I hope
A different fate attends you.
Du. Go to the church!
Perform your rites there, and return again
As fast as you can.
Gas. I could e'en expire
With contemplation of his happiness.
Lio. What old man's that?
Pet. This is my father, sir.
Lio. Your own father?
Gas. So please your Grace.
Lio. Give him a pair

Of velvet breeches, from our grandsire's wardrobe.
  Gas. Thrice noble Duke! Come, son, let's to the church.

  [*Exeunt Petrutio, Gasparo, and Angelia.*

  Enter ANTIQUARY *and* PETRO.

  Lio. How now! what new-come pageant have we here?

  Du. This is the famous Antiquary I told your Grace of, a man worthy your grace; the Janus of our age, and treasurer of times past: a man worthy your bounteous favour and kind notice; that will as soon forget himself in the remembrance of your Highness, as any subject you have.

  Lio. How comes he so accoutred?

  Du. No miracle at all, sir; for, as you have many fools in the habit of a wise man, so have you sometimes a wise man in the habit of a fool.

  Ant. Sir, I have been grossly abus'd, as no story, record, or chronicle, can parallel the like, and I come here for redress. I hear your Highness loves me, and indeed you are partly interest in the cause, for I, having took somewhat a large potion for your Grace's health, fell asleep, when in the interim they apparell'd me as you see, made a fool, or an asinigo* of me; and for my boy here, they cogg'd him out of his proper shape into the habit of an Amazon, to wait upon me.

  Lio. But who did this?

  Ant. Nay, sir, that I cannot tell, but I desire it may be found out.

---

  * Assinego. A Portuguese word, meaning a young ass. Hence applied to a silly fellow, a fool. Shakespeare has the word in Troilus and Cressida, ii. 1, and it is not unfrequently found in the Elizabethan writers as a term of reproach. Ben Jonson, in his Expostulation with Inigo Jones, makes a severe pun on his name, telling him he was an *ass-inigo* to judge by his ears.—*Halliwell.*

Du. Well, signior, if you knew all, you have no cause to be angry.

Ant. How so ?

Du. Why, that same coat you wear did formerly belong unto Pantolabus the Roman jester, and buffoon to Augustus Cæsar.

Ant. An I thought so I'd ne'er put it off while I breath'd.

Lio. Stand by ! we'll enquire further anon.

Enter AURELIO, LORENZO, MOCCINIGO, BRAVO, ÆMILIA, LUCRETIA, OFFICERS.

Now, who are you ?

Aur.   Your Highness' officers.
We have brought two murderers here to be censured,
Who by their own confession are found guilty,
And need no further trial.

Lio.   Which be the parties ?

Aur. These, and please you.

Lio.   Well, what do you answer ?
What can you plead to stop the course of justice ?

Moc. For my part, tho' I had no conscience to act it,
I have not the heart to deny it ; and therefore expect
Your sentence. For mercy I hope none, nor favour.

Lio. What says th' accuser ?

Luc. Please your Princely wisdom,
He slew a man was destin'd for my husband ;
Yet, since another's death cannot recall him,
Were the law satisfied, and he adjudg'd
To have his goods confiscate, for my own part,
I could rest well content.

Moc.   With all my heart ;
I yield possession to whomsoe'er
She shall choose for a husband.   Reach a paper

Or blank, I'll seal to it.
   Luc. See, there's a writing!
   Moc. And there's my hand to it:
I care not what the conditions be.
   Lio. 'Tis well! whom will you choose in place
     of the other?
   Luc. Then, sir, to keep his memory alive,
I'll seek no further than this officer.
   Lor. How, choose a common serjeant for her
     husband!
   Æm. A base commendadore? I'll ne'er endure
     it!
   Aur. No, lady, a gentleman I assure you, and
Suppos'd the slain Aurelio.   [*Discovers himself.*
   Moc. A plot, a plot upon me! I'll revoke it all.
   Lio. Nay, that you cannot, now you have con-
     firm'd it.
   Moc. Am I then cheated? I'll go home and die,
To avoid shame, not live in infamy.   [*Exit.*
   Lio. What says the villain Bravo for himself?
   Bra. The Bravo, sir, is honest, and his father.
   Aur. My father? bless me, how comes this
     about?
   Bra. That virtuous maid, whom I must always
     honour,
Acquainted me with that old lecher's drift:
I, to prevent the ruin of my son,
Conceal'd from all, proffer'd my service to him
In this disguise.
   Lio. 'Twas a wise and pious deed.

     Enter PETRUTIO, ANGELIA, *and* GASPARO.

   Pet. Room for the Duke's kindred!
   Lio. What, you are married, I perceive.
   Pet. I am, royal brother.
   Lio. Then, for your better learning in our
     service,

Take these instructions.—Never hereafter
Contemn a man that has more wit than yourself,
Or foolishly conceive no lady's merit
Or beauty worthy your affection.
 Pet. How's this ?
 Lio. Truth, my most honour'd brother, you are
  gull'd ;
So is my reverend uncle, the Antiquary,
So are you all ; for he that you conceiv'd
The Duke, is your friend and Lionell ;
Look you else.
 Pet.   'Tis so.
 Gas.   'Tis too apparent true.
 Lio. What, all drunk ? Speak, uncle !
 Ant. Thou art my nephew !
And thou hast wit, 'tis fit thou should'st have land
  too.
Tell me no more how thou hast cheated me,
I do perceive it, and forgive thee for 't ;
Thou shalt have all I have, and I'll be wiser.
 Lio. I thank you, sir. Brother Petrutio,
This to your comfort ; that is my sister,
Whom formerly you did abuse in love,
And you may be glad your lot is no worse.
 Pet. I am contented ; I'll give a good Wit
Leave to abuse me at any time.
 Lor. When he cannot help it.
 Gas.   This 'tis
To be so politic and ambitious, son.
 Pet. Nay, father, do not you aggravate it too.
 Lor. Well, signior,
You must pardon me, if I bid joy to you ;
My daughter was not good enough for you.
 Pet. You are tyrannous.

    Enter LEONARDO.

 Leo. Save you, Gallants !

Lio. You are very welcome.

Leo. I come in quest of our noble Duke,
Who from his Court has stol'n out privately,
And 'tis reported he is here.

Lio. No indeed, sir,
He is not here. 'Slight, we shall be question'd
For counterfeiting his person.

Du. Be not dismay'd,
I am the Duke!

Leo. My lord?

Du. The very same, sir,
That for my recreation have descended,—
And no impeach, I hope, to royalty,—
To sit spectator of your mirth. And thus much
You shall gain by my presence; what is past,
I'll see it ratified as firm as if
Myself and Senate had concluded it.
And when a Prince allows his subjects sport,
He that pines at it let him perish for 't.

FINIS.

www.ingramcontent.com/pod-product-compliance
Lightning Source LLC
Chambersburg PA
CBHW022050230426
43672CB00008B/1131